15
08/16

# TO CATCH A
# TARTAR

# TO CATCH A TARTAR

## Notes from the Caucasus

## Chris Bird

JOHN MURRAY
*Albemarle Street, London*

First published in 2002
by John Murray (Publishers) Ltd,
50 Albemarle Street, London W1S 4BD

A catalogue record for this book is available from the British Library

ISBN 0-7195-6027-6

Typeset in Monotype Bembo 12/13.5
by Servis Filmsetting Ltd, Manchester

Printed and bound in Great Britain by
Creative Print and Design (Wales),
Ebbw Vale, Gwent

*For Sasha Stancliffe Bird and Matt Stancliffe Bird*
*and for*
*Thomas Dworzak*

# Contents

# Contents

# Illustrations

*(between pages 146 and 147)*

The author and publishers would like to thank the following for permission to reproduce illustrations: Plate 2, Mary Evans Picture Libary; 7, 8, 9, 11, 12, 13, 14, 15, 16 and 17 © Thomas Dworzak/Magnum Photos. Plates 3 and 4 are taken from John F. Baddeley, *The Russian Conquest of the Caucasus* (London, Longmans Green, 1908). Plate 5 is taken from John F. Baddeley, *The Rugged Flanks of Caucasus*, vol. 1 (Oxford, Oxford University Press, 1940).

# Acknowledgements

I would like to thank the following for their company, support and generous sharing of ideas, on and off the road:

Editors: Charles Meynell of Russia Briefing, who set me on the road; Deborah Seward of The Associated Press; and Boris Bachorz of Agence France-Presse.

Colleagues in the Caucasus: Gayane Afrikian, Shakh Aivazov, the journalists at Black Sea Press in Tbilisi, Chris Booth, Heidi Bradner, Thomas Dworzak, Misha Dzhindzhikhashvili, Didier François, Carlotta Gall, Thomas Goltz, Lika Gracheva, Peter Graff, Andrew Harding (whose valiant Niva jeep should be mentioned in dispatches), Nino Kirtadze, Isabelle Lasserre, Steve LeVine, Paul Lowe, Anders Saeter, Lawrence Sheets and all at Reuters in Tbilisi, Sebastian Smith, the journalists at the Turan news agency in Baku, Hasman Umarova, Sasha Zemlianichenko.

Books and papers: Lady Cicely Nepean (great-niece of John Baddeley) for her kind permission to quote from Baddeley's work, and also Michael, Barbara and Annabel Baddeley for invaluable directions in my researches; Lisa Seager, who took great trouble to track down books, papers and photographs from the Baddeley Bequest at the London Library; Caroline Hoyle at the library of the Royal Geographical Society; Moshe Gammer at the University of Tel Aviv for drawing my attention to his essay *The Imam and the Lord*; Thomas Dworzak for the contemporary pictures and the loan of much Caucasiana; Carlotta Gall for her generous loan of Maskhadov's memoir of the war of 1994–96 and for sharing her kaleidoscopic knowledge of Chechnya; Tom de Waal for the kind loan of notes from an interview with Dudayev's relatives; the London Bureau of The Associated Press for their kind permission to access their database; Kit Bird for innumerable book, article and etymological searches way beyond the call of duty and for passing on a love of Tolstoy; Hilary Jenkins for the lead to David Urquhart.

The book: Adam LeBor for listening to the idea; Laura Longrigg at MBA Literary Agents for running with it; Gail Pirkis at John Murray for great patience on some false starts; Caro Westmore at John Murray for patience with my technical glitches; my editor, Antony Wood, who enabled me to write the book I wanted to write, who also corrected my Russian cases and points of Russian history and who translated a stanza from Lermontov's *Cossack Lullaby*; Philippa Fletcher for listening.

The people: the many Chechens who with humour and patience took great risks to look after journalists and their impossible demands, even in the complete absence of western reaction to their suffering; the many Russian soldiers who courageously told us what was really happening; Kyril Zinoviev for my first steps in Russian; the late Sergey Novikov in Moscow and Natasha Grechenko in Grozny; Drs Vasily Chachibaya and Elena Chachibaya in Tbilisi; and Natelo for looking after the heroes of these times – Rachel Stancliffe, Sasha Stancliffe Bird and Matt Stancliffe Bird.

I thank Penguin Books for their permission to quote Chapter 17 of Leo Tolstoy's *Hadji Murat* from *Master and Man and other stories*, translated by Paul Foote (Penguin Classics, 1977; Copyright © Paul Foote, 1977).

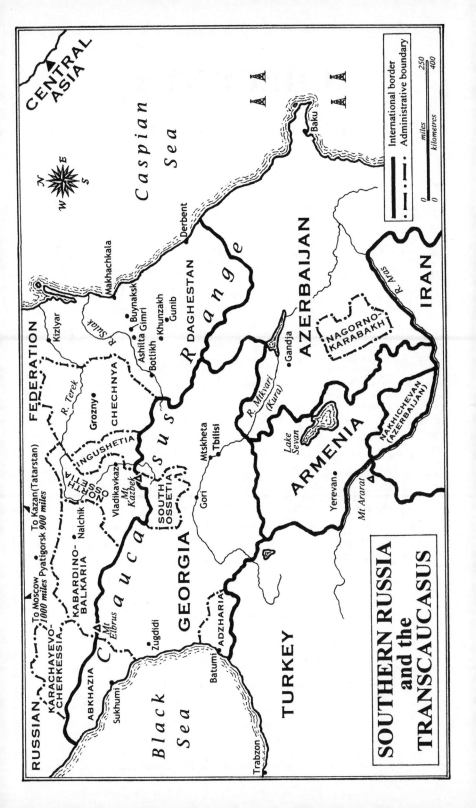

SOUTHERN RUSSIA
and the
TRANSCAUCASUS

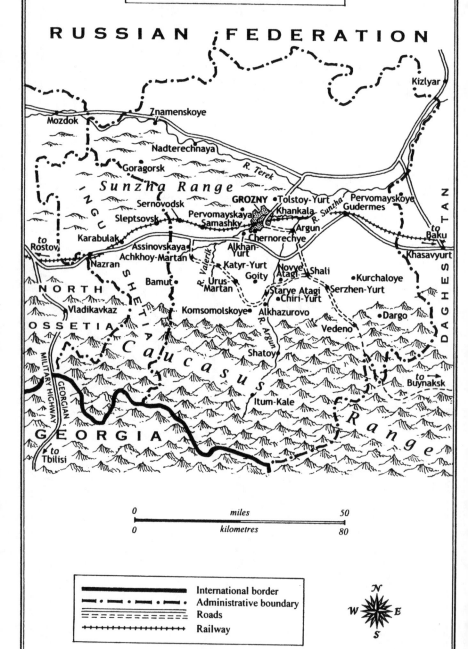

'If everyone would only fight for his own convictions, there would be no wars,' he said.

'And a very good thing that would be,' said Pierre.

Prince Andrey laughed.

'Very likely it would be a good thing but it will never happen.'

'Well, what are you going to the war for?' asked Pierre.

'What for? I don't know. Because I have to. Besides, I am going . . .' He stopped. 'I am going because the life I lead here – is not to my taste!'

Lev Tolstoy, War and Peace

There was in romance great virtue in unequal odds.

Evelyn Waugh, Men at Arms

# The unretired colonel

*Perestroika* is revealing the real Lenin to us.

Mikhail Gorbachev, 1990

THE METRO ROARED and clattered to a halt at Oktyabrskaya Station. I hurriedly folded away my copy of the daily *Izvestiya*, of which I understood about one-tenth, took the stairs two at a time and barged my way through the heavy, opaque glass doors to the icy Moscow street outside. The cloying smell of sweat and vodka breath dissipated instantly in the intense cold outside. A big black Lenin marched ever onwards on a red marble plinth, like a hamster in a wheel, in the middle of the square. A grey sky lidded the surrounding brute office blocks like a tin tray. Cyrillic letters on grimy street signs danced and ached in my head as I walked to Sergey Novikov's 'office', a small flat tucked away behind the French Embassy off Bolshaya Polyanka Street. Mothers in elegant coats guided children into the backs of cars after the end of classes at the French school next door. Up a musty stairwell and past a row of battered metal postboxes, I rang the bell to the flat.

In December 1993 my loyalties were spread between various impecunious news outlets which printed stories on anything from Russia's secretive oil and gas industry to its once revered and now impoverished scientists. The previous month, a 'minder' at the Russian foreign ministry's

3

press centre, a deserted concrete tomb on Zubovsky Boulevard, had looked dubious before he handed me my first press card, accrediting me as the Moscow bureau chief of *Metal Bulletin*, a commodities journal that I had worked for in London.

Days measured out by the tumbling price of nickel and London's wet clinker pavements had weighed heavily on the young man dreaming of snowbound forests and adventure. K—, from the Slav exile of Chiswick, with its conspicuous Orthodox church, helped me escape by taking me through my first faltering steps in Russian. I first caught sight of K—, a tall, stooping man with a proud aquiline nose and a piratical patch over one eye, during a weekly seminar at London University's School of Slavonic and East European Studies. He described to the audience a trip back to Russia where he said there seemed little hope of reviving pre-Communist traditions. Young couples, he said, still seemed to prefer marrying at the town hall and laying a bunch of crimson carnations at the foot of a Soviet war memorial to going to church.

All became clear during my first lesson in his dim, book-lined study as *K—* recalled hearing, as a young boy, the shouts of the women textile workers protesting against bread shortages in the streets of Petrograd in February 1917. A Georgian in his hospitality, *K—* refused payment for the lessons and was dangerously liberal with his vodka. He once told me off for signing a postcard with *poka*, an informal Russian *ciao*, which he said was not the kind of word used by polite St Petersburg society. This was our only contretemps. K— was an encyclopedia of fascinating details and observations about my Russian heroes: how no male characters in Tolstoy's novels ever have a selfless motive (this was a truth that somehow hurt); how Isaac Babel, the mysterious author of the clinical Russian Civil War story-cycle *Red Cavalry*, was so curious that he would demand, without explanation, to look through a lady friend's handbag simply because he wanted to know what was inside. The result of these lessons was a poor grasp of Russian grammar (entirely my fault as I never prepared for them) and a galloping enthusiasm for all things Russian. The Russia of Tolstoy's *War and Peace*, devoured as an undergraduate, was so powerful and real that I longed to join the young Rostovs on their star-spangled, hoar-frosted sleigh journey to the Milyukovs' Christmas party in fancy dress. I would go as a Kazan Tartar and join the lively Natasha, disguised as a Cossack, young Petya got up as a Turkish woman and Sonya, dressed as a Circassian with a burnt-cork moustache under a sable hood.

Such was my preparation for the meeting with the Russian press minder.

'So, you'll be setting up an office here?' he had asked, playing with the magic green press card in his hand which opened the sides of many a Russian mountain. The minder, on the basis of this interview at the press centre's dark, empty bar, would decide whether I could stay and work. I nodded an emphatic 'yes' and garbled something about the important place Russia had in the world metals trade and how *Metal Bulletin* was the magazine to bring Russia to the market.

'How many staff will you be employing?' he pressed. Staff? My own monthly retainer only came to £200. My 'office' was whatever room my two sons, two-year-old Sasha and three-month-old Matt, were not in. I often typed on the floor. My wife Rachel and I had been sublet a flat on the seventeenth floor of a diplomatic block by a departing Moscow-based journalist. The flats, in a supposedly posh Moscow suburb, were the province of the UPDK, the Soviet service which housed all foreign diplomats, journalists and trade representatives living and working in the Soviet Union and which had survived – or had been forgotten – in the new Russia.

The journalist kept the small side office – against my wishes – as he said he still had business in Moscow. This turned out to be a voracious appetite for Russian women, who would call the flat and ask in ringing giggles, '*Zhaka, mozhno?*' – 'Is Jacques in?' With a paunch and receding silver hair, the journalist liked to be called 'Jacques' as this fitted his self-image of an ardent French lover (he was not French). He had wandered into the kitchen in a long dressing-gown one morning while I was away on an assignment and related to Rachel, as if recalling a memorable gourmet meal, how he had bedded a mother and her daughter simultaneously. He had followed the account with pointed questions about my absences. The boys proved excellent protection from this demon-eyed libertine. In the web of impossible Russian bureaucracy and huge prices foreigners were automatically charged (hotels, rail and air tickets, everything had a separate price for foreigners), it was the safest flat I could rent on my unsteady income.

The minder had not been entirely convinced of the title's seriousness as he handed me my press card.

After the bell to the flat rang, there was a grating of locks and a short sucking sound as Sergey Novikov opened the front door, which was padded in dark brown vinyl. He clicked his heels in mock courteous attention. His round, moon-like face smiled shyly. His trousers, old sweater and slippers were of Soviet vintage. Yellowing newspapers lay in piles all over the tiny one-room flat. A bare table held a blackened glass ashtray overflowing with cigarette butts. An ageing computer stood on another table, unplugged and thick with dust. A mug was half-full of oily black instant coffee. A mustard-stained sideplate lay unwashed in the sink. A sofa doubled as a bed in the corner.

Despite the drab surroundings Sergey, in his early forties, carried himself with the mien of a Russian count. The cheap cigarettes were inhaled as if they were pipes holding the choicest Turkish tobacco. The stomach-burning coffee was sipped delicately as he frowned, legs crossed, over a newspaper. Sergey was my partner on one of my 'strings', a series of precarious attachments to various journals, of which *Metal Bulletin* was one. I was supposed to edit what he wrote for an English-language newsletter but we soon dispensed with that formality. I sat at the feet of the master and learned.

Sergey worked for the First Chief Directorate of the Committee for State Security – the foreign arm of the KGB – where he was an Arabist with the rank of Colonel. He treated me as if I were a trainee spy, the lessons delivered with paternal humour. He had waited on the Finnish border to escort me and an old Volvo full of books and baby clothes south to Moscow. We spent the night in a drunken stopover with one of his KGB pals in St Petersburg. Emotional at the end of a bottle of vodka and rough *zakuski* – sour bread, gherkins, herrings and sausage – Sergey declared in carefully enunciated English (he preferred French and was forever quoting Napoleon): 'I am your Russian father!'

A typical editing session saw Sergey pace the room, puffing away on a cigarette, all the while explaining the fiendishly complicated ins and outs of the Kremlin while I frantically typed them down. He turned to me one day and suggested I spend time driving round Moscow to get the lie of the city. 'The first thing an agent does,' a barely perceptible smile on his lips, 'is to get to know a city's streets like the back of his hand. It's useful for drops and the like. But you have to be careful. If your host sees you moving around a lot, then they usually see through your diplomatic cover.' Sergey had learned his craft as a KGB agent in Cairo and Algiers. He talked of tailing American agents round these cities as of much-loved teenage pranks.

His current duties on the newsletter had not changed much from his job at the First Chief Directorate's leafy headquarters in Yasenevo, just outside Moscow. Instead of drinking coffee and reading the papers there, where he was a colonel in the KGB's Middle East section, he now drank coffee and read the papers at the flat. He said he was happy to have given up commuting from the bus stop outside Yasenevo, where men in long leather coats, carrying flash attaché cases bought with precious amounts of hard currency on jaunts abroad, waited for the long ride home.

Sergey put his addiction to newspapers down to Kim Philby. As a trainee he had attended a lecture by the retired double agent in Moscow. 'He said the secret to being a great agent was to read the papers.' Old KGB friends and political contacts would drop by for coffee or vodka. Sergey had instilled into the flat, of monastic emptiness, the atmosphere of a gentlemen's club. It was a retreat from a failed marriage. Only his young mistress was allowed in to wash the mustard-stained plates and coffee cups.

The rambling talks did not feel like work. Sergey, always ready with a Russian proverb, answered any jibe about his meanderings: 'Work is not a wolf – it won't run off into the forest.' But this tough shrub in Moscow politics had roots and tendrils winding in and out of government offices and his old firm, which provided the newsletter with what I thought at times was dangerously accurate information. He cut it a bit fine in one edition when he revealed that a colleague on his way to London during a brief period of openness – when spies were supposedly 'declared' to the host government – passed on useful intelligence to Iraq during the Gulf War. The officer in question threatened to kill Sergey, only half in jest, when they met at an officers' reunion party. The officer did not get his cushy London post.

Sergey was surviving because he had something to sell in a Russia where the sausage and vodka certainties of Soviet times had vanished. Men and women in coats of charcoal and brown, the colour of smoke from a steel plant, lined the streets in neat rows around the cavernous Kiev railway station, each with one thing to sell: an old pair of shoes, sausage filched from a factory, a child's worn winter coat. I first visited Sergey's place in October 1993 to hear Russian soldiers shelling the parliament. The sounds of President Boris Yeltsin's tanks lined up outside the White House building, where he had made his own stand against the Soviet coup plotters in 1991, were echoed by the live television coverage from CNN, rebroadcast on Russian channels. Sergey treated the violent ups and downs of Russian politics as if he were once again station chief in Algiers. Perhaps that was the most comfortable way of handling the new Moscow – the shoot-outs, poverty, the littered roads and the incongruous billboard models for Italian fashion houses thick in one's head like the cheap vodka – now a foreign city to most of its inhabitants.

KGB officers like Sergey had travelled, were sophisticated and used their old state and Party networks to ship metals, oil and anything else to make money. But for Sergey, there was something faintly distasteful about *beeznees*. He once recounted how two ex-KGB colleagues, who had gone into partnership together, had fallen out over the use of a fax machine. Each of them came to him separately and told Sergey they planned to order a contract killing of the other. A contract hit was probably cheaper than a new fax.

That autumn Sergey took me to interview Leonid Shabarshin, his old boss and head of the KGB for only one day following the Communist Party old guard's 1991 coup. We found him sitting in an empty, white-washed office under the terraces of the Moscow Dynamo football club. Young men in suits, which strained over their heavy bodies, respectfully passed on messages and papers. Shabarshin, in an expensive tweed sports jacket, treated them like an impatient headmaster. Shabarshin was now involved in a little *beeznees* himself, in the shape of a security agency. He barked at me, made Sergey feel nervous and at first refused to speak to us. He harrumphed and growled bearlike for a bit longer and then spoke matter-of-factly about the potential for growth in the security business in the new Russia and how ex-KGB officers like himself were the best qualified to provide it.

It was not what he said but rather the setting that told his story. This senior officer, who had dashed around on secret missions in Iran and Afghanistan and who had delivered sensitive reports inside the Kremlin walls, had been reduced to running a seedy security agency with offices begged, borrowed or stolen from the KGB's football club. His security business sales pitch was spat through clenched teeth. The bear turned playful cub when I asked him to sign his recently published memoirs – *In Moscow's Web* – which Sergey, in Jeeves mode, had quietly suggested I bring along to the interview.

Sergey was an aristocrat of sorts. His father had been KGB station chief in Cuba, and Castro had tried to expel him after he was instructed to block the *guerrillero*'s 'adventurism' in foreign affairs – nothing should rock Brezhnev's leaden ship of détente. His great-grandfather had been a senior official in the Tsarist finance ministry, but Sergey was always rather vague about that. He resurfaced during the Civil War as an officer in the All-Russian Extraordinary Commission for Struggle Against Counter-Revolution and Sabotage: the *Cheka* for short. Sergey took an ironic pride in 'Iron Feliks' – the ruthless leader of the Cheka, Felix Dzerzhinsky – and thought the removal of his statue after the August coup outside the KGB's Lyubyanka head-quarters a nonsensical swipe at Russian history. Sergey liked to quote the revolutionary poet Mayakovsky to sum up Russia's political *modus operandi*, an allusion to the Bolsheviks' weapon of choice: 'The word is yours, Comrade Mauser.' The countless Lenins still striding forward on cracked concrete plinths across the former Soviet Union and the millions of words of Leninist hagiography often obscured the fact that it was Lenin, not Generalissimo Stalin, who sent Russia down the path of a violent and crippling totalitarianism. 'The Bolshevik seeds pro-duced such poisonous shoots that it is hard to say when they will be brought under control,' wrote Dmitry Volkogonov, a colonel-general in the Soviet Army and a historian, in 1995. Sergey's grandmother waited until she was on her deathbed before telling him what she had seen as the daughter of a Cheka officer in Tbilisi. Chekist officers resorted to cocaine to help them get through the thousands of executions ordered by Lenin. Every morning there were bodies floating in the River Kura following a night of executions.

Such were the small packets of history handed down through Sergey's family, which was more privileged than most, a bright thread running through the grey army blanket of Soviet citizens' barracks life. It was this proximity to violence, civil war, the famines, the purges, the *Gulag*, the official glorification of the vio-lence, the millions dead, that numbed one to any sense of the human cost of this experiment, which allowed an arrogant and feeble Communist Party to march into Afghanistan. Sergey remembered how under Brezhnev he had been told to make his reports shorter and shorter 'for the old men upstairs'. The days senior functionaries could actually lift a Mauser, let alone fire one, were long gone. But the mindset of the leather-clad Bolshevik died hard inside the Kremlin. The same walled-in arrogance would see the lives of tens of thousands squandered recklessly inside Russia's own shrinking borders, in a tiny autonomous republic north of the Caucasus Mountains called Chechnya.

It was in writing for humdrum commodity journals in Moscow that I glimpsed the mechanism behind the former Soviet Union's spectacular and dizzying collapse. The once mighty military industrial complex haemorrhaged the country's valuable raw materials through new republics like tiny Estonia which, though it did not mine any copper or nickel, was suddenly the world's fourth largest exporter of non-ferrous metals. A greying metals trader from London spoke to me about this over whisky and cigarettes in a dimly lit lobby bar at the Mezh hotel, a hard currency trough for foreigners on the Moskva. Like Woland, the devil who descends on 1930s Moscow in Mikhail Bulgakov's novel *The Master and Margarita,* he took a Faustian pleasure in watching this once powerful empire collapse, the hopes raised by glasnost now lying like a discarded silver wrapper off an imported stick of gum in a Moscow gutter. Companies like his, and the elite Party hacks who jumped with what they could before the system collapsed underneath them, were making a killing out of the teetering Soviet industrial behemoth.

For years the trader had dealt with the faceless and predictable state monopolies in Moscow to prise out quotas of rare earth metals, fed in drips to keep world prices high. 'The senior officials might get girls, a holiday, or a few grand in dollars, but the state trading house always delivered. It was all very civilized.' The hard currency went to keep Party high-ups in a comfort the Soviet experiment could not provide for all the other citizens. Now the trader went straight to the factory gates in towns like Sverdlovsk, recently given back its Tsarist name of Yekaterinburg, and shipped his goods out by the truckload. 'We have the anarchy of the civil war here. The union has collapsed, leaving a hodge-podge of semi-independent republics.'

Police officers paid $60 a month were hopelessly ill-equipped to fight the mafias – some of them ex-KGB people – doing the deals. The head of the anti-mafia squad in Yekaterinburg had his office hit by a rocket-propelled grenade shortly after I interviewed him. The survivor of two previous shootouts, he was not in his office at the time but the squad's only computer was destroyed. He told me that even when he had the computer, donated by a Western European anti-mafia squad, he could not hope to compete with the sophisticated computer-hacking technology and American-made monitoring devices used by his quarry.

The money surfaced in the oddest ways. In the town's main casino, the ceiling in one of the rooms was completely covered with small plaster harpies, their breasts bare above their wings and talons. Their nipples were wired up with small electric lights which twinkled like a galaxy in the casino's dark, velvet-lined interior.

Some of the metals factories still used plant looted by the Red Army – literally whole smelting complexes – from Germany in 1945. Once-secret tank factories now had a right to sell complex and expensive alloys direct to wherever they wanted. In the chaos, no one knew where they had gained this right. 'People are not interested in political parties, they are just interested in surviving,' said the trader, 'whether it's selling their place in the petrol queue or their body.' Achingly beautiful women in furs floated around the lobby and sat blankly at nearby tables, dropping their lashes in an elegant tout. This new Woland and others as fantastic as Bulgakov's walking, talking black cat stalked the streets of Moscow paying out fabulous sums in dollars that changed alchemically into increasingly worthless roubles.

Moscow's dark winter days; the short-tempered staff in the state shops selling heavy bread, sour milk and sausage; the ingenuity required to cook decent meals from the few tins on sale in the new, private street kiosks which sold a dazzling array of vodka and liquers of dubious provenance; all took their toll on my family. Driving home one evening, we found a drunk sound asleep on a traffic intersection, his face buried in the snow. He smiled dizzily as we shook him awake and helped him totter to an apartment building where at least he could sleep it off in the relative warmth of a communal staircase. A middle-aged woman tut-tutted as she passed.

Rachel sank to the floor in shock one day when she found out the child minder we had hired had left Matt on his own in the flat. Sasha would cry with fear when we left him at the Russian kindergarten opposite our flat, across a dual carriageway groaning with filthy trucks and banked high with slate-coloured slush. Columns of cream-white steam from an aged heating plant nearby diffused in the sky like milk in ditchwater. To enter the kindergarten, Sasha had to pass a medical test. A frumpy, overweight school nurse insisted on jabbing a swab into his bottom, seemingly for no other purpose than to humiliate him, a violent ritual to instil fear of authority from an early age. The nurse pulled a rusty surgical blade from a dusty glass with the intention of drawing Sasha's blood. '*Nyet! Absolyutno nyet!*' I said, shaking. The nurse hesitated, smiled ironically and withdrew the blade.

'It seemed to me that these people with their fresh, cruel Slavic faces ate and slept in a photographer's prayer room,' wrote the poet Osip Mandelstam of 1930s Moscow; he disappeared into the Stalinist maw in the same decade. The hard edges of those times had never been properly smoothed over. The wide avenues you could not cross, the vast apartment blocks you could not enter and the massive factories walled up, save for a tiny enquiries counter less than a foot square on an unnamed sidestreet, made you an ant. 'Nowhere, never, have I felt so strongly the watermelon emptiness of Russia,' Mandelstam wrote.

After finishing the newsletter that evening, I left Moscow for Tatarstan to report on the territory's bid for independence. Sergey insisted on accompanying me to Moscow's Kazan Station. From there I planned to take the overnight train east across the steppe to the region's capital, after which the railway station was named. Sergey shrugged on a blue overcoat, wrapped a large scarf round his neck, placed a mink *shapka* above his moon face, zipped on his winter boots, pulled on his gloves – tensed in anticipation of the unforgiving Moscow rush hour – and moved stiffly out through the door. After the tobacco fug and heart-squeezing coffee, the sharp cold outside was a dash of icy water in the face. Sergey's dowdy Zhiguli, once exported to Britain as the Lada Riva, coughed, purred and crunched out over the frozen ruts behind the apartments and into Moscow's frosted streets, lit the lemon yellow of French headlamps.

I had to pinch myself.

A decade earlier, Russia had seemed as remote and strange as the oriental cupolas of an Orthodox church. I was once told as a child that I would be able to spot an invading Russian on the London Underground as he would have snow on his boots. I wondered for ages afterwards why the snow wouldn't have melted by the time he'd got to London. News programmes showed maps of Europe cut in half, Nato on one side and the Warsaw Pact countries on the other. The black silhouettes of tanks in the east far outnumbered those on my half of the map. My French teacher revealed he spoke Russian when he decorated his classroom during a special culture week with posters from the Komsomol youth movement. The apple-cheeked youths in shorts and red scarves were a mix of 1920s soap advertisements and Hitler Youth.

When I was a boy, my father worked for the military government in divided Berlin. As the West did not recognize East German authority over the military authorities, it was young Russian conscripts who examined our identity cards – *not* our passports as that would be to recognize East Germany – when we drove down the 'corridor', an empty motorway, to Helmstedt in West Germany. The Russians would send us back if one letter from the identity cards was out of place on the 'flagging order', a travel document typed out by a bored British NCO which authorized us to drive from the capitalist enclave through East Germany and out to the West.

The Soviet guards at the checkpoints, in long grey coats, grey caps and black boots to the knee, looked like tin soldiers, their high cheekbones red with cold adding to the effect. Some would look round furtively, move a bit of earth from a nearby flowerpot, pull out an army belt buckle emblazoned with a Soviet star and hold it up, whispering urgently: '*Zwanzig Deutschmark!*' In Helmstedt, where watchtowers glowered over the wall, I once reported excitedly to a kindly British sergeant how I had seen a column of East German army trucks dithering down the

*Autobahn* – my bit part as a Cold War warrior. From the British 'military train' that ran the same route on to Braunschweig, you could see into the back of a Russian tank park, pointed out by a British army captain who accompanied the passengers. The French military train, which clattered up to Berlin from Strasbourg, was welcomed into the divided city to the crackling strains of the *Marseillaise* over the station tannoy.

The Communist Bloc was only a stone's throw from the sparkling shopfront of the Kaufhaus Des Westens on the Kurfürstendamm, across the minefields, searchlights, barbed wire and machineguns fired by trip wires which shored up the wall dividing east and west. A cigarette brand called *West* plastered the city in advertising posters which exhorted smokers to 'Go West!' But I felt I would sooner fall out of the back of a cupboard into frozen Narnia than gain entry into the strange, cold, enemy land on the other side of the wall.

As I walked into the Kazan Station with my own Mr Tumnus, the nervous Faun waiting under a lamp at the back of the wardrobe, Sergey's anxieties rubbed off on me. A true Muscovite anywhere outside the city's main ring road feels he is in Indian country.

The station was a sea of tired and unwashed travellers. The surface of this human ocean rippled in places as families and traders packed and repacked flimsy check-patterned bags bulging with goods. In a dirty white-tiled underpass, lit with a flickering neon tube, two interior ministry troops held a man with a dark skin against the wall at gunpoint and demanded i.d. A dull voice echoed round the gloomy interior over a tannoy announcing departing trains, the destinations indistinguishable to my ear. A blue cloud hung over the station and caught at the back of the throat as large samovars were heated with brown coal in each of the waiting carriages on the platforms.

Trains have a special, intangible frisson in Russia, where adventure, change and new possibilities open up along the thousands of miles of wide steel tracks that leave Moscow and cut their way through eleven time zones of snow, steppe, desert and forest. Anna Karenina meets Vronsky alighting from a train; and meets her end when she places her head under the wheels of another. Rival armoured trains, like fire-breathing dragons, shunt back and forth across a frozen, snowbound Ukraine in Bulgakov's civil war novel *The White Guard*. Sergey told me friends of his in the KGB had to travel in southern Russia in armoured trains to fend off railway bandits. Armed and balaclavaed guards rode shotgun on top of the carriages. I pleaded with Sergey to arrange a trip on an armoured train but the promised chance never materialized. I sensed a Muscovite reluctance to leave town. While the country's rusting airline network could strand you for days – a common question at check-in in Russia's Far East was to ask if the airport had any jet fuel – the trains for the most part still ran on time.

The past crackled like the pages of an old book inside the carriage as you sipped lemon tea from a glass in a metal *podstakanchik*, or holder, watching the steppe float by. Small Russian villages of creaking wooden *izby* painted a jaunty blue would flash past, giving out onto men crouched on stools holding fishing lines over holes in the ice in the middle of a frozen river; they carried large hand drills to bore holes in the ice. You could imagine the novelist Turgenev walking out of a forest, a gun in the crook of his arm, thinking up the next episode of *A Sportsman's Sketches*. You slept as Mandelstam imagined the bourgeois slept, 'lulled on the springs of Pullman cars, tucked into envelopes of snow-white railway sleep'.

I had a ticket booked in 'soft class', a compartment comprising four bunks. The Kazan Station is Moscow's gate to the east. As in E.M. Forster's description of London stations in *Howard's End*, Moscow's stations tend to take on the characteristics of their final destinations. The Leningrad Station's yellow and white baroque breathed the culture – and snobbery – of St Petersburg, a night's journey away on the *Krasnaya Strela*, or Red Arrow. On the opposite side of the road, the Kazan Station's sprawling, dark interior, full of oriental faces, spooled out into Russia's vast Siberian hinterland, spread like a white cloak to the Pacific Ocean and the ice-capped volcanoes of Kamchatka. 'Leningrad is civilized,' said Sergey, who tended not to keep up with post-

Soviet rebaptisms. He looked unenthusiastically at the Kazan Station entrance. 'Kazan is full of Central Asian bandits.'

Sergey found my carriage, a faded army green, and waded ahead down the narrow corridor to my compartment. He delivered a strangled 'Good evening' into the compartment, turned round hastily and squeezed his way back past the other passengers settling in, sweating from the sudden warmth.

'You don't have to go right now, tonight,' Sergey said, his forehead damp under his mink cap.

'What do you mean?'

'I'm saying, you don't have to go tonight.' No explanation was forthcoming.

'Sergey, why? I've got meetings tomorrow, I must go tonight.'

'The two men in your compartment, they're Chechens,' he said.

South of Moscow lie the Caucasus Mountains, a sudden electrocardiac trace after a thousand miles of dead flat steppe. The region was up in arms, in anarchy. The reports in the Moscow media of violent excesses and hostage-takings in the new republics of Georgia, Armenia and Azerbaijan, and in would-be republics like Chechnya, took on the tone of we-told-you-so. We Russians, went the line, established order and prosperity. The wars, the lack of electricity and gas, were the price of throwing off colonial rule. The Chechens, still nominally 'Russian' citizens, were the most detested. The mobs busy carving up Moscow and other cities were for the most part Russian but the Chechen gangs were more visible and seized on by Russians as proof of an innate wickedness.

Newspaper small-ads in the new flats-for-rent columns in Moscow told all those who were *LKN* – the insulting Russian initials which stand for those of 'Caucasus National Appearance' – not to bother enquiring. In the state of emergency in 1993 following Yeltsin's decision to shell his recalcitrant parliament into submission – a Leninist tactic if ever there was one – Moscow's mayor decided to expel the *LKN* from the city. It was the equivalent of trying to throw out London's Asian and West Indian community. The fact that Chechens, Azeris and others had had nothing to do with the political row, even if the rebellious parliamentary speaker, Ruslan Khasbulatov, was a Chechen, was largely ignored. Muscovites, who had seen their once quiet city crumble and be subjected to rocket attacks by rival gangs, were jubilant. The mayor's popularity soared. Foreign observers went along with the clichés. Chechnya was regularly written up as the former Soviet Union's 'first mafia-controlled state'. As if a large and powerful mafia hadn't long been at work inside the Kremlin.

With the Chechens, something older was at work. Russian children are rocked to sleep with the words of Mikhail Lermontov's *Cossack Lullaby*. The second stanza runs:

> Over the stones careers the Terek,
>    Its muddy waters play;
> Up the bank the evil Chechen
>    Creeps and whets his blade;
> But your father is a fighting man
>    And he has battled much;
> So sleep serenely, little one,
>    Hushaby, hush, hush.

I knew nothing of this. The Chechens were just a fearsome people who had brought their own clan warfare from their distant mountain republic to the streets of Moscow, much to everyone's alarm and annoyance. Like the settlement under the magnifying glass at the beginning of each *Asterix and Obelix* adventure, Chechnya was a little 'indomitable' Gaulish village surrounded by nervous Russian legions, the whole people having apparently fallen into a cauldron of magic potion. The Chechens did themselves no favours by swaggering around in shaky television footage carrying guns and knives, the very picture of Lermontov's unshaven, dagger-sharpening bandit.

Sergey was still sweating and a little out of breath, symptoms of a heart condition. I was now uneasy but insisted on my journey. I walked into the compartment where a slim man in his thirties, with dark hair, was sprawled on one of the bunks. He flashed a wolfish grin, some of his teeth a dull gold. Opposite him sat a younger man who also looked Chechen. I remember returning to my car one evening in Moscow to find a group of young men from the Caucasus – all immaculately dressed in Loden coats and sharp leather jackets – huddled round it. We all froze for an instant when they realized it was my car. They hesitated, then melted into the frozen dark when they saw Matt in my arms and Sasha toddling beside Rachel. When Sergey said goodbye and left me in the train compartment, I felt as if I had been abandoned at boarding school and had met the house bully while unpacking in the dormitory.

The train moved slowly out of the station and into the night, the backs of factories and flats outside a jumble of indistinct geometry in pools of muddy lamplight.

The older man was a Chechen from the republic's capital, Grozny; the younger was from the newly independent republic of Azerbaijan further south. They spread out an old newspaper on the sidetable, pulled out a knife and started slicing sausage. They bid me eat with them but I turned them down: everyone knew that on such journeys food and drink were laced. Your apparently generous fellow passengers would then rob you while you were out cold in a drug-induced sleep. I was famished, having drunk only coffee all day with Sergey but was too embarrassed to haul my luggage to the restaurant car.

The two men immediately asked me how many dollars I was carrying and offered to change some for roubles. I declined nervously. They asked me how much I earned. I never learned how to field this question, a perennial, without looking sheepish. Even the dowdiest British journalist's income was a fabulous amount to one of the empire's citizens. A Victorian governess, Lucy Atkinson, on meeting a drunk Russian officer on her way to Siberia in 1848, gave her interlocutor the benefit of the doubt in her *Recollections of the Tartar Steppes*: 'A Russian, without the slightest intention of being rude, often asks whence you come, where you are going, and your business, and some, even, what your resources are; and just as freely they give a sketch of themselves.'

The Chechen told me patiently – my Russian was terrible –

that he was on his way to the Siberian oil town of Tyumen to sell cosmetics in a street market there. He patted a suitcase full of lipsticks and powders. The conversation tailed off. The Chechen broke the silence.

'I have a gun in Grozny, a Kalashnikov,' he said enthusiastically, in apparent compensation for the contents of his suitcase. He mimed shooting it with a big grin. 'I know Dudayev,' he added proudly.

Dzhokhar Dudayev, an ex-Soviet air force general, had left the strategic bombing unit he commanded in Tartu, Estonia, to declare Chechen independence in 1991. His wide lapels, thin black moustache, slim hips and wide-brimmed hat gave him the air of a Latino dance star. His heavily armed entourage gave him the weight of a Chicago gangster.

'You should go to Grozny and meet him!' the Chechen traveller insisted. 'He is a great man. You will come to meet Dudayev and you will stay with me as my guest, *nyet problem*.' He asked for a piece of paper. On it he wrote in pencil his name and his address and telephone number in Grozny. 'Come! You are welcome!'

My two companions changed into thin tracksuits for the night. I slept fitfully, fully clothed, as the train rattled eastwards to the Tatar capital. I kept feeling for my wallet. I awoke as the train crossed the frozen River Volga early the next morning. Through the window I could see, at one end of a steel bridge, a guard in a sentry-box. He stood to attention, a bayonet fixed to his rifle. Below him, mothers and fathers pulled their children jerkily across the ice on small toboggans. I jumped off the train in Kazan tired but relieved, the cold morning sun hurting my eyes. I screwed up the piece of paper with the address on it and tossed it on the ground. Grozny was one place in Russia I was sure never to visit.

# The blood of Genghiz

Scratch a Russian and you'll find a Tartar.

Russian proverb

WHERE DO THE borders of Russia begin and end? The question is cobwebbed by a decades-old view which conflated 'Russia', in western minds a geographical cloud of unknowing, with the 'Soviet Union'. To this day I still have to explain to people that when I lived in Georgia, Kazakhstan and Ukraine, I was *not* living in Russia. My eyes were opened to the problem the morning after Sergey reluctantly left me to take the train to Kazan. Only one night's journey east from Moscow, I found myself in the middle of landlocked Tatarstan's little known struggle for independence. Like Chechnya, it was an 'autonomous republic' which wanted to free itself from the Kremlin in the early 1990s, finally agreeing a deal with Moscow for considerable self-rule in February 1994.

Kazan was a revelation. Buses donated by Turkey cruised the freezing streets of the Tatar capital. Snow stuck precariously to the curved, shiny roofs of the mosques, some boxed in by scaffolding for repairs which had stopped for the winter. Islamically correct women's apparel filled the buckled windows of a state clothing shop, the dummies stiff-armed fantasies from *The Thousand and One Nights*. Tolstoy studied oriental languages at the university, a white stucco building glazed in snow and which stood in elegant contrast to the modern concrete faculty buildings across the street. Another student of privileged birth,

Vladimir Ulyanov, enrolled to study law there but was expelled for participation in radical student politics and withdrew to his mother's estate. From 1901 he stuck with one of his aliases – 'Lenin'.

The pattern of would-be independent statelets across the old Union was well represented in Kazan: a nationalist government, run by its former Communist Party first secretary, Mintimer Shaimiyev, used apparently legal means on the surface and bullying tactics out of sight to push independence; a more radical nationalist grouping shouted from the sidelines what the government itself would not dare say in public; and a large minority who did not speak the proposed new 'language of state' – largely Russians – feared that if the dreams of the radical nationalists were realized, they would lose their homes and futures.

Relations were uncertain between Tatars and ordinary Russians, the latter mostly oil workers unsure of their future as other Soviet republics broke from the empire like great plates of ice which snapped off in the post-colonial thaw of 1991. The Kamaz truck factory outside Kazan had blown up in mysterious circumstances, said to be a warning to Tatar leaders from Moscow, the explosives rumoured to have been planted by Sergey's KGB colleagues.

The Tatar government was grappling with its status, claiming to be subject to both Russian and international law at the same time. R. Khakimov, an aide to the Tatar 'president', Mintimer Shaimiyev, had an elegant, high-ceilinged office inside the town kremlin, a fairy-tale fortress encrusted with decorative stars. He spoke with the articulate languor of a Jesuit. 'Our position is that we want recognition from Russia, that we are a sovereign state, but that we also want to preserve cultural and economic relations. We propose a *confederative* union.' He insisted Tatarstan conduct its own foreign policy, even though the republic did not have a single customs post.

'Aren't you a bit in the same situation – geographically – as Lesotho?'

'We have air links,' Khakimov ventured.

'And your oil?'

If independence meant flying out the landlocked republic's declining oil wealth over jealous Russia, then so be it.

I had travelled through southern Central Asia the previous summer but Russian and Soviet colonialism there was more obvious. The states born of the old Khanates of Turkestan were only conquered a little before the last-minute scramble for Africa at the end of the nineteenth century and were always considered foreign lands in the minds of those in Moscow. Off the beaten track, which outside the Central Asian republics' capitals was never that far, Russian was not spoken. Life there was syncretic: the loyal Uzbek Communist Party functionary would think nothing of driving out to the countryside in his black government Volga sedan to attend a nephew's circumcision ceremony performed by a Moslem cleric. And like other successful colonial rulers, Moscow did not dig too deep lest the cotton, metals and oil of the classic colonial exchange stopped flowing.

But the territory comprising present-day Tatarstan, ever since the capture of Kazan by Ivan the Terrible in 1552, has been regarded as Russian territory.

Kazan is the fulcrum over which Russian identity teeters between Europe and Asia. The Mongol horsemen who followed Batu Khan, grandson of Genghiz, settled on the banks of the Upper Volga in Kazan, and further south in Astrakhan on the Caspian Sea, after razing Moscow and then Cracow in 1241 (the *hejnal*, the warning of the Mongol horsemens' approach, is still sounded from the top of St Mary's, overlooking Cracow's main square, cut short to mark the point where the trumpeter took an arrow in his throat). The Tatars are the Golden Horde's Turkic-speaking descendants. Ivan built the cathedral of St Basil the Blessed on Red Square to celebrate his victory, its garish domes and cupolas said to represent the turbans of his slain Tatar enemies. Napoleon is reputed to have ordered 'that mosque' to be destroyed in 1812, the church saved, not for the last time, by 'General Winter'.

Tatar legend has it that Ivan demanded he marry the vanquished khan's wife. She agreed but only on condition that a tower of seven tiers be erected in seven days. The Syuyumbike tower was duly built – it now stands as part of the Kazan kremlin's wall. The khan's widow then asked permission to climb the tower to bid farewell to the city. Permission was granted and, according to the legend, she threw herself from the top rather than share her bed with her Slav conqueror.

Ivan IV set some important precedents. He shared with Stalin a murderous paranoia (both were further unhinged by the death of their first wives – Ivan's, Anastasia, poisoned by an unknown assassin, and Stalin's, Kato Svanidze, dying of tuberculosis when the Bolshevik revolutionary was twenty-seven). After Anastasia's death, Ivan created the *oprichnina*, the 'special realm' – it actually comprised half the Russian realm – the ancestor to the KGB. The *oprichniki* wore black cloaks, rode black horses and were given unlimited powers to investigate and crack down on sedition, real or imagined. The dog's head and broomstick they carried were said to represent their snarling bite and their orders to 'sweep away everything superfluous out of the land'. Ivan showed himself a match for the Mongol khans when in 1570 he sent in the *oprichnina* to sack Novgorod, a rich merchant town where the Slav *boyar* elites still enjoyed a small jot of independence from Muscovy. Almost the entire population was slaughtered, and lands were seized and divided up by the *oprichnina*.

It was Ivan IV's conquest of the Khanate of Kazan that heralded Russia's newfound imperial ambitions. From Kazan, Cossack adventurers like Yermak opened up Siberia, the 'sleeping land', to send back silver, gold and precious furs, placing even Alaska, across the Bering Straits, under the tsar's dominion (until sold to the United States in 1867 to pay off debts at two cents an acre). In 1547 Ivan IV was the first ruler to be crowned as 'tsar' – 'caesar' or 'emperor' – over a nebulous territory which constantly expanded and contracted as political and military fortunes waxed and waned. The vast and vulnerable steppe remained a constant prey to the piratical raids of nomad slavers centuries after the Mongol Khans were driven back east.

'Tartars', 'Tartary', 'Tartarin'. The words breathe banditry, old maps and silk.

English language dictionaries give conflicting definitions and spellings of the word *Tatar*, but for Russians and outsiders, spelt *Tartar* in older English spelling with an *r*, it became a generic term for anyone inside the Russian Empire who was not a Christian, usually Muslim, and was applied to Chechens, Azeris and even Slav-speaking Cossacks as well as ethnic Tatars, regardless of ethnic identity. The word *Tatar* or *Tartar* conjured up the 'grey wolves', Batu's 'heathen Tatars', who galloped out of the mouths of the Don and Dnieper rivers with a swiftness as terrifying as the arrows shot from their compound bows of horn, sinew and wood.

'**Tartar**: A strolling vagabond, a thief, a beggar . . . A person supposed to resemble a Tartar in disposition; a rough, violent-tempered, or irritable and intractable person,' says the *Shorter Oxford English Dictionary*. It also contains an antique phrase: '**catch a Tartar**: encounter or get hold of a person who can neither be controlled nor got rid of; meet with a person who is unexpectedly more than one's match', or, as it is revealingly phrased in a 1924 pocket edition, 'find intended victim more formidable than expected'. Further entries in the *Shorter Oxford* have '**Tartarly**: rough and fierce'; '**Tartarean**: of or belonging to Tartarus in Greek mythology; pertaining to hell or to purgatory; infernal; hellish.'

'I'll tell you what I am,' Dickens's loathsome headmaster, Mr Creakle, whispers to David Copperfield, twisting the boy's ear until his eyes water: 'I'm a Tartar.'

In the summer of 1992, I interviewed the chairman of Kazakhstan's privatization committee on the future of the oil-rich republic, which had been independent for only a few months. He was an ethnic Kazakh. The Kazakhs, like the Tatars, are also descendants of the Mongol hordes but from further east, with Kazakh society to this day divided into the 'junior', 'middle' and 'senior' hordes. The minister rolled up his sleeve and proffered the bunched veins on the inside of his forearm. 'The blood of Genghiz Khan runs through my veins!' he shouted at me in triumph, as if to clinch all arguments about the Central Asian state's future. 'I'm descended from him, you know.' You could see his imagination whirl out of the stuffy Soviet office block he had inherited in the capital, Alma-Ata, leap onto a horse and put some imaginary foe to the sword. A spick portrait of Lenin, the picture of a Tartarly Twenties oil baron, gleamed behind the chairman's desk.

The same feeling of exultation filled Professor Marat Mulyukov, a Tatar nationalist (without the extra 'r' as the Russians and ethnic Tatars themselves spell it). As he spoke, you could see the colour flooding back into a sepia past of fezzes, delicate spectacles, Tatar language newspapers and national pride that surfaced with the liberal 'Jadidist' movement, whose democratic ideas threatened the Empire at the end of the nineteenth century.

Professor Mulyukov was head of the Tatar Civic Council, a radical if politely spoken nationalist group. A crumpled Tatar flag with a sharp crescent was pinned to the wall behind a cluttered desk, a splash of colour in the brown, aquatic gloom of his office off a Kazan side street. 'We want to recreate the Tatar state,' said the professor, peering through pebble spectacles. 'We lost our independence in 1552 and ever since then we've been a Russian colony. As a result of Russian colonial policy, and the totalitarianism of Soviet times, we are on the verge of disappearing as a nation. You may say from the diplomatic point of view that we are in a state of war with Russia.'

He lit a cigarette and brushed some wayward ash off an ancient suit, the same mud brown as the walls and furniture. His surroundings were humble but his case for independence was – and is – as strong as Kazakhstan's, particularly as both territories have large Russian minorities. 'The autonomy we were given in Soviet times was a present to keep the people quiet. Tatarstan has a large industrial base and used to produce far more than independent republics like Moldova or Tajikistan. Russia has always sucked people's blood – even Britain didn't carry out such robbery.' He smiled at the jibe, then frowned. 'Russian historians have made the Tatars out to be Barbarians.'

Or servile. Vladimir Nabokov, in an acid aside to his literature students at Cornell University, described the Tatars as a people from the 'province' of Kazan, 'a few thousand of whom migrated in the nineteenth century to Petersburg and Moscow where some of them pursued the calling of waiters'.

Professor Mulyukov spoke of another Russia, a Russia that has only ever existed as an empire, even if its territories are separated by seas of steppe instead of salt water. If you took away successive historical layers like those of the proverbial matryoshka doll and threw in all the mixed marriages and progeny from centuries of warfare and conquest, you would be no closer to solving the riddle of what constitutes Russian national identity. As the Russian proverb has it: 'Scratch a Russian, and you'll find a Tatar.' Lenin was part Kalmyk, Jewish, Swedish and German. Under strict orders from Stalin (himself a Georgian national) Lenin's hagiographers suppressed his Kalmyk and Jewish ancestry because, as the historian Orlando Figes has noted, 'this was inconvenient to a Stalinist regime peddling its own brand of Great Russian chauvinism'.

Sergey told me once how in Algiers the KGB tried to make contact with a CIA agent there. An officer was chosen to go and knock on the American's door and was instructed to introduce himself as a Swedish businessman. 'The officer chosen was an Uzbek who could hardly string two sentences of English together,' said Sergey, wheezing with laughter. The agent had the door slammed in his face. The attempted inclusion of the Turkic Uzbek officer in Soviet service and Sergey's ridicule of him said much about both the Russian and then the Soviet empire's schizophrenic attitude to its non-Russian peoples.

As such peoples were never fully trusted or respected, an ethnic Russian was usually the real power behind the local Party first secretary nominally in charge of the empire's 'republics' and 'autonomous' territories. Yet even so, a non-Russian leader like Dudayev, who called on the Chechens to fight a *ghazavat*, or holy war, against Moscow, had previously risen to be a general in the Soviet air force, commanding a fleet of aircraft which bombed mud *kishlyaki*, or villages, in Afghanistan (on his foreign trips, in imitation of Jordan's King Hussein, he insisted on flying his own Tupolev 134 passenger jet).

The substance of the idea of *Homo sovieticus*, a Soviet man devoid of national identity – a popular Soviet song went: 'My address is not a house or a street, My address is the Soviet Union' – was around centuries before the Revolution. Even after the fall of Kazan, Russians greatly respected the Tatars' system of government, and they were still threatened by the Tatars' swift cavalry armies until Peter the Great. When the Muscovite dynasty died out in 1598, a converted Tatar prince descended from Genghis Khan, Boris Godunov, was elected tsar by a council of notables in a desperate attempt to stave off crisis in the empire.

The inclusion or exclusion of non-Russians – or perhaps more accurately non-Christian Orthodox – became increasingly problematic as Russia's borders widened to the east and to the south. Influenced by the Swedish naturalist Carl Linnaeus, imperial administrators, soldiers and travellers set about classifying Russia's diverse new subject peoples, much like their British colonial counterparts. They were often scornful of what they found. A traveller returning from Russia's Arctic tundra described the people he came across as 'worse than animals, for even dumb animals do not eat beasts, fowl, or grass that God has forbidden them to eat, while these people, not knowing God who dwells in Heaven and refusing to accept his law from those who bring it to them, are raw-eaters who eat the meat of beasts and vermin, drink animal filth and blood as if it were water, and eat grass and roots.'

Kurban Said (the Turkic *nom de plume* of Lev Nussimbaum, a Jew who escaped the former Soviet republic of Azerbaijan after the 1917 Revolution) starts the novel *Ali and Nino* with a pre-revolutionary geography lesson in the capital, Baku. Most of the class at the Imperial Russian Humanistic High School are Turkic Azeris, with a sprinkling of Armenians, Poles and one Russian. Their priggish teacher, a Russian, tells the class that it will be their responsibility whether Baku 'should belong to progressive Europe or to reactionary Asia'. One of the Azeri pupils raises his hand and says: 'Please, sir, we would rather stay in Asia.'

The teacher curses his pupils under his breath for mocking Russia's imperial might. Russia professed to follow the enlightenment and western codes for religion, culture and manners, but this classroom clash underlines the insecurity of the Russians' belief in their own cultural superiority over their 'subjects'. A literate Russian would only have to travel a few versts outside town – in fact, to the bottom of his or her estate – to find fellow Russians living in the most primitive conditions and far from the western mores espoused by the French-speaking court in St Petersburg. Until the emancipation of the serfs in 1860, most Russians were slaves.

Turgenev, whose own heart turned west but whose name has Turkic roots, concluded: 'The trouble with us Russians is that the Tartar is so close behind us. We are a semi-barbarous people still. We put Parisian kid-gloves on our hands instead of washing them. At one moment we bow and utter polite phrases, and the next, flog our servants.'

Tsarist officials zigzagged between bloody subjection and public tolerance of these new-found 'wild, unruly, and disloyal peoples', termed *inorodtsy*, or 'foreigners', by the imperial administration. Ivan the Terrible destroyed Kazan's mosques and built churches in their place, instructing Kazan's new Orthodox bishop in 1556 not only to convert the 'pagans' but to teach them to read and write in Russian also. But few Tatars converted to the Orthodox faith. Of those that did, many converted back to Islam in later periods. In 1782, echoing official sentiment in the time of Catherine the Great, a Russian law professor argued belatedly: 'We believe it is better to spread civilization, public order, and culture, and to settle a province, than to exterminate the peaceful inhabitants of an empire and to destroy them by fire and sword.' Extermination won over 'civilization' in the following century.

Today's Russian Academy of Sciences is diplomatic in the classification of its peoples. It lists 138 different nationalities in its 1994 edition of *Narody Rossii* (Peoples of Russia), from the 33,000 Abazin in the Caucasus at the beginning of the encyclopedia to the 380,000 Yakuts in eastern Siberia at the end, with old-fashioned illustrations of folk costumes and vernacular architecture that succumbed long ago to the drab five-storey flats built in Khrushchev's time, known as *Khrushchevki*. Careful to decry the horrors of Stalinism, especially against the smaller peoples, the encyclopedia's editors argue with Sunday school primness that 'the richness and strength of Russia is secured in its cultural variety'.

But what if, like the Tatars, you still wanted to set up on your own? It was Russian guns, not high-minded notions of *le citoyen*, that kept the Tatars inside Russia and all other peoples before them. Lenin's solution to the puzzle was world revolution, after which peoples would be 'national in form and socialist in content', having no longer to worry about independence in a happy-ever-after global socialist entity.

Lenin soon ran into problems after the Revolution when Georgians, Ukrainians and many other peoples took Bolshevik promises at face value and proclaimed independence from the old empire. Attacked for being a 'great-powerist' by Marxist rivals, out to preserve the empire, Lenin retorted: 'We hardly mean to urge women to divorce their husbands, though we want them to be free to do so.' Lenin did not grant any divorces. But as soon as the Soviet empire started to crumble in the late 1980s, many of its 'peoples' walked out as soon as they could. The borders of the Russian Federation have today shrunk back to roughly what Peter the Great inherited three centuries ago.

Yeltsin, triumphant after clambering onto a tank to face down the Communist putsch in August 1991, found himself in exactly the same predicament as Lenin. In trying to win over non-Russian nationalities in his duel with Gorbachev for the Kremlin between 1990 and 1991, Yeltsin famously told the Tatars and other peoples to 'take as much sovereignty as you can swallow'. He presided over the Russian parliament's own 1990 declaration of sovereignty for the Russian Soviet Federated Socialist Republic which flew in the teeth of Gorbachev's flailing attempts to keep the Soviet Union from disintegrating. But fearful of losing any more territory, Yeltsin copied Lenin by promptly reneging on his promises of sovereign largesse as soon as he came to power in 1991.

The 'near abroad', the name Russians give to the ring of former Soviet republics which broke away in 1991, keeps a wary eye on the Kremlin, no matter that this time their independence, unlike the short-lived declarations after the Revolution, has been internationally recognized. In March 1996 the Russian parliament voted to declare the break-up of the Soviet Union illegal. Power in Russia (still) rests with one man, the president, but the ballot sent a shiver through Moscow's former colonies. At the time of the vote, a Georgian friend asked me incredulously: 'Can you imagine the British parliament voting to restore its old empire?'

# Cowboy of the Caucasus

'It is wonderful to be a Georgian, even if Georgia
perishes. You sound hopeless. But has it ever been
otherwise in the Land of Tamar? And yet our rivers run,
our vine grows, our people dance.'

Kurban Said, *Ali and Nino*, 1937

ONE OF THE last epics of decolonization was taking place.
What shape would this once mighty empire, cracking and
breaking in the violent torrents of a nationalist spring, eventually take? Millions of Russians and other peoples were on the
move in one of history's largest ever but least reported population movements. In the Central Asian state of Tajikistan, I
queued up with ageing Russian *babushki* who had waited for
days in a hot railway station in the capital, Dushanbe. A train
was supposed to travel down to the Afghan border and loop up
to the relative safety of neighbouring Uzbekistan. Civil war had
broken out and the Russians there had about them the air of
Belgian families fleeing the Congo. Only there were no paratroopers to protect them. The Soviet, and then by default
Russian, 201st Motorized Infantry Division sat holed up in their
Dushanbe barracks, unsure of what to do. Russians did not have
much of a future in the cold north even if they managed to
leave. Much like the Algerian *pieds noirs*, they were looked
down on and made to feel uncomfortable among their hard
drinking cousins in European Russia and Siberia. Everyone was
cut adrift. Magbola was a Sudanese student studying agriculture
in Dushanbe. The streets were hot and empty. Her clammy concrete institute had closed months ago. She had no money to
return home to Khartoum. She was doubly anxious to leave

after one of her Sudanese friends, also stranded, was knifed by a gang of Tajiks.

My reporting trips took me not only to Tatarstan but also to Sakhalin Island in the Pacific, where I gorged myself on red salmon eggs and Japanese beer, the Urals steel town of Nizhny Tagil, where my throat burned from the plant's yellow fumes, and the capital of Azerbaijan, Baku, where the casinos and bars opening for US oilmen framed another round of the 'Great Game' over the oil-rich waters of the Caspian Sea. The real story appeared to be not in Moscow but in the outposts of empire, where peoples and nations were waking like Rip Van Winkle from decades of Soviet sleep.

Moscow was also hard on the family. Rachel, who had given up her job in London, was stuck at home in the flat with the children and a new language to learn. The flat flooded one night when a pipe burst on the floor above. The new white paint I had hauled out from Britain to slop over the turd-brown wallpaper was wrecked. The light switches stabbed us with electric shocks. We were both tired of being told by *babushki* that Sasha and Matt were underdressed for the Moscow winter when they both moved like stiff Michelin men in their coats, hats, scarves and snow trousers. Something had to change if I was to persuade the family to stay in the empire.

We had originally thought of setting up in Georgia, reputedly a Transcaucasian Tuscany. The 1991–92 civil war had put paid to that idea. My problem now in early 1994, however, was not war but a perceived peace in Georgia – the Caucasus story was considered 'over' by news editors and journalists I spoke to in Moscow.

I tried the news agencies, who want news from all over the world all the time – even from places like Georgia. I put on a jacket and tie to see one agency chief. He wanted to send me to Tbilisi immediately. Money came last in the enthusiastic conversation.

'How much do you pay?' The editor looked around the room. 'We can pay $20 a story.'

No matter how desperate I was to leave Moscow, I could not feed my family on that. I walked away from the meeting to catch the metro home on a dark grey March afternoon, fed up. But a few days later I eagerly accepted an offer of $40 a story from Agence France-Presse. I left their cramped bureau on Moscow's noisy Sadovaya-Samotechnaya Street aglow, and mentally brushed the bureau chief's stiff words about expenses under a carpet woven of the gaudiest optimism. I now had a proper credential, a name I could conjure with: Caucasus Correspondent for AFP or, as one of the editors from Paris dubbed me, 'Cowboy of the Caucasus', his flattery neatly sidestepping an impassioned plea for my own jeep.

If you put Tbilisi at the centre of an imaginary Caucasian clock, the various conflicts and would-be independent statelets in my journalistic empire would run somewhat as follows. At four o'clock, Nagorno-Karabakh was a self-proclaimed independent republic inside Azerbaijan, not even officially recognized by its main state sponsor and gunrunner, Armenia. But the Karabakh Armenians' small representative office in the 'neighbouring' Armenian capital Yerevan stapled a visa into your passport, enabling you to remove it before leaving Armenia and entering Azerbaijan, which claimed Karabakh as its own; separatist Abkhazia on Georgia's Black Sea coast was at ten o'clock; the South Ossetians in central Georgia, who claimed that one day, like the two Germanies and Koreas, they would unite with their brothers in North Ossetia across the border with Russia, was at eleven o'clock; the 'Chechen Republic of Ichkeria' was across the North Caucasus range at one o'clock.

The only language that knit any of this Babelish, spiky territory together was Russian, the imperial tongue except – in the Tsarist era – the Arabic learned by peoples who had converted to Islam. Georgia and Armenia have their own alphabets and philologists have hit numerous dead ends trying to link the mountain languages to the outside world, save for Azerbaijan's Turkic language and the Armenian tongue's Indo-European roots.

These little-known points of Wilsonian self-determination did not include autonomous 'republics' like Adzharia, also on Georgia's Black Sea coast at nine o'clock, and a string of autonomous territories north of the Caucasus Mountains, running from west to east: Adygeia, Karachayevo-Cherkessia, Kabardino-Balkaria, Ingushetia and past Chechnya, Daghestan, where at least 40 different languages are spoken, from the estimated 500,000 speakers of Avar to the 200 speakers of Ginukh high up in the Caucasus near the Georgian border. Pliny wrote that 'we Romans conducted our affairs there with the aid of 130 interpreters'. In 1834 German was added to the list after a large party from Württemburg turned up and settled after losing their way to Mount Ararat where they had hoped to witness the Second Coming.

In the region's long struggle against imperial dominion by Persian, Turk and Russian, geography was both a help and a hindrance. It is worth quoting from John Baddeley's history published in 1908, *The Russian Conquest of the Caucasus*:

It may be said without exaggeration that the mountains made the men; and the men in return fought with passionate courage and energy in defence of their beloved mountains, in whose fastnesses, indeed, they were well-nigh unconquerable. Yet, by one of those strange contradictions that meet us on all sides, strength and weakness went hand in hand. The very height and ruggedness of the great ranges, the profound depth and steepness of the valleys, the vast spread of the primeval forest, made union impossible; and without unity the tribes in the long run were bound to fall before the might of Russia.

As Gorbachev's hold on the empire weakened, ethnic and nationalist tensions among its subject peoples from the Baltic to the Black Sea, locked up for decades by the Soviets, were sprung free. A massacre of Armenians by Azeris in the drab industrial city of Sumgait in February 1988 started a movement of peoples which would uproot more than a million souls in the Caucasus by the mid-1990s. Poorly led Soviet troops were sent in to impose martial law and quell nationalist demonstrations in Nagorno-Karabakh, Tbilisi and Baku which were bloody, only exacerbating hatreds, frustrations and violence. All this was set against an economic collapse far worse than the Great Depression of the 1930s. Armenian refugees from Baku were pressured by the Armenian authorities to live in villages abandoned by Azeris in territory captured by Armenian forces, the walls of the mosques daubed with male genitalia. An empty parking lot was all that remained of an Armenian church in Baku. A quarter-million Georgians fled separatist Abkhazia on the Black Sea coast between 1992 and 1993. Russians in Chechnya who were young enough, had relatives elsewhere or enough money started to leave Grozny, fearing the gun law there. Russian meddling, especially in Abkhazia, continued after the Soviet collapse but the Kremlin's half-hearted and at times contradictory attempts to hold on to its colonies looked like the last spasms of a being that was clinically dead. Yeltsin had enough trouble holding on to Moscow to worry about 'bandits' and *LKN* over a thousand miles to the south when in March 1994 I went ahead of the family to Tbilisi to scout out the possibilities. I travelled two hours and twenty minutes south on a screaming, straining Tupolev 154 passenger jet which had crammed in about thirty extra passengers who stood in the aisle throughout the flight.

During my first week in the city, armed police stormed the parliament in protest at the sacking of their interior minister. 'Don't, whatever you do, go inside the parliament,' an editor at the agency told me on a hissing line from Moscow. I was touched by his concern until he added brusquely: 'You might not be able to file.' The siege was over by the time I ran the mile to get there. I spoke to a few dazed members of parliament outside, who described the police as waving pistols. It was not clear if any shots had been fired. I dialled Moscow for an hour, repeating the number of the agency over and over again, to try and file my story. My heart leaped when – finally – a crackly pause gave way to a ringing tone which echoed back from a different planet. The editor answered to say a Georgian stringer the agency had not told me about had reported the story a few hours before. I went home unpaid.

That evening, I was invited to a party at the house of an

American journalist, one of three foreign correspondents based in the whole of the Caucasus. Getting to the party posed a problem. Tbilisi's gun law meant few dared go out after dark. The journalist had recently helped a pregnant woman hit in crossfire near his house to a hospital. The US embassy advised the handful of its citizens in the city that if they absolutely had to walk the streets at night, they should carry a baby doll, swaddled to look like a real infant. They argued that gangsters respected people with children.

Life in Tbilisi had collapsed. Telephones no longer worked to the next town, let alone abroad. There were constant power cuts. Russia cut off natural gas later in the year as it no longer wanted the country's wine or tea in exchange. The Kremlin now wanted *baksi* – dollars. I thought seriously about buying a gun. My father, who knows about these things, advises that a gun only increases the likelihood of a violent encounter. You would have to be prepared to use it. And heaven knew what would happen if Sasha or Matt found the thing.

But shortly after I arrived, the ministries of defence, security and the interior told the rowdy parliament that they could no longer guarantee anyone's safety in the country. The nightly shoot-outs made that obvious. But for a government, no matter how ragged, to admit publicly it can do nothing to maintain law and order was unsettling. A debate on guns, dear to most men's hearts in the Caucasus, ensured a full house at the parliament. A vote was taken on a law proposing that all citizens should be allowed to own guns for self-defence. There were 140 votes for the law and six against. The six who voted against argued the law did not go far enough as it did not allow for the possession of automatic weapons. This small technicality was overlooked by my neighbours on the upper floors of the courtyard where we eventually settled. They took the oil cloths off their Kalashnikov assault rifles at New Year to fire off a few celebratory rounds.

Sergey had set me up with an introduction in Tbilisi to Vasily Chachibaya, a friend of his brother's from student days, and his wife Yelena, now both doctors at the city's Number Four Hospital. I slept on a sofa-bed in a room I shared with a grand piano. Both were experienced surgeons; their state salaries were worth about 50 cents a month. I asked how they survived. Vasily opened a polished cabinet to reveal several cases of vintage Georgian cognac, the colour of strong tea. 'This is what the patients give me – it's a currency of sorts,' he said. I volunteered to him Winston Churchill's preference for Armenian brandy over French cognac, thinking anyone from the Caucasus would be proud of such a fact. Vasily took offence. 'Everyone knows Stalin sent him Georgian brandy.'

One evening at home with the Chachibayas, after a dinner of *tsatsivi*, chicken served with a delicate walnut sauce, several bursts of machinegun fire cracked and rattled for several minutes a couple of blocks away. I went to the window, my nerves tingling with excitement, as this was more than the usual lazy 'Piff! Paff!' of previous nights. 'I must go out – it sounds serious,' I said, adding self-consciously: 'I have to call the agency.'

Both Yelena and Vasily were making the most of a sudden burst of electricity and completely ignored the exchange. Yelena, having put their small daughter to bed, sat in an armchair under a standard lamp and sewed. Vasily watched Russian television news beamed down from Moscow and which still carried the next day's temperatures for the whole of the former Soviet Union, as if nothing had changed.

'Don't be crazy. It's nothing,' Vasily said distractedly of the shooting. 'It happens all the time. Wait until the morning.' He turned back to the flickering screen. I obeyed with what I thought was indecent readiness.

On the evening of the journalist's party, Vasily walked me to a street corner near his flat to stop a taxi. The sun hurried in a blaze of orange behind the mountains ringing the town. Dust rose and hovered in the air. Russia had turned out Georgia's lights – no *baksi*. Only car headlamps lit the streets. Vasily stopped the first car that approached – virtually every car-owner was by force of circumstance a part-time taxi-driver – and allowed me to climb in only after giving the driver a thorough grilling to ensure his intentions were honest. He took down the registration number just in case.

At the party, great court was paid to a group of young telephone operators. The journalist paid them a retainer, guaranteeing instant access to any of Georgia's six international lines. The worthless interim currency, the *kuponi*, which had stabilized at about 1.5 million to the dollar, meant a five-hour call to Australia was virtually free. Russian roubles, themselves sliding against the dollar, were considered hard currency.

On the way back, the cars on the dark streets swerved like fireflies. The passengers inside them and the barrels of their rifles were dark, spidery shadow puppets, cut-out devils sent by some god of chaos.

The traffic police – the former Soviet Union's ubiquitous GosAvtoInspekt, the State Car Inspectorate, or 'GAI' for short – were off the streets before dark during the city's self-imposed curfew. But even during the day, the drivers of dilapidated Ladas and Volgas, with farting exhausts, dented body work and smashed headlights like black eyes, ignored the traffic cops' whistles and striped batons whirled about in an accented plea to stop. No car in Tbilisi, neither the traffic inspectorate's own vehicles nor President Eduard Shevardnadze's wheezing Chayka limousine, would pass muster with a hungry traffic cop wanting to feed his family from on-the-spot fines. But most drivers could bet safely that the police had no petrol to give chase.

Stained tankers parked on the roadside were the closest Tbilisi had to petrol stations. Weeds grew on the forecourts of the old state-owned pumps. The tankers carried fuel filched from Russian military supplies to top up soldiers' starvation wages north of the Caucasus Mountains. I regularly replenished four 20-litre jerrycans stored in my damp cellar along with firewood – to fuel a car and a generator – as insurance against shortages. The scent of low grade fuel, which sloshed around in leaky canisters stopped with plastic bags, deadened even the smell of cheap Kazbek cigarettes inside a car's rancid interior. Lee Miller, a photographer for *Vogue* who followed the Allies into liberated France, understood perfectly the sense of squirrelish well-being in a store of fuel. In an earlier incarnation she was Man Ray's silver bromide muse but there was nothing surreal in the loving portrait she took of a jerrycan and a champagne bottle wedged in the snow on her hotel balcony in Paris. Along with cigarettes, they were simply the most prized wartime commodities.

A 20-litre jerrycan was usually enough for a petrol dealer's business for the day. The seller, squinting from the smoke of a badly packed Kazbek cigarette jammed in the corner of his mouth, would carefully measure out one or two litres in a clear plastic lemonade bottle so the driver was able to look at the piss colour of the petrol he was buying – usually a filthy 76-octane. The petrol was sniffed, sometimes dabbed on the tongue, to check its vintage. But for all the rituals, contraband petrol was often mixed with water and the driver's car would shudder and die a kilometre down the road.

On one of my first mornings in Tbilisi I travelled on the metro to Rustaveli Station in the city centre, which is crossed by two underground lines. The carriages, the same solid square boxes that screamed through the tunnels deep below Moscow, were packed as electricity had been switched back on not long before. A sullen crowd outside the entrance to a metro station signalled one of the city's regular outages.

The train hummed loudly as the rubber-edged doors slid open for a few seconds and banged shut. As I left the carriage, there were shouts and scuffles. A young man ran out, bobbing up and down in the crowd like a dog breaking up a flock of sheep. He ran for the stairs. A group of young men, cursing and waving pistols, bolted after him. A relieved 'tut-tutting' bubbled up from the shuffling crowd when they were sure they were no longer in danger of being fired on.

Outside the metro station, Tbilisi was bathed in hard spring sunshine which hurt one's eyes but failed to warm, like a tepid bath spiked with disinfectant. The people on the streets, after a winter without electricity, looked pale and tired, as though they were venturing outside for the first time after a wracking fever. People walked slowly up and down Prospekt Rustaveli, the main avenue named after Georgia's twelfth-century poet whose epic verse story of chivalry, *The Knight in the Panther's Skin*, is always presented to a newly married couple: 'The lover must be constant, not lewd, impure and faithless; when he is far from his beloved he must heave sigh upon sigh; his heart must be fixed on one from whom he endures wrath or sorrow if need be. I hate heartless love – embracing, kissing, loud smacking of lips.'

Men with puffed eyes, unshaven, sat on small side walls on the avenue selling piles of newspapers, the headlines printed in the Georgian alphabet, an extravagant, black filigree. Grubby, cracked shop windows let in a wan light onto empty display shelves.

The younger women promenaded in black microskirts carefully sewn at home with long, black knitted socks pulled over their knees, their thin, pale legs incongruous in a country where it is the height of shame for men to wear shorts. Teenage girls were still 'kidnapped', bundled into the back of a possessive boy's car for a night outside the town, a wheezing Lada the unromantic replacement for the Kabarda thoroughbred of pre-revolutionary times. The girl was still forced, for the sake of her imperilled honour, to marry her abductor.

In Kurban Said's novel *Ali and Nino*, the heroine, Nino, is a Georgian and a Christian. She sobs as she tells Ali, the Muslim from neighbouring Azerbaijan she has promised to marry on the eve of the Russian Revolution, that in Tbilisi she is not forced to wear the veil as she would be in Ali's home. 'Seven times Timur the Lame destroyed Tiflis,' Nino complains. 'Turks, Persians, Arabs and Mongols have overrun the country. We stayed. They devastated Georgia, raped it, murdered it, but never really possessed it. St Nino came from the West, carrying her vine, and it is to the West we belong. We are not Asiatics. We are the furthest eastern country of Europe.'

Vine branches lashed together with the hair of St Nino of Cappadocia, reputedly the daughter of a fourth-century Roman governor who brought Christianity to Georgia, is the origin of the Georgian Orthodox cross's shape. A jug of cloudy white Kakhetian wine is still placed with defiant pride on the table. But centuries of invasions have left their mark.

'You must understand, we say we are Christian,' my elderly neighbour, Natelo, later explained. Swathed in black, a widow, and gesturing to the closed, Turkish-style courtyard of which the flat I eventually found for my family was a part, she said: 'But none of this is Christian. We are all really Moslems in disguise.'

The Persian Narikala fortress disintegrated gently above the town on a hill overlooking the fast-flowing River Mtkvari – the Kura in Russian – which cut deep through the town. Near the fortress, on the Sololaki Ridge, stood a 25-metre statue of 'Mother Georgia', her voluminous skirts and conical breasts a creation by Jean-Paul Gautier in aluminium plate. She looked down stiffly over the city like a lost part of an enormous chiming clock. She held in one hand a goblet of hospitality, a sword in the other for her enemies. Otherwise, the 'Tiflis' of imperial times, depicted in the brooding nineteenth-century lithographs of the Russian prince Alexander Gagarin, looked remarkably unchanged given seven decades of mountain-moving Soviet rule, the faceless apartment blocks on the outskirts left as so much residue from the experiment.

At no. 13 Prospekt Rustaveli, the Hotel Tbilisi was a burned out shell, giving the avenue a gap-toothed smile. The pale, honey-coloured walls belonging to the church of Kashveti next door had been repaired following the shelling in 1992, when the then nationalist president, Zviad Gamsakhurdia, was blasted out of the city by rival warlords. It was the only building that radiated a solid warmth that morning. Elderly women and young mothers lit spitting tapers to oval-faced icons in its hushed interior.

Opposite stood the white stucco palace that once belonged to Tbilisi's nineteenth-century Russian viceroys, where grandees like the silver-haired Prince Mikhail Vorontsov dined, danced and dealt cards for an after-dinner game of *l'hombre*. The palace, its walls the texture of ersatz icing on a sickly Soviet cake, was empty. Drama students hung around in bored groups near the Paliashvili opera house opposite, another Russian oriental confection dating back to 1896.

At one end of the avenue, strange loops of concrete, nicknamed 'Andropov's ears', dominated the empty Republic Square. The space was overlooked by the Hotel Iveria, a Seventies tower block built for tourists and located just past the parliament and the post and telecommunications building. The hotel's metal balconies were draped with flapping white squares. The laundry was fussed over by women in mourning, their dull black clothes dusty as crows' feathers, their dark eyes brilliant pools of grief. They were Georgian refugee women who had lost their subtropical gardens, spacious balconies and their men in Georgia's western republic of Abkhazia in 1993. The refugees were despised by the townspeople for supposedly taking their jobs and bringing new 'mafias' to the town. But really because they served as a humiliating reminder to Georgians of their rediscovered weakness. Camping out in hotels like the Iveria, in disused factories or tents across the Caucasus, they represented all that had gone wrong after nearly two centuries of Russian rule had collapsed.

As Nino complains to Ali in Said's novel, ancient Christian Georgia, a powerful civilization under Queen Tamara, was first prey to the Mongol hordes in medieval times and then suffered successively the jealous attentions of Persia in the east and the Sublime Porte to the west. A population of five million in the mid-thirteenth century had withered to just half a million when King Giorgi XII, dying in Tbilisi in 1800, sought protection from Russia and handed the Georgian crown to Tsar Paul I, convinced Russian imperial rule was the only means of escaping the attentions of the Muslim south.

Giorgi XII's request for protection from Russia was not the first. In 1658, Taimuraz, the 'Iberian tsar', pleaded in person at the Kremlin for Russian aid against the Turks and Persians but to no avail. Paul's mother, Catherine, showed keen interest in Georgia's strategic value and dispatched General Todtleben to Tbilisi in 1769 on the outreak of war with neighbouring Turkey. He crossed south through the mountains through the treacherous Dariel Gorge with four artillery pieces and 400 men, expelling a Turkish army 12,000-strong from Georgia's second city of Kutaisi the following year. Todtleben went on to try and take the

Black Sea port of Poti but failed and he was recalled by Catherine.

Georgia's Irakli II appealed to the Kremlin when the Persians again demanded Georgian subjection. This time, Catherine sent Lieutenant-General Count Paul Potemkin, a cousin of Catherine's favourite. The Count built a fort at the northern foot of the Caucasus Mountains, Vladikavkaz ('ruler of the Caucasus'), and heading up the crashing headwaters of the Terek, set about improving the rough track – mentioned in Strabo's *Geography* – through the Dariel Gorge across a pass of 7,977 feet.

Pushkin's poem 'The Avalanche', written in 1829, describes the track through the gorge to Tbilisi, the Georgian Military Highway:

> Beaten by jagged rocks to steam,
> Before me pours the boiling stream;
> Above my head the eagles scream,
>      The pine-wood speaks,
> And through the mist there faintly gleam
>      The mountain-peaks.
>
> From where the snow-clad summits soar
> An avalanche in days of yore
> Thundering down with mighty roar
>      The channel filled
> Through which the river Terek tore
>      Impetuous-willed.

Despite its remoteness, the gorge was for centuries the main trade route across the rocky spine of the Caucasus Mountains. The only other routes north (even today) hug the Black Sea or Caspian coastlines. I commuted from Tbilisi along the 'A301' for many months as war loomed in Chechnya, hitching in a BBC journalist's Niva jeep on several journeys to the Chechen capital, Grozny. On a breaking story, we would leave at four or five in the morning, allowing us to get there by lunchtime the same day.

We would pass the small town of Mtskheta, Georgia's ancient capital, in darkness. I fumbled like a drunk with DTs trying to pour cups of coffee from a steel thermos as the jeep hit pothole after pothole on the unlit road. A few petrol-sellers setting up shop for the day would swim out of the dark by the roadside in the Niva's weak headlamps. As we headed north, dawn broke over the reservoir fed by the Aragvi and guarded by the seven-teenth-century fortress of Ananuri. The cupola of the Ghvtismshobeli (Mother of God) church, a honey-coloured stone drum topped with a sheet-metal cone which rose up from inside the fort's crenellated walls, seemed to sing – the country's ancient, warm polyphony rendered in stone.

After Ananuri, the road steepened and worsened. Floods and landslides had taken great chunks out of the paved road, reducing it to the dirt track it once was. The trees thinned out and gave way to sparse, rocky green uplands which tapered up to cragged, grey peaks of jurassic lime, partially covered with a snow like flaking whitewash.

We would pull over on one of the switchbacks an hour before the Russian border to give the jeep a rest, next to an unpromis-ing, battered trailer with no wheels and whisps of smoke curling up out of a metal pipe on its flat roof. A large, wolf-like moun-tain dog slept next to the door. Inside, a Georgian couple pre-pared us a breakfast of bread and tender pork *shashlyk*. On one return journey from Chechnya in late autumn we rounded a corner to find the whole mountainside a sea of sheep. Three mountain dogs ran, leapt and barked, deeply happy in their responsibilities. Lord and master of this enormous flock was a leathery Pan in filthy tweeds. He embodied a tradition of trans-humance thousands of years old. We stopped and asked him where he was headed. He pointed southeast and said he was planning to sell the sheep in Armenia, a walk of several hundred miles.

Count Potemkin entered Tbilisi on the new 'highway' with two battalions and four artillery pieces on 3 November 1783, Irakli having already signed an act in July acknowledging himself a vassal of the Empress. John Baddeley wrote of Potemkin's entry into Tbilisi: 'The day was cold and gloomy, and the shivering Georgians remarked that their new friends had brought their climate with them; but they had brought something else it was thought, or at least hoped – permanent protection, that is, against the Tartar and Persian – and the sorely-tried inhabitants of Tiflis rejoiced accordingly. They were doomed, however, to bitter disappointment.'

Almost as soon as he got there, Count Potemkin was called back and Tbilisi was left undefended. In 1795 Agha Muhammed, the 'Persian eunuch', sacked the city, massacred many of its inhabitants and marched off with 20,000 slaves. His troops were said to have hamstrung the right leg of every woman they had raped.

Although Georgia was incorporated into the Russian Empire in 1800, Russian attitudes to the newly acquired territory differed little from those of its Moslem rivals. Russia saw in Georgia less a Christian ally than an exotic odalisque. The early nineteenth-century Russian writer Alexander Shishkov painted Georgia as a 'beautiful woman, lying luxuriantly on a multi-coloured carpet, her head resting on the snowy Caucasus as on a white pillow, while the fragrant roses of Gilan bloom at her feet!'

There is a telling postscript to Georgia's voluntary vassalage which goes to the heart of the country's hot-cold relations with Russia. General Tsitsianov, a Georgian by birth but by upbringing a Russian, was one of several Georgians in the tsar's service. Tsitsianov distinguished himself in the war with Poland, capturing Vilna in 1795, and was made Commander-in-Chief in Georgia in 1801. Baddeley wrote:

> As a Georgian, and the scion of a princely race, he had that country's best interests at heart; but, born and bred in Russia and serving the Tsar, he was in honour bound to devote his energies and abilities to the furtherance of Russia's aspirations, the attainment of Russia's political aims. To many Georgians it must have seemed, as we know it did to members of their royal house, that patriotism in this case must necessarily war with duty. But Tsitsianov held otherwise, and the impartial historian can neither

question his motives nor impeach his judgement. He found his unhappy country, untaught by the bitter past, still a prey to internal dissension, still, after the oppression of centuries and the recent horrors of the Agha Muhammad's incursion, at the mercy of Tartar, Turk, and Persian the moment the grey-coated Moscovite soldiers should turn their backs at the caprice of an autocratic master.

Giorgi XII's widow, Queen Marie, and her children thought differently and schemed frantically to hold on to the throne – against her husband's dying wish – determined not to hand her children's patrimony over to the northern tsar. The old king's brother had already run off to try and win over the Persian court to wrest Georgia back from Russia. The queen caused General Tsitsianov constant trouble with intrigues of her own. Tsitsianov ordered her arrest. The Russian general sent to carry out the arrest found Marie in bed, feigning illness and refusing to move. After argument ended in stalemate, the general left the queen's room to find more men to remove her by force. When he left the room, he heard a violent struggle and returning, found a son and daughter of the queen stabbing their *kinzhaly* (daggers) into a junior officer he had left behind. When the general rushed up to the queen's bed commanding her to call off her children, Marie pulled her own *kinzhal* from under her bedclothes and stabbed him in the side, wounding him fatally. Marie was arrested and marched to Russia as a common criminal, immured in a convent in Voronezh for seven years and then allowed a modicum of freedom as an exile in Moscow. She was buried with full royal honours in Tbilisi in 1850.

Her violent spite was given new life as the hold of Lenin's heirs over the empire, expropriated from the Romanovs, began to crumble. In April 1989 Soviet troops crushed a nationalist demonstration on Prospekt Rustaveli using trenching tools – nineteen Georgians, mostly students, were clubbed to death. President Gamsakhurdia – a Queen Marie – came to power on the surge of Georgian nationalist sentiment pent-up for two centuries. But his extreme nationalist pronouncements were a self-inflicted disaster given the country's multi-ethnic character. The son of a celebrated writer, a translator of English and French literature and a nationalist dissident in Soviet times, Gamsakhurdia's democratically elected presidency quickly became a dictatorship under his crazed leadership. Tellingly, he remained silent and refused to condemn the Communist old guard during the attempted Moscow coup in 1991, after which many of Georgia's new National Guard deserted him in disgust and formed a rival paramilitary group which ousted him in street battles during Christmas of that year. Gamsakhurdia fled and was granted political asylum in Chechnya.

Moscow's hand could be seen stirring the resulting separatist wars in Georgia's 'autonomous republics' of Abkhazia to the west of the country and South Ossetia in the centre. Georgia disintegrated into corrupt fiefdoms controlled by avaricious warlords who had broken into – or who had been handed the keys to – the Soviet arsenals still staffed by stranded, unpaid Russian troops. The price for a Kalashnikov rifle on the black market in Georgia at this time was about $250.

By 1994, Georgia's clichéd playground reputation of Kakhetian wine, kohl-eyed women and delicate song, preserved in thick, Soviet aspic by Intourist, was smashed by ethnic and civil strife. 'Georgia has woken up after 200 years,' Natelo told me later in the yard one day. 'Look what has happened . . .' she sighed. The anarchy suited Russia, determined to keep Georgia inside the imperial fold. Russian troops, alongside Cossack and Chechen irregulars, went into Abkhazia and helped the separatists push out Georgia's hopelessly divided and ill-equipped armed forces.

The Kremlin also kept up the pressure by rationing once plentiful gas and oil – the desired hard currency was only half the story. And while Russian troops departed from bases in Germany and the Warsaw Pact states, Moscow ordered thousands of once Soviet, now Russian troops to stay in Georgia, a move completely at odds with the country's new-found sovereignty. Portraits of nineteenth-century Russian generals, sporting chintzy epaulettes and broad sashes curved over their paunches, still decorated the officers' mess at the Russian army headquarters in Tbilisi. The Russian defence minister, General Pavel Grachev, was a constant visitor to Tbilisi, earning him the Georgian sobriquet of 'Russia's real foreign minister'. He had the same paunch, Napoleonic tufts of hair brushed forward and the pugnacious military countenance of his Tsarist forbear, General Alexey Yermolov. But he lacked his predecessor's cruel intelligence and came across like an overbearing Soviet traffic policeman. Gia Nodia, an owlish intellectual who ran a poorly funded think tank in Tbilisi, was depressingly frank: 'I think Georgia will only be semi-independent for some time, like Poland was in Soviet times.'

Russian conscripts would soon rue Georgia's collapse. The Abkhazian bid for independence fed the Chechens' own separatist claims inside Russia itself. Georgia's knock-down arms bazaar fed Chechnya's own weapons market. By December 1994, Moscow's last-ditch *divide et impera* had come full circle when these guns were turned on Russian troops invading Chechnya.

Eduard Shevardnadze was modern Georgia's Tsitsianov. For thirteen years he was the republic's all-powerful First Party Secretary under the Soviets. He was then Soviet foreign minister and Mikhail Gorbachev's grinning sidekick in the 'Gorbymania' days. In the chaos following Gamsakhurdia's fall, Shevardnadze was invited back by Gamsakhurdia's opponents, despite his tough Communist past, to rule his chaotic homeland in March 1992 (a pretender to the Georgian throne, Jorge Bagration de Mukhrani, an employee of Fiat and a part time racing-driver living in Marbella, declined a similar offer). He rarely smiled now. His struggle to keep Georgia together was forgotten. A Foreign Office official with a flat blond mane explained to me that Georgia was of no interest to Britain as it had nothing worth buying. I thought how Napoleon had chaffed about 'a nation of shopkeepers'. Germany, which felt some debt to Shevardnadze for reunification, gave him an armoured Mercedes after he was nearly blown to bits in an assassination attempt in 1995. Russia was suspected of having ordered the bombing through one of Shevardnadze's own subordinates, who had formerly been a colleague of Sergey's in the KGB. Sergey told me before I left to look him up: 'We still have a hotline straight to his office from Yasenevo.'

Shevardnadze's suits said it all: ill-fitting and crushed. Shevardnadze's writ did not run further than the doors to his fifth-floor office in the Georgian parliament, guarded by exhausted and nervous bodyguards (their US trainer had been shot dead in Georgia just before I arrived). Real power lay with men like Dzhaba Ioseliani, who in Soviet days had served eighteen years in a St Petersburg gaol for manslaughter and robbing a jewellery shop. Ioseliani, also a published poet, was now head of the Mkhedrioni, or 'Cavaliers', a paramilitary group which helped oust Gamsakhurdia in 1992. His forces were sent to Abkhazia to battle the separatists there but they stopped well short of the front and sacked Georgia's western town of Zugdidi instead. He sat one floor down in the parliament guarded by men in tight-fitting designer black, the dress code set by Mussolini for paramilitaries. They had drug-red eyes and fondled pump-action shotguns. Ioseliani's only display of nerves in his lazy, arrogant banter was to run his hands continuously through a string of semi-precious prayer beads.

Shevardnadze stepped out of the parliament building to walk down Prospekt Rustaveli on an April morning to mark the fifth anniversary of the 1989 Soviet crackdown. As a Politburo member at the time, he had played an unwitting part. A crowd of mourners wore black. Shevardnadze stood like a block of granite in a shabby woollen overcoat, strands of lichen silver hair blown up in the breeze on top of his pink scalp. After several near-death scrapes in Abkhazia the previous year, he looked exhausted. I barged my way up to him through the crowd on the avenue and demanded to know if he was in control of the country.

He fixed me with fjord-blue eyes, paused and said humbly: 'No, I cannot say that I am.'

He retreated. Prospekt Rustaveli was taken over by noisy pro-Gamsakhurdia demonstrators, one of them whirling a black, white and cherry-red Georgian flag in the manner of Italian jockeys before a *pàlio*. Someone threw a hand grenade into the editorial offices of a pro-Shevardnadze newspaper opposite the parliament the same afternoon. A stunned editor, in the room when the grenade went off, stood gibbering by the desk that had shielded and saved him. The blast left a strong, sweet smell of cordite.

To try and understand what was going on, I wandered into the offices, also on Prospekt Rustaveli, of Giorgi Chanturia, leader of Georgia's National Democratic Party. The party's support in a country with such ravaged communications and instability was difficult to measure but Chanturia was Shevardnadze's most outspoken and well-known critic. His business card showed a traditional Georgian wine cup embossed in silver on an oblong card, black and shiny as a gravestone. He had served time in prison under Gamsakhurdia for his party's moderate, democratic views. He now saw in Shevardnadze, whom he had helped back to Georgia, a weak servant of Russia. Chanturia dreamed of founding a state like the ones he saw when attending Christian Democratic party conferences in Western Europe.

'Empire is the only political progeny of the Russians and is as precious to them as democracy is to the Americans,' he told me in one of his short lectures. There was a note of hurried boredom in his voice at having to talk to someone so ill-informed. 'The naivety of the west, the low political culture of the captive nations, Russian chauvinism and the masterly activities of the Russian secret services made the preservation of the Russian empire inevitable. Many of our politicians lack knowledge of Russia. Outward changes in Russian policy we once considered as radical changes are nothing of the sort.'

We sipped grainy, tepid Turkish coffee.

'The failure of Rutskoy and Khasbulatov (respectively the nationalist and left-wing leaders who defended the Russian parliament against Yeltsin in 1993) did not mean an end of empire but an end of ideology. Yeltsin is free of Marxism-Leninism and strengthened with western credits but he is still an imperialist – an imperialist with a human face. The head of state [Shevardnadze] and our nation haven't much time. A social explosion could put the state and even our nation's very existence in question.'

Shevardnadze had a real opponent in Chanturia. Nicknamed the 'silver fox', Shevardnadze had cunning but he was a man of the past. His international credibility would last him only so long. Chanturia was young, his vision of a democratic Georgia fresh. As if to underline the shortage of time, which seemed in plentiful supply everywhere else in Tbilisi, Chanturia nodded to indicate the interview was over. He had turned to his computer screen before I had left the room.

In December of that year, I saw his body laid out at party headquarters. His nose was pinched and grey above his soft black beard. The room was bordered in black-clad women who rocked back and forth, dabbing their red eyes with white handkerchiefs. He had been gunned down outside his home. Irena Sarishvili, his wife and who later replaced him as leader of the party, was with him and carried a Kalashnikov bullet millimetres from her heart. I visited her a few weeks later, climbing several flights of stairs as there was no electricity to power the lifts. After laughing away her own wounds with jokes about setting off airport metal detectors, her face, porcelain from weakness, quickly refocused in hatred and fear. In her eyes, Shevardnadze was the prime suspect behind her husband's killing. She sat up in bed, a black shawl around her thin shoulders emphasizing the January chill, a Queen Marie of sorts whom somebody wanted out of the way. Chanturia's ideas had many enemies. Too many people profited from the lawlessness.

I confronted Shevardnadze the same day with Sarishvili's suggestions. He had refused repeated requests for an interview up until that afternoon, when it was mysteriously granted. The same fjord-blue eyes focused in an intense Arctic glare. 'People say I am responsible for many things,' he said.

# The de-electrification of the Georgian Republic

'He abandons me here, and the Lord knows why . . .'

Princess Lisa in Tolstoy's *War and Peace*

VASILY AND YELENA took me off for a long Sunday lunch with friends who lived in Georgia's ancient capital of Mtskheta, about fifteen miles north of Tbilisi. Despite the hardships of those times, the table was full: fried aubergine with pomegranate; bunches of herbs and spring onions to crunch on; soft white cheese; fried potatoes; pork fat; *khachapuri*, a fried cake of dough with melted cheese inside; *lobio*, a hot stew of mashed red beans; *khinkali*, spicy meat dumplings; little pots of *tkhemali*, a sour plum sauce; and jug after jug of cloudy white wine made from the vines coming back to life on the trellis above the cold spring table. The cloudiness comes from the stalks which are thrown into *kvevri*, amphorae, along with the grapes.

Miriam, the husband and head of the household, was the *tamada*, or toastmaster, an ancient tradition in Georgia and after a few months of living there, the bane of my existence. A succession of toasts drunk to Georgia, peace, women, children, the family and increasingly complex combinations of all the above were delivered in florid rhetoric before the final *Gaumarjos!*, 'Health!', when a whole glass of wine was downed in one go. I sometimes had to get up half-way through a meal and find a place to lie down to fight off the vomit-inducing 'spins' I last experienced as a student. To have refused to drink would have been to cause serious offence. But this lunch, in cool spring sunshine, was special and – by Georgian standards – relatively sober. The wine and talk of family made me sentimental. The lunch was rounded off with gritty coffee, sweet pastries called *khada* and a series of Georgian songs sung in three-part harmony over the top of a tinny piano on the bare floorboards in the farmhouse living-room afterwards.

To sober up, Yelena and Vasily took me to the centre of the town to see the Sveti-Tskhoveli Cathedral, 'The Church of the Life-Giving Pillar'. Its biscuit-coloured walls were built in the eleventh century on the site of a church constructed earlier, around AD 330. Sveti-Tskhoveli is the holiest church in Georgia but the modest three-aisled basilica is smaller than most British wool churches. The Georgians say Elias, a Jew from Mtskheta, was in Jerusalem when Jesus was crucified. A Roman soldier sold him Jesus's robe. When Elias took it back to Georgia, his sister Sidonia died instantly on touching the cloth, overcome by such a sacred object, her grief compounded by the death of her mother who herself fell dead on hearing – all the way from Mtskheta – the nails being hammered into Christ's wrists. Sidonia was buried with the robe – she would not let it slip from her grasp, even in death. On her grave grew a large cedar. In the fourth century, King Miriam chose Sidonia's grave as the place to build the church and had the tree cut down along with others to be made into columns to lay the church's foundations. One of the columns – the cedar tree – flew up and hovered in the air. It was brought down to earth again only with an all-night prayer session from St Nino of Cappadocia. From this possessed column, a liquid with strong curative powers was said to flow.

The church was adorned with sensual carvings of animals, bunches of grapes and saints. Most of the old frescoes inside have been destroyed by invaders. Tamerlane's men ripped the gold from the baptismal font in the fourteenth century. But one fresco has survived on the south transept depicting sailing ships, sea monsters, dragons, mermaids and a haunting creature with a leopard's body and the head of a young woman. A small stone church built inside is a copy of the Holy Sepulchre in Jerusalem, to underline Sveti-Tskhoveli's (self-proclaimed) rank as the world's second most holy place as the guardian of Christ's robe.

Inside there was a queue of nervous, giggling brides in shiny white satin dresses waiting to get married. They were upstaged by the grumpy-looking priest, with a long wire-wool beard, who officiated. A red silk cloak was thrown over his dirty black cassock. A sugary crown encrusted with semi-precious stones coloured a milky blue and pink was scrunched onto his head. Snakes of greasy hair escaped underneath. He jabbered through the ceremony as quickly as he could, grimacing as he walked around the bride and groom who continued to giggle. People walked about the church's plain stone interior and chatted. A small choir, half-hidden round the back of a pillar, sang what must have been the closest earthly representation of the music of the spheres. It was music that physically warmed you like whisky and made the hairs stand up on the back of your neck. The wedding guests were not to be cowed by the cathedral's 1,700-year history, refusing to walk about the ancient building with falsetto whispers and hesitant coughs. Here was a God that was an equal of his flock. I said as much to Vasily.

'We are close to our God, we understand each other,' he said.

Outside the church Vasily pointed to an iron chain hanging down from the top of the coned steeple and recounted a new version of the fall. The monks, he explained, used to have a chain running from the church up and over the River Aragvi to the wind-blown monastery of Dzhvari on the steep hill opposite. They would descend on the chain for mass. One day, halfway down the chain, a young monk spotted a young maiden swimming naked in the river below. Overcome, he lost his grip and fell to his death and the rig, Vasily said with a wink, was taken down.

Despite the violence and my hand-to-mouth existence with the agency, I wrote home to the family who were on a break from Moscow in England:

*Tbilisi*

Am writing a letter as virtually impossible to get an international line here unless aquainted with the international operators. Was at a party a couple of nights ago at the Reuter correspondent's house where they were practically the guests of honour – apparently around $60 a month guarantees you unlimited access to Georgia's *six* international lines. So will attempt to fax this via sat from the horrifically expensive Metechi Palace Hotel!

What a complete and totally utter change from Moscow this place is. Instead of row after row of dilapidated tower blocks dotted amidst the city's ubiquitous grey sludge, a Middle-Eastern style town with cobbled streets, small gardens with trellises for vines, ancient churches – I could go on – set among dramatic, rugged mountains. There's a possibility I might get the office of the departing *Liberation* correspondent, a wonderful room with a good tel. line in an old house complete with oriental-style balcony for $50 a month. It's not only the difference in appearance but the difference in attitudes; as the Georgians are proud of saying, 'We are a southern people', and – so far, touch wood – lack the awful, pompous and stifling bureaucratism of Moscow – my accreditation here was arranged in a couple of days flat . . .

The situation here is extremely unstable. On my first day I saw a bunch of youths giving chase to someone, all brandishing pistols. It's virtually impossible to go out after dark unless you have a car – the blackouts and gangsters make it too dangerous. I've heard shooting every night, although I believe most of the shots are fired into the air after a good few brandies. The economic problems are enormous – Vasily, a qualified surgeon, earns (officially) about 50 cents a month. The rouble is considered hard currency here. That said, fresh food is available at the central bazaar here – chicken, lamb, cheese, all sorts of fresh veg and fruit and – this is the best part – fantastic wine. The red wine here is good, but sweet, while the white wine is dry. It's v. difficult to describe but it's slightly cloudy, light and refreshing, reminding me a bit of the wine we drank in Santiago de Compostela . . .

. . . Am not going to make any great decision yet about work – much will depend on whether AFP think I'm any good . . . Vasily and Yelena think you all look beautiful, and many toasts were drunk to your health today. I've asked a lot of people whether it would be safe for you to come here – the water is cleaner, the air better, Italian-style weather, better food, and a sizeable town *house* for about $500 a month are all good – but it would be a bit of an adventure – no hot water, power cuts, etc (although sturdy Japanese-made kerosene stoves can be found in the market while I noticed the Reuters man's house has a wonderful open fire-place). But I know another move would be unsettling for the kids and that anything could happen here . . .

To this day I am haunted by my total lack of responsibility in dragging the family south. The arrival of some of the international aid agencies meant Rachel, who was trained in public health, quickly became the family's main breadwinner. But as she soon found out, healthcare was virtually non-existent in Georgia. I had no insurance. If anything serious had happened to the boys, I should have been completely reliant on the goodwill of the International Red Cross, who kept a light aircraft at the airport, to fly them out. Guns and poverty had put Georgian society into a tailspin. Spring and summer in 1994 would give way to Georgia's worst winter yet. We were conspicuous, no matter that we lived with the same hardships as everyone else. But I felt in the Caucasus for the first time unexplainably free, as if all the fears and responsibilities of the past had shrunk in size like a visit years later to a childhood classroom.

I bagged the office for $50 a month, a room in an old town house shared with two other journalists with large windows and a curved iron balcony painted a chipped viridian that gave out onto the Narikala fortress. The address: No. 4, Lermontov Street. After the gastronomic deprivations of Moscow, the fresh cheese, tomatoes, herbs and bread brought across at lunchtime by an elderly woman living next door – I paid her a small retainer to shop and cook – were indescribably delicious.

I returned to Moscow to help the family pack. Sergey clucked and fussed and insisted on squeezing us and all our bags – including the high-chair – into his Lada Zhiguli to escort us to Moscow's Vnukovo airport, the empire's gateway to the south. We argued with the Russian customs officers, jostled with anxious passengers and bribed the baggage-handlers to ensure our possessions were stored in the hold.

Sergey was appalled at my decision to move to Tbilisi. 'You'll be kidnapped down the first side street. You have kids – there is no water, no electricity, there's shooting all the time. All the big stories happen here. Stay here.' He set my head spinning once more with nagging doubts. But after Tbilisi, Moscow seemed as flat as a Potemkin village.

Sergey and I shook hands. He looked at me as if I were joining some dubious cult. Before pushing through to Departures I caught his eye briefly. His glance was unsettled, as if he wanted to tell me something but could not. I knew he had been to a heart specialist in London, arranged by the newsletter's editor. The doctor had lectured him at length about his nicotine and caffeine addictions. He ignored the warnings, continued to smoke and to sip his bitter black instant coffee, and occasionally boiled up some pale frankfurters for sustenance.

He was one of a gifted generation left stranded by the changes. To grasp what was going on and stay decent was emotionally and physically exhausting. He laughed at the inconsistencies of Communism and the Kremlin theatricals that followed its fall but he was inordinately proud of his Russianness. I would later see the same among the Russian officers dealt a losing hand in Chechnya. Sergey was too old to adapt but had the years strung out ahead of him like telegraph poles down an empty prairie road. He called a couple of times when I was in Tbilisi to say he had read some of my stories, and that I was known (Russian radio and television stations often picked up what foreign journalists wrote, at times reading out entire reports verbatim). The telephone in the Tbilisi flat would ring in longer bursts to indicate a long-distance call. His voice, across the seashell hiss, was far away. Thoroughly engrossed in the Caucasus, I did not think to call him back and ask him how he was. His trainee was too busy growing up. I received a telephone call in Tbilisi a few months later while doing the washing up. Sergey was dead.

Noisy families and short men urgently hissing 'Taxi! taxi!' crowded a metal pen where we waited for our bags. The sky was black and chill despite the onset of summer. It was two in the morning. We had waited on the tarmac in Moscow in a hot, airless Tupolev 154 for eight hours, Sasha and Matt squirming on our laps, while the air crew haggled and cut deals to ensure a full aircraft before flying south to Tbilisi. The other passengers came well prepared and began laying out picnics of bread, cheese, chicken and Georgian wine on crumpled copies of *Izvestiya*. The stewardesses, with hard faces heavily made up like the grey boiled eggs spread with congealed caviar in the airport restaurant, ignored all pleas for information as to when – or if – we were going to take off.

A friendly face focused itself in the crowd and the driver I had arranged to meet us beckoned to an elderly Volga sedan with a roofrack. The children slept on the soft back seats while we strapped luggage to the roof. We drove for five minutes before the driver pulled over on a deserted stretch of highway. I only relaxed when I saw a man walking over to the car out of the dark with a jerrycan. The driver bought just enough petrol to get us into town.

We pulled up at no. 10 Kakabadze Street (named after the modern Georgian painter), near the parliament, a little way up the hill of Mtatsminda. The driver only remembered the street I was talking about when I called it by its Soviet name, Moskovskaya ulitsa. We carried the children in through a small gateway into a compact courtyard, surrounded by three floors of wood and glass-fronted balconies, a bit like an Elizabethan theatre, with a walnut tree shading a wooden bench and a table forming a sort of stage in the middle. Worn iron steps, which buckled underfoot, led to the upper floors.

The dark green door onto the yard led into a small kitchen with a bathroom tucked down a narrow corridor out of sight. A heavy iron door which gave onto a staircase and out onto the street was bolted shut and hardly ever used. Through the kitchen was a large L-shaped room, with a neat parqueted floor, a high ceiling, a springy sofa, a low cupboard carved in Turkish fashion and a heavy, glass-topped dining table. In the walled-in blank of the L was a dark, windowless bedroom. Through the dining/sitting-room was a light room at the front with windows that looked out onto the sloping street. Along with a small box-room next to it, this was where I planned the boys should sleep and play.

Avrora, the owner, waited for us in the courtyard. She was tall, with jet black hair, doughy arms and a powdered face, and carried her prominent bosom under a long tent dress. She spoke in a booming voice. She had been named after the battleship which fired the blank round signalling the start of the October Revolution. After a saccharine greeting from her, I started for the bedroom where I planned to put the children to sleep. Avrora sailed close behind and expressed surprise as I prepared to put Sasha in the bed. 'I thought this was going to be my room,' she said, feigning suprise and hurt. 'Where will I go?'

The rent I was paying in *baksi* was a significant sum. I had rented the flat on the understanding that my family and I would be the sole occupants. I told her, politely but firmly, that she had to find somewhere else to live. But when we woke the next day, Avrora was anchored in the courtyard, talking excitedly to the neighbours, waiting for me. 'You will need someone to look after the children,' she barked. 'I don't want simply anyone coming into *my* flat. So I will look after them. It will be an extra $250 a month.' She stood over us, her brown eyes sparking defiance, daring Rachel and me to disagree. We were newcomers to the subtle blend of emotional blackmail and veiled threat used by tough, wheedling landladies across the former Soviet Union. We should have made to walk away in the dance of the bazaar. We compromised instead and hired her niece to look after the children. She was pleasant enough but she took no interest in them. So after the first month, with the stealth of the wiliest diplomats, we ejected Avrora from the flat.

The potholed courtyard was the centre of our lives for the next two years. Kids bounced and clanged up and down the paper-thin iron staircases. Our closest neighbour, Nunu, sat on the bench in the summer, grinding coffee in a small brass cylinder, unchanged from Ottoman times. She earned a pittance at the education ministry. Her husband, Gogi, was a dynamo of crazy business ideas which were always short of money. Their nine-year-old daughter Nino was the oldest child in the yard. She beamed constantly, teased Sasha and Matt and would hang upside-down from the iron bars on our kitchen window like a bat.

Nunu's mother, Natelo, was the *begum* of the courtyard. Hers was a gentle, firm and never spiteful authority. She would carefully steer Avrora away from me when she cruised into the courtyard to collect the rent. A widow, she always wore black. Her thick hands were criss-crossed with cuts and scars and chafed by half a century of washing and peeling vegetables. She wore a scarf, a Moslem in disguise, over a head of thick, curly white hair. Her blue eyes, darting around constantly to track an errant child or a thieving cat, were as keen as a hawk's. Natelo took on the task of looking after the boys when Rachel left for work at the aid agency and I left for my 'bureau'. She taught Sasha, now just three, and Matt, a year old, to speak faultless Georgian (it was Matt's first language), talking to them in a constant sing-song voice, accented with the odd staccato burst of anger when either of them was out of line. At the breakfast table in the kitchen, munching on bread and jam, Natelo and the boys would speak Georgian, I would exchange a few words with Sasha and Matt in English and discuss the plans for the day with Natelo in Russian.

Natelo quietly despaired when I dressed the boys for nursery school as I had no patience to find matching socks, which probably reflected badly on her when they kicked off their shoes in the classroom. Holding their hands, talking to first one, then the other, she would walk them down the street to a small flat with high windows and bare wooden floorboards. Many of the state schools were closed as there was no money to pay the teachers or heat the classrooms. The boys learned Georgian songs plinked out on an ageing piano, played games and listened to stories. In winter they huddled round a single kerosene stove in thick leather jerkins, lined with oily sheep's wool that smelt of mutton, which I had bought from an Ingush man from the boot of his car near a Russian military checkpoint on my way back from Chechnya. Whatever the material shortages, the kindly women who ran the nursery were a far cry from the fat lady Bolsheviks that Sasha had encountered in Moscow. Sasha no longer cried when he left the flat for the morning.

Food was never a problem as we were lucky enough to have money to pay for it. The stalls in the large, echoing hall that served as the food market were full, even in winter: fresh fruit and vegetables, nuts, meat, sacks of spices, cheese, honey and a dubious array of roots and herbs to boil up as bitter, medicinal teas. We bought bread from a nearby bakery where *puri*, long strands of dough, were thrown onto the sides of a hot, clay cylindrical wall to bake. A Georgian in rough country clothes would cart a beaten-up leather shopping cart into the courtyard and bawl at the top of his voice, '*Mazoni! Mazoni!*', a creamy yoghurt with a tart aftertaste. He refused to sell you any if you had no empty glass jar to swap it for the one the yoghurt came in. Later in the autumn, Rachel and Natelo cleaned jars and boiled great pans of fruit and sugar to bottle supplies for the winter.

When there was no electricity, which was much of the time, the flat was lit with candles and hurricane lamps which burned stolen jet fuel sold near the airport. While queueing up to mount the stairs for a flight to Moscow, I once watched a mechanic in oil-stained overalls walk up to the wing of the plane, unscrew a small bolt and bleed the aircraft of a few litres of kerosene into a filthy metal paint can. The passengers in the queue remained stony-silent. If the electricity came on at home, there would be a spontaneous and happy cry up and down the courtyard of '*Shuki!*', the Georgian word for 'power', and everyone would rush to turn on a television set, a boiler or a stove. There was a theory that if you rented a flat on the same grid as a hospital or a government building, electricity was no longer a problem. The

Reuters correspondent had paid for a thick black cable to be hung across Rustaveli Avenue to siphon power from the PTT building to supply his office but even then he had to keep a back-up generator on the roof in reserve. I knew of nowhere with constant power. After my pleading and pleading, the agency agreed to buy a small generator with enough power to run a computer and a couple of lamps. It would cut out if I tried to boil water for coffee. Often away, I kept the generator at home instead of the office so the kids around the courtyard could watch *Zorro* outwitting the fat Sergeant Garcia before they went to sleep. But it buzzed and spluttered like a noisy lawnmower so we used it rarely for fear of souring relations with our neighbours.

When there was water in the taps, we filled buckets, a large plastic dustbin and the bath with enough water to wash, flush the lavatory and cook for a few days. Before finding an electric boiler which warmed about 80 litres of water whenever the electricity was turned on, we heated water on a stove fashioned from scrap metal that I had bought for five dollars from a thin, elderly Armenian in Stepanakert, capital of the self-styled independent republic of Nagorno-Karabakh. A metal pipe came with the stove to take the smoke up a chimney – or as in many Soviet-era flats, through a hole cut in the living-room window, lined with a small amount of heat-proof putty. The children were still small enough to splash about in a plastic tub of hot water in front of the fire. A laager of chairs draped with sheets encircled the fireplace to keep out the draught. They would jump out onto a purple Daghestani *kelim* to dry off. All we could manage was a quick, luke-warm sponging down in the same plastic tub after throwing off several layers of clothes that we had worn for a week, especially in winter when clothes took longer to dry in the damp air.

Below the Narikala fortress, the hammam, or Turkish baths, were much in demand by the townspeople now starved of hot water. The prospect of a long, hot soak with gallons of deliciously warm water to thaw out our cold bodies drew us there one winter's day. On the way to the changing room, Sasha spotted a large rat. I ordered everyone out. The family were cross with me, disappointed that my squeamishness had stopped their long, hot wallow.

The cold was ennervating and mercilessly stalked the old. I had never seen death so regularly and so close up before but after a few months in Tbilisi, I barely glanced at the open trucks carrying a body strewn with a few flowers at the front of a slow-moving funeral procession, the mourners walking behind. Vera, an elderly Russian-Armenian woman, lived in a tiny, bare flat across the courtyard from us. Chicken wire covered her windows. A stained sheet was drawn across at night as a curtain. She was bent with arthritis and suffered from dementia. Her unkempt grey hair and her toothless anger, a mad Madam Mim, scared the children. Natelo would scold her for slopping out her urine into the middle of the courtyard. Vera's daughter would slink into the yard with a parcel of food. Natelo would pounce on her like a cat. 'Shame on you!' Natelo scolded the daughter. 'Your mother should live with *you*! She can't be on her own and we can't look after her!' A musical, angry chorus picked up Natelo's refrain and poured out of the windows around the courtyard. The daughter tidied up the flat a little, left the food and bolted as soon as the disapproving voices in the courtyard had died down.

Magli, another elderly woman on her own, lived in a similarly austere flat next to ours. A photograph of her dead husband, a young man in uniform placed on a scratched kitchen table, was all she had by way of decoration. She wore a faded black robe like a nun and wrapped herself in woolly shawls in winter. Her own dementia was sunny, not angry like Vera's. Magli had few visitors so it was Natelo and the rest of the courtyard who quietly kept her alive by bringing her plates of food. It was difficult to keep eye contact with Magli when talking to her as her grey, tangled hair was alive with a thick infestation of lice.

My constant worry in the courtyard was of fire. The city's precarious and dangerous heating arrangements consisted of leaky gas cylinders, overloaded electrical connections, kerosene lamps and stoves made of paper-thin metal and were often tended by people like Vera or Magli. I bought a smoke alarm on one of our trips back to Britain.

Despite their extraordinary capacity to make do and survive, the cold and the poverty of a war economy were a shock to the once recently well-to-do Georgians. They had enjoyed one of the highest standards of living in the former Soviet Union. Sergey's mouth watered at the food and wine Vasily, when a medical student, had brought up to Moscow. Now, if I wanted a hot cup of coffee in the morning, I had to chop wood for the stove. I had rented the flat for its pretty, open fireplace, but an open fire was too wasteful of precious heat, hence the ugly iron box put in its place.

A stream, commaed by a waterfall, bubbled down through the middle of Tbilisi's sloping Vake Park, about ten minutes' walk from the flat. It was a place of hushed green and of grandmothers steering grandchildren from the city's smart Vake district on morning constitutionals. One winter morning I met a fifty-year-old teacher playing truant to gather fallen branches from the sides of a gravelled path. She stuffed the branches into a shopping cart, struggling under a heavy coat to snap the greener ones. 'If my husband knew about this, he'd kill me.' Her hands were prematurely cracked and calloused. Her face had the pale, wan look the city's inhabitants carried as they shivered through winter in their unheated apartments. 'We built all of this with our own hands.' She looked about the park, a feeling of emptiness compounded by the bare trees and a cold, muddy sky. 'Now we're cutting it all down with our own hands.'

# A *is for Abkhazia*

We always were English, and always will be English, and
it's just because we're English we're sticking out for our
right to be Burgundians!

*Passport to Pimlico,* 1949

I TRAVELLED BY bus and by Lada Zhiguli to get the lie of the
land as Sergey had taught me. I was filing expenses of $10–20
a day – dirt cheap – so the agency did not complain about my
wild succession of datelines, hopping back and forth across the
snow-capped mountains like a flea in crumpled bedsheets.

One of my first reporting trips in the Caucasus was to witness
the arrival of Russian 'peacekeeping' troops in Abkhazia. This
subtropical territory, less than half the size of Wales, has a sizeable
mandarin harvest. Lulls in fighting during Abkhazia's war to
break from Georgia in 1992–93 were attributed to both sides
stopping to bring the fruit in. The air smelled of lemons and of
woody tea. Small abandoned bushes were now chewed by goats
in the old Soviet tea plantations. Dark, forested mountains swept
down to the glass waters of the Black Sea which sluiced gently
up and down on the stone beaches of the provincial capital,
Sukhumi. The United Nations was not prepared to field the
peacekeeping force Georgia had asked for (in the hope of maintaining some semblance of its tattered sovereignty). Russia deftly
volunteered its own troops which, ignoring UN protocol,
painted eggshell-blue bands round their helmets and called
themselves 'peacekeepers'. They were not an impartial force. It
was Russian troops that had tipped the balance in favour of the
Abkhaz separatists in the first place.

The Abkhazians recount a legend that when their leader turned up late to receive land that God was parcelling out to various tribes, God had nothing left. The Abkhazian leader put down his lack of punctuality to guests he could not abandon without showing them the requisite hospitality. Much impressed, God is supposed to have then handed over the land He had saved for Himself. Sukhumi was once an Imperial and then a Soviet resort over which, thanks to the height of the North Caucasus range, the shadow of Communism was said never to have fallen. Nevertheless, Stalin had a dacha a few kilometres up the coast in Novy Afon, where Nikita Khruschhev claimed to have heard him mumbling to himself in the garden: 'I trust no one, not even myself.'

Mandelstam described the town in the 1930s as 'a city of mourning, tobacco, and fragrant vegetable oils. This is the place to begin studying the alphabet of the Caucasus: every word begins with an *a*.' The Caucasus correspondents would tease the proud staff in Abkhazia's 'Ministry of Foreign Affairs' by simply adding the letter *a* to a Russian word and pronounce themselves fluent in Abkhaz. The word for restaurant was indeed '*a*restoran' and nine-tenths of an Abkhaz dictionary really *is* devoted to words beginning with *a*. Mandelstam described the sound of the language as being as if it had been 'torn out of a larynx overgrown with hair' (also an accurate description of the Chechens' Vainakh tongue).

Shevardnadze was nearly killed in shelling when he personally took command of Georgian 'government' troops to try and retake Sukhumi in 1993. His scrappy, ill-equipped forces, the self-serving bandits of the Mkhedrioni and other freebooters, were no match for the Abkhaz fighters, their Chechen and Cossack allies and the not so covert help provided by the Russian military. Georgian reinforcements brought in by passenger jets were easy targets, the planes lucky enough to land leaking kerosene from wings sieved by machinegun fire.

When I turned up in the summer of 1994, buildings on the palm-lined seafront were blackened and roofless. Weeds and bushes grew inside many of the houses. Thousands of monkeys from the Soviet Academy of Sciences' experimental breeding centre had escaped, a few surviving in the forested foothills near the town and captured occasionally for export to the pet markets of Istanbul. Wandering around the empty villages in Abkhazia, you bumped into armed Cossacks – blond, hard-faced and with rifles over their shoulders – who still found plenty to loot from houses and garages months after a 'ceasefire' had been agreed in the spring.

The three battalions of Russian paratroopers did not patrol the predominantly Georgian villages on the western side of the River Inguri, which had been ethnically cleansed by looting Cossacks, Abkhaz and a group of Chechens under the command of one Shamil Basayev. Georgian refugees wanting to return to their homes got no protection. Instead, they reinforced what was in reality Georgia's new border, with Abkhazia sliced off Georgia's northwestern tip by the waters of the Inguri.

Abkhazia, like all territories in the Caucasus, was granted a bogus autonomy in Soviet times as part of Stalin's malicious geographical equations which entrapped the region in a permanent feud. The cheque written out for sovereignty by the Bolsheviks was always meant to bounce. The Abkhaz were doubly aggrieved. Half the Abkhaz population is thought to have emigrated to the Ottoman Empire when Russia annexed the territory in 1864, along with 600,000 Cherkess, or Circassians, who were forcibly deported to Turkey. Their number of 100,000 was further diluted by the flood of Georgians sent into the territory by the Soviets to skew population figures. The Russian 'peacekeepers' deployed in 1994 were simply a means of continuing Moscow's centuries-old policy of divide and rule. Georgia, and her rebellious Abkhaz subjects, were once more caught in Moscow's web, the Kremlin starting to refasten its grip – momentarily lost – on a strategically vital region sitting next to billions of barrels of oil under the Caspian Sea.

The Georgian president faced Lenin's and Yeltsin's sovereignty problem in miniature.

At the Abkhaz 'border', there was an annoying performance with a couple of armed thugs who passed themselves off as

Abkhaz border guards. Green and white striped Abkhaz flags, like mint humbugs, were sewn to the shoulders of their baggy combat jackets.

Beforehand I had rung a Moscow number to call Otar Kakalia, the Abkhaz 'foreign ministry' press secretary, to tell him I was coming. 'Do you have a visa?' he asked over a terrible line, a *spetsliniya*, or 'special line', routed in a giant zigzag to Sukhumi via Moscow.

'No!' I shouted. 'Can't I get one from you when I arrive?' Kakalia was non-committal but seemed to think it was all right. An Abkhaz representative in Moscow sometimes stamped passports at his flat. Abkhazia still boasts an honorary consul in London, a Yorkshireman who teaches at the School of Oriental and African Studies.

One of the guards on the border repeated the question.

'Do you have a visa to enter the *independent* republic of Abkhazia?' he snapped.

'No, of course not. But I'm expected by your foreign ministry and your president and you will have to explain everything to *them* if you turn me back,' I replied.

'No visa, no entry,' said the bearded troll, unimpressed, at the western end of the bridge spanning the Inguri. A few cows munched grass in the rich green meadows, strewn with mines, divided by the river below.

'They'll give me a visa in Sukhumi,' I said.

'It's *"Sukhum"*! *"Sukhum-i"* is the Georgian imperialists' name,' he spat. 'You can't go to *Sukhum*, you don't have a visa,' and so on for an interminable half-hour. Then, for the sake of appearances, the other guard cranked up a field telephone and shouted in larynx-ripping Abkhazian for a few seconds. 'You can cross,' he said in Russian. 'But get a visa in *Sukhum*,' he said sourly, 'or we won't let you back out.'

In a nearby village now virtually empty of Georgians I climbed into a minibus headed for Sukhumi. Its passengers were Abkhazians. One of them, in her fifties and wearing a black woollen dress and thick black tights in the subtropical heat, started a conversation with the other passengers about recent attacks. She blamed Georgian fighters. 'I'm ready for them, just let them stop us now,' she said, leering through the window at the thick scrub forest slipping past. She fished in her handbag and pulled out a Makarov automatic pistol. She twirled it about like Calamity Jane. 'I'm ready for them,' she said, acknowledging the hard nods of approval in the minibus which now seethed with hate for all things Georgian.

I rode in the minibus as it was impossible to take a car into Abkhazia with Georgian licence plates. As in Italy, all cars across the former Soviet Union had a series of letters – and more recently in Russia, a number – which told you in which region or city the vehicle was registered. A car with Tbilisi plates was an instant target inside Abkhazia. A colleague and I once took the plates off his jeep and stuck on a large 'PRESS' sign instead. We were stopped by Abkhaz irregulars who melted out of the bushes on a dusty side road fifteen minutes after crossing the river. They had Kalashnikovs strapped across their chests or hanging from their hands. We wound down our windows and forced a smile.

'Where are your number plates?' said one of them, looking the jeep up and down with the air of a sniffer dog after drugs. He turned to his comrades. 'This is a Georgian vehicle.'

'We're international journalists – I'm from the *B–B–C*,' said my colleague.

'Rubbish. This is a Georgian car. Out while we search it.' The Abkhaz irregular took about 30 seconds to find the plates, each sporting a cherry-red Georgian flag, stashed under one of the front seats. 'Ha! Georgian!' exclaimed one of the fighters in triumph. 'Back you go!'

That I lived in the Georgian Babylon of Tbilisi was more cause for complaint so I quickly adopted the fiction that I was actually based in Moscow but just happened to be in Tbilisi for a reporting trip – to rebuff the automatic question as to why I had not come across the River Psou from the Russian side on Abkhazia's western tip. They did not believe me. But they accepted it for form's sake.

I waited for my visa at the foreign ministry. Considering the paucity of Abkhazia's international relations, it took quite a long time. The would-be republic's visas, like its gaudy stamps (prized by collectors and unrecognized by the Swiss Postal Union that polices global philately), were recognized only by Moldova's own breakaway republic of Transdniestr, Georgia's other rebel republic of South Ossetia and Chechnya, none of which bordered the other. Kakalia picked up an ageing rubber stamp which had not seen ink for some time. He breathed heavily on the underside of the stamp and pressed, with meticulous care, an aquamarine circle onto the green, yellow and white visa stamp which read: 'Arespublika Apsni, VISA No. 04761, $10'. I asked Kakalia to bump it up to a multiple entry visa as a hedge against future red tape which he arranged without blinking for an extra $25 and more heavy breathing.

Kakalia, a slick young functionary with an eagle's nose, handed me leaflets on Abkhazian history and a lengthy explanation of the layout of the flag – green stripes for Islam and white ones for Christianity, 'an indication of the religious tolerance of Caucasian peoples'. The open palm in the top left hand corner is a symbol taken from Sukhumi's past as a fourteenth-century Genoese trading port, also frequented in previous eras by Greek and Roman ships.

The recent passions of the Abkhaz war appeared to blind the proud Abkhazians to their unwitting re-enactment of the 1949 Ealing comedy *Passport to Pimlico*. In the film a delayed bomb explosion reveals to the denizens of the south London borough an ancient document giving title of the land to the Duke of Burgundy. Fed up with the strictures of postwar rationing, the inhabitants of Pimlico, led by the grocer Arthur Pemberton (played by Stanley Holloway), declare themselves 'Burgundians' and keep their own laws: the pub stays open out of hours with the happy consent of the local bobby; the high street bank expropriates funds from head office and the dressmaker turns down clothing coupons. Barbed wire goes up, Whitehall lays siege until the sorry Burgundians, clutching new ration books, are readmitted to the United Kingdom – in a shower of rain. Far-fetched, perhaps, but the film's director, Henry Cornelius, based the tale on the Canadian government's decision in January

1943 temporarily to cede the suburb of Rockcliffe, Ottawa, to the Netherlands. This was done in order to enable Princess Juliana of the Netherlands to give birth to her third child, Princess Margriet, on 'Dutch' soil during the German occupation so as to ensure exclusively Dutch nationality to meet the country's laws of succession, although Princess Juliana ended up with four girls anyway.

The Abkhazians' willingness to fight for their independence from Georgia was unquestioned. But the Abkhazians' weaponry and fighting talk concealed a deep-seated insecurity over Abkhazia's dubious status. I was reliant on Kakalia for a telephone line to Moscow to file stories. The line was always of terrible quality and I had trouble dictating the dateline, 'Sukhum*i*', in a way that would not attract Kakalia's attention. 'It's *Sukhum*! Tell your editors it's *Sukhum*!' he shouted at me across his desk, hands on hips.

One of Kakalia's foreign office colleagues, after confidently painting a future for Abkhazia as 'a Monaco on the Black Sea', asked tentatively what the prospects were of finding a job in Germany. You could not blame the bureaucrat and hesitant patriot for wanting to leave. Russian border guards, not Abkhaz soldiers, checked passports at the River Psou and at Sukhumi's small port. Russia, now building up to a war with the Chechens, had put Abkhazia under a partial blockade in a fit of remorse at having encouraged separatism.

The only imported food on sale consisted of packets of grey macaroni and blue tins of meat stamped as food aid from the European Union. Russian border guards stopped cars from crossing the Psou. The airport was closed. The Russians allowed one tiny passenger boat from the Turkish port of Trabzon, the *Ritsa*, to chug in and tie up at a small concrete pier in Sukhumi once a week. The boat was Abkhazia's only link with the outside world. In the summer of 1995 Abkhazia's recently founded 'state' tourist company, Abkhaz Kurort, collapsed almost as soon as it tried to get off the ground when Russian border guards turned back 10,000 Russian tourists who had booked holidays.

Moscow had betrayed the Abkhaz. But they were still a useful stick with which to beat Georgia if that country got ideas above its station. The Abkhaz remained beholden to the Russian 'peacekeepers' for what was left of their sovereignty. Russian roubles formed the territory's currency. And Russian soldiers continued to arrive with their families to holiday in Sukhumi's elegant but empty sanitoria – those undamaged in the fighting – as if the sun had never set on the Soviet Union.

In Soviet times, the Party elite, the mines and military bases located in cold, inhospitable parts of the empire 'owned' sanitoria in warmer climes further south. The sanitoria in Sukhumi belonged to the empire's elite Rocket Forces, in charge of the nuclear arsenal. The Rocket Forces' area of responsibility might have shrunk but they were not about to relinquish control of their timeshare on the Black Sea. The sanitoria, sensible white-washed boxes set about with palm trees which looked out onto the sea, were surrounded by a tall iron fence. The main gate carried a large Russian flag and a strict notice to keep out. The sanatoria were deemed Russian territory and I needed my pass-port and a Russian foreign ministry press card to get inside. Megaphones on wooden poles, giant plastic foxgloves, relayed muzak to the sun-dazed soldiers playing handball on the beach. Dour matrons in starched white overcoats walked stiffly between the buildings or manned desks in the sanitorias' hallways, giving the place a touch of the asylum.

I went to see the duty officer in charge of handing out rooms. I found him in a sanatorium building past a sandbagged entrance and an armed sentry. He signed a chit, accepting only Russian roubles in payment. On the way to my room I stopped a Russian colonel in cut-offs, a military issue matelot vest and plastic sandals. His tan accentuated the pallor of his wife, a frail Siberian lily, uncertain in her light cotton dress. She kept casting about to make sure her two small sons were in eyeshot. 'There *is* a block-ade against Abkhazia,' said the colonel. 'But here conditions are optimal. It's quiet, peaceful, and secure.' They said they were planning an excursion the next day to a mountain lake.

I went to bed early. Occasional bursts of unexplained gunfire broke the monotonous, hot rasping of the cicadas.

As for the fate of millions of its own Russian nationals, the imperial foot soldiers left behind, the Kremlin cared little. Outside the Rocket Forces' Eden, elderly Russians moved across Sukhumi's weed-choked pavements like slow-moving turtles. They sold *papirosi*, cheap Russian cigarettes, to earn enough roubles to buy bread. They did not boast the extended family networks of the Abkhazians to feed them. 'We're hungry, there's no food and we haven't received our pensions for two years,' said sixty-five-year-old Raisa, one of the cigarette-sellers. Married to a Georgian, she refused to change back to her maiden name despite the trouble it brought her from the Abkhaz. 'Everywhere nationalism – they say I should change my name but why should I?' she asked defiantly. A couple of Abkhaz men glared at us. She wore black to mourn the death of her twenty-year-old daughter, killed fighting Georgian forces, on the Abkhazian side, in 1992.

# Letters of credit

*Journalist*: Excuse me, Mr President, what's the price on your head?
*Dudayev*: It started at around 5 million roubles and today it's up in the billions, and in greenbacks – a few million.

1992

BORIS YELTSIN, President of Russia, was sent the following missive on 29 October 1991 from one D. Dudayev in Grozny:

Esteemed Boris Nikolayevich!
With the aim of widening and strengthening our mutual links, deepening contacts and coordinating mutual relations in political, economic and social spheres, it has been decided to open in the city of Moscow a representative office of the Chechen Republic in the RSFSR [Russian Federation].

Comrade Sharip Takhayevich Yusupov has been appointed and accredited as the personal representative of the Chechen President.

I ask that you provide Comrade Yusupov with the utmost assistance on all questions related to the normal functioning of the Chechen Republic's representative office (in particular the granting of lodgings and a bank account).

I would like to take this opportunity to convey, esteemed President of the Russian Federation, my best wishes, hope and belief in the future development of bilateral relations for the well-being of our people and the Republic.

President of the Republic of Chechnya   D. DUDAYEV

The day before, Dzhokhar Dudayev had been elected president of Chechnya, a territory half the size of Holland with fertile plains ending in beech forest and rising to sharp, ice-covered peaks to the south, in a ballot Moscow had refused to recognize. Four days later, Dudayev signed a decree declaring the Chechen Republic of Ichkeria – 'Ichkeria' is the name of the Chechen highlands – a sovereign state. The representative office was never opened. As with Tatarstan, Yeltsin, like Lenin, refused to grant any divorces.

Events had made Yeltsin and Dudayev allies. In Grozny, the National Chechen Congress, which had elected Dudayev its chairman in November 1990, moved quickly to bring Chechens out on the streets to support Yeltsin against the Communist old guard's putsch in August the following year. The Congress, under the direction of the schoolteacher and leader of the small nationalist Vainakh Democratic Party, Zelimkhan Yandarbiyev, set up an operations centre in Grozny almost as soon as news of the putsch got out and issued a written appeal to the interior ministry troops based in the republic: 'Let us not be fooled again by a corrupt pro-Communist clique. The Executive Committee of the National Chechen Congress appeals to you personally to follow its instructions and to come to the defence of democracy in order to avoid bloodshed in our republic.'

As in much of the Soviet Union, Party bosses took their telephones off the hook or feigned illness. By sitting on the fence, they were swept aside in Chechnya in what quickly developed into an almost bloodless revolution. Dudayev sent in his 'National Guard' to take the pro-Communist town council in September and in the ensuing mêlée, the chief of the council, Vitaly Kutsenko, was killed after falling from a window. It is unclear whether he jumped or was pushed.

The Chechen historian Abdurakhman Avtorkhanov saw through Yeltsin's earlier promises of sovereignty immediately: 'When the Chechens took his words seriously and made known their wish to leave Russian structures and make their republic independent, the Yeltsin team reminded the Chechens and other peoples in Russia: the Russian Federation is one and indivisible.'

Now that he had all but won his battle with Gorbachev, Yeltsin, within days, had the Russian Federation's autonomous republics and regions declare that they wanted to remain inside Russia, the new oath of allegiance being carried in a communiqué put out by the official news agency TASS. But Tatarstan, Chechnya-Ingushetia as it still was (before the Ingush set up their own tiny republic a few months later, which was committed to remaining inside Russia) and four other republics refused to sign the communiqué.

Dudayev's proclamations and letters maddened the Kremlin. Russian Vice-President Alexander Rutskoy, who piloted fighter aircraft in Afghanistan, was sent to Grozny to remonstrate with Dudayev and the Congress leaders. He shaped all further debate in Moscow on Chechnya's future by declaring: 'This isn't a revolution, this is banditry.' Yeltsin declared a state of emergency in Chechnya. Back in Moscow, Rutskoy organized the dispatch by air of several hundred interior ministry troops to reimpose Moscow's authority. The attempt was a fiasco. Dudayev's National Guard surrounded the airport. Three days later the interior ministry troops got back into their military transports and flew out.

'The language of ultimatums is not the kind of language which is understood by such an explosive and proud people,' Avtorkhanov warned. After that, the Kremlin took little action except for a half-hearted economic blockade which hit only the vulnerable. The clique around Dudayev and Russian businessmen, among them the Mercedes-owning elite inside Russia's defence ministry, made money out of the embargo. Russian troops did not return until the invasion in December 1994.

I travelled to Grozny in July 1994 as the rest of the region was quiet, so quiet that the BBC correspondent and I paced the office we shared on Lermontov Street wondering if we would make enough to eat that month. A Georgian driver we sometimes hired underscored hard times by sitting in the corner of the office in a pose of such tortured dejection – he only got paid when we had work – that we had to ask him politely to wait outside in his car.

To get to Grozny, which without my own transport this time took about a day, I took a bus north to Vladikavkaz in North Ossetia over the Georgian Military Highway. Georgia was still ostensibly at war with the South Ossetians and, cursed with the wrong number plates, Georgian drivers did not like travelling to the town. I then climbed into a taxi driven by an Ossetian who took me as far as a Russian military checkpoint built in the middle of a crossroads on the Rostov-Baku highway to the east of the town. Its sandbags, camouflage netting, corrugated iron roofing, searchlights and machinegun emplacements retained the flavour of a nineteenth-century Cossack fortress. The Russian soldiers here also described themselves as 'peacekeepers'. The Ossetians and Ingush had fought a brief but bloody war over the disputed Prigorodny district, another of Stalin's geographical booby-traps, which was tripped in 1992. In 1993 the rude Afghan War veteran in charge of restoring order in the North Caucasus, Major-General Viktor Polyanychko, was killed in his car in a defile near Vladikavkaz. His assassins reportedly closed in on horseback.

The driver left me with a young conscript, sweating in a flak jacket, a great iron bib. He wrote down my press card number in a tatty logbook. He tut-tutted in disbelief when I told him I was headed for Grozny.

'They're killing each other there!'

Another region, another conflict on ice, another driver, all within less than an hour of each other. An Ingush man on the other side of the checkpoint was driving to Grozny so I hitched with him. I looked out eagerly for signs of Moscow's blockade against Chechnya. There was nothing. Not even a placard to say we had entered Chechnya. Only the Cyrillic letters *ChI* denoting the Soviet-era republic of Chechnya-Ingushetia on the numberplates told you where you were on the highway that rolled gently through low hills parched a tobacco brown. We were pulled over once by a couple of Chechens in uniform who claimed to be the 'ecological police', who made us pay a fine for using either a petrol- or diesel-driven vehicle. There was no alternative fuel. I noticed these bogus environmentalists had disappeared on subsequent visits.

In Grozny, a dowdy Soviet city of shabby tenements and curling Thirties stucco, of some 400,000 souls, Ladas with black tinted windows peeling at the corners and Mercedes limousines swam like lazy sharks up and down the dusty streets, occasionally jerking to a halt to talk to friends or aquaintances by the side of the road. Money-changers waved thick wads of roubles as if they were football rattles in front of the passing cars at the end of Victory Avenue. The business was not hidden as it was elsewhere in Russia. I made my way across Freedom Square to a large, imposing concrete block, the Presidential Palace. A few young men, unshaven, loitered in the square, squatting by the kerbsides. They looked up and down the street, absent-mindedly plucking sunflower seeds from paper cones and spitting out the black husks. Groups of bearded elders, grey lambskin *papakhas* set back on sweating foreheads, talked in groups. Women in gaudy print dresses and neat kerchiefs tied over their heads were the only people apparently headed in any particular direction – to the sprawling market a few hundred metres on from the Presidential Palace. No one seemed to be killing anyone.

At the doors to the Presidential Palace, more women in head-scarves were leaving for the day at two pm. The two guards on the door swaggered a little in front of the women as they flicked through my passport. The lifts did not work so I climbed the steps at the side of the building in search of the Chechen Press office, home to Dudayev's spokesman, on the fourth floor (it didn't print any news, official or otherwise). I walked in to find a bearded man in jeans and a combat jacket chatting on the telephone behind a desk with a long table drawn up to it to make the shape of a T. The bank of telephones to his left and the dreary metal cabinet to his right completed the classic furnishings of a middle-ranking Soviet bureaucrat. The man ended his conversation, put down the receiver and looked at me with distaste. He introduced himself as Movladi Udugov, the Chechen information minister. I drew myself up. I said my agency wanted an interview with Dzhokhar Dudayev (they had not asked for one) and would it be possible to see him that afternoon.

'The Chechen *President* is very busy right now,' he said, 'and I really don't know if he'll see you.' Udugov gave no lecture about Chechen independence. There were no visa or press accreditation forms to fill out as there were for the busy clerks in Sukhumi. He lifted his eyes and sighed with a mixture of boredom and exasperation as yet another journalist lectured him on how important it was that world opinion get to hear the Chechen *President*'s side of the story and not just Moscow's. 'Come back at six o'clock and we'll see,' he said, making to leave the room by stuffing a pistol into his belt.

'But my deadline's at four.'

'Six.' And he kicked me out of the office.

To kill time, I went to check the market to see how Moscow's economic blocade was biting. It didn't appear to be. It was as big as any market I had seen in the former Soviet Union. Long lines of stalls with claustrophobic paths set haphazardly between them were set out in rough department store order: piles of gaudy print dresses, the leather coats that nearly all Chechen men wore in winter, a section full of enamel pans and glass crockery and another selling televisions and stereos. The food section smelled of brine from buckets of bitter gherkins and cheese. Women also sold pails of *manti*, a kind of ruffled pasta stuffed with spiced meat, a dish probably picked up by Chechens in exile in Central Asia, where I have seen the same dish. There were bottles of vodka from Moscow and flat-packs of tinned beer brewed in Turkey.

Near the smoke from the *shashlyk* stands, which hissed as their attendants sprinkled water on the embers with priestly grace, was Grozny's arms bazaar. This was not obvious at first glance. There were no rows of Kalashnikov assault rifles or RPG7s (rocket-propelled grenades) laid out for inspection. Ruslan, a Chechen arms dealer in his teens who had taken me under his wing, explained that the Chechen justice minister had recently spoken on Chechen television vowing to crack down on illegal arms dealers.

'Which is something coming from the government — they're the biggest arms dealers of the lot. Their people come here and confiscate the weapons and then sell them off themselves.'

We walked over to his car nearby which was watched by his twelve-year-old brother. Ruslan pulled out a cloth bundle from between the front seats, unwrapped it and, careful to keep it below the level of the car windows, showed me a cut-down Kalashnikov for close-range fighting. It could be mine for $1,200. On the way out of the market he bumped into a friend carrying a smaller object in a handkerchief. He unwrapped it to reveal a small gambling pistol he had bought.

'Fifty dollars,' he said smiling, and added with a sly grin: 'I'm just off to get it registered.'

I left Ruslan, who extended me a warm invitation to go bear-hunting with Kalashnikovs in the nearby mountains.

Other people I spoke to – doctors and nurses at a local clinic, stallholders in the market – were disappointed with how little independence had brought them. The affluent-looking market survived through the *perekupshchiki*, shuttle traders. They flew all over the world from Grozny's main airport – Russian air traffic controllers turned a blind eye – buying up goods cheaply and selling them at the market back home. The air tickets cost little and the professional shoppers brought back hundreds of kilos of goods on charter flights specially set up for the trade. During the war you would often meet a peasant woman up in the hills slaving away in a kitchen who would relate her visits to quiet, stuffy shops in Vienna or the glitzy malls of Dubai. But their margins were small. Much of the population had trouble finding cash to pay for food, let alone CD-players. The blockade hurt state employees, who had difficulty working out exactly which state it was they were working for. Both the Russian and Chechen states took advantage of the confusion and did not put aside money to pay teachers and health workers. Most had not received a salary in over a year. The elderly could draw their pensions in the steppe town of Mineralnye Vody but the bus trip there and back of about twelve hours cost almost as much as the pension was worth. Dudayev's one economic policy, a Soviet-style subsidy to keep bread priced at a symbolic one rouble, failed.

Dudayev wrote to international figures and institutions asking for support. He was a regular pen-pal, sending letters and telegrams to world leaders – and even meeting them on occasion – to try and gain a gram of recognition. As in Tatarstan, Chechnya's fast-declining oil refining capacity and its dwindling oil reserves were the calling cards used to open doors. This 'from the government postbag of the Chechen Republic':

HIS EXCELLENCY
PRIME MINISTER OF LUXEMBOURG
MR JACQUES SANTER

13.08.92

The Government of the Chechen Republic:

1) Has the honour of bringing to your attention a request for a grant of a credit in the region of 25–30 million US dollars for a period of 6–8 months.
2) We pledge to spend this sum of money exclusively for the payment of salaries for the citizens of our country, a delay in payments of 4–5 months having occurred because of a lack of ready cash in the Russian Central Bank [sic].
3) We guarantee to return the credit with the delivery of petroleum products on favourable terms.

PRESIDENT          DZHOKHAR DUDAYEV

While it is not known whether M. Santer stepped in with the cash on this occasion, a few Chechens behind Dudayev made millions on petroleum deals. In a free economic zone in all but name, Russian businesses were perfectly willing to break the Moscow embargo to do business with the rebel republic. One group of Chechen fraudsters carried out what was thought to be the biggest bank heist in Russian history, making off with the equivalent of $700 million in roubles. Members of a Chechen gang turned up in banks around Moscow and cashed promissory notes issued by banks in Grozny. After the Moscow banks had issued the money, different members of the gang dropped by shortly afterwards posing as 'police detectives' from Grozny who confiscated the promissory notes as part of their 'investigation', ensuring no evidence of the fraud was ever found.

The real arms trading took place well out of sight of the *shashlyk* stands in the bazaar. The trade brought millions of dollars to the republic and shame to the Russian armed forces which colluded massively. In rare arrests made in January 1993, three Russian officers belonging to the Siberian Military District were caught trying to sell radio-controlled mines to arms traders reportedly from the Caucasus. The following month, Grachev announced on Red Army Day the court martial of 46 senior officers for corruption.

Not much of the money went to the republic's one million Chechens or its 300,000-strong minority of Russians. Much of it went into large new houses for the few, the gothic brick creations nicknamed '*vozdushnye*', or 'out of thin air'. Some trickled down to placate family and friends or sluiced into a new village mosque, like the oil expropriated in small amounts by freebooters who shot holes in the ageing pipeline network.

The Russians in Grozny, who had grown up with the oil industry since before the 1917 Revolution, left if they had money to do so or relatives outside who were willing to take them. As in Abkhazia, few of them had either. Stooped, lonely old women, who had survived the terror and hunger of the 1930s and the horror of the eastern front, made up the meagre congregation at the city's small Russian Orthodox Church of the Archangel Michael, a subdued waiting-room for death. The small church, with cream cornicing piped over raspberry walls and a cool, whitewashed interior, was a bright anomaly amid the concrete apartment blocks that lined Lenin Avenue just over the River Sunzha from the Presidential Palace. Opposite the church on one side of an apartment block was a large Soviet mural depicting a naive, Picasso dove in flight over the word *mir* – 'peace'. After a service that July, the priest, a tall man further elongated by his black soutane, did not want to talk about how the Russians 'staying on' were faring in independent Chechnya. We sat in the dark vestry after the service in awkward silence. I got up to leave.

'We don't want any trouble,' was all the priest volunteered. His eyes, liquid coals, said more.

By the summer of 1994, many Chechens, whatever their feelings towards Moscow, felt Dudayev had turned Chechnya into a parody of a state. Invitations for asylum handed out to East German leader Erich Honecker (declined) and the ex-president of Georgia, Zviad Gamsakhurdia (accepted), did not help, even if Gamsakhurdia thoughtfully issued a decree from his Chechen guesthouse recognizing Chechen sovereignty on behalf of the country he had just fled.

While much of the Chechen political opposition ranged against Dudayev was just as dubious, the ex-general greatly weakened his support by dissolving the parliament and declaring one-man rule. Chechnya's dashing and witty stand against Moscow in 1991 ran into the ground. The territory had become the epitome of a banana republic. Dudayev strutted for the local cameras in the glitzy tunic, polished belts and peaked cap of a cheap Latin American *caudillo*. The bodyguards ranged around him dressed and pouted like the pictures wrapped around the Arnold Schwarzenegger 'Terminator' bubblegum on sale by the boxful in the market. His writ still ran in many of the mountain *teips*, or clans, south of Grozny. But his authority was confused over the low summits of the Sunzha Range that rose north of the city. In three other towns inside Chechnya, rival warlords, with not so covert help from Moscow, had come forward to challenge Dudayev.

The Chechens' own palpable dissatisfaction with him, and their equally palpable anxiety about complaining out loud for fear of being overheard by the DGB, Dudayev's secret police, went entirely against the grain of a people who for centuries had seen each other as equals and had stood up to generals and dictators far more menacing than their current leader. The Chechens and Ingush, while distinct peoples, say they are Vainakhs, who speak a similar language and share many of the same traditions, including no history of feudal or class distinctions, unlike the Kabarda and Cherkess, or Circassian, princely castes to the west.

The traveller and historian Baddeley was told a cautionary tale by the Ingush in which the *gortsy*, mountaineers, get together to choose a prince to rule over them. The most notable mountaineer does not bother himself with the meeting and is, of course, chosen as prince. The notable turns down the first two appeals to rule over his fellow mountaineers but at the third request reluctantly agrees. He appears in a gorgeous silk *khalat*, or robe, belted with a donkey's girth. When the notable's new subjects object, saying that a donkey's girth goes ill with a silk *khalat*, their unambitious ruler replies: 'And so would a prince with the Ingush people!' Baddeley concludes: 'And indeed the Tchetchens and Ingooshee have ever been democratic to an extreme degree, ignoring class and rank though not merit.'

It was difficult to square Dudayev with a people who proclaimed to be 'equal and free like the wolves'.

At a quarter to six there was no sign of Udugov. I worried that I might have got the appointment wrong as Dudayev had moved the clocks forward to be one hour ahead of Moscow. Most Chechens, keeping to Moscow television schedules, ignored this. I was ushered up to the ninth floor an hour later. Dudayev looked shorter, greyer and older than in the photographs of him. I thought he must have put on kohl for the cameras but his eyes were grey with sleeplessness. He was unable to sleep until four or five in the morning and then would wake late. His moustache was clipped meticulously. In fact everything about him was meticulous: the words he chose, where he rested his hands, when he lifted them up and brought them gently crashing down to make a point. His grey suit trousers were cut to obscure a pair of Cuban heels. He smiled, shook my hand and waited to be seated while his sheepish personal cameraman set up the room for a television interview. The office was spacious, panelled but unremarkable save for a striking full-length portrait of Sheikh Mansur, the first to declare *ghazavat*, 'holy war', against Russian rule at the end of the eighteenth century. The Sheikh was depicted in a long white *cherkeska*, a Circassian tunic, a straight *kinzhal* at his belt and a curved sabre unsheathed in his left hand. The finishing touch for the interview was to place on a low table in front of him a modest sign embossed in Latin, not Cyrillic, script:

> *Jokhar Dudayev*
>
> *President*

The Chechen President said nothing new. Asked what he was doing to curb illegal arms sales, he pointed to the justice minister's 'crackdown'. On accusations that his was a 'mafia state', Dudayev tossed back his standard rejoinder: 'The mafia are in the Kremlin.' To some extent he was right. Dudayev on this occasion was uncharacteristically cautious, leaving the gate slightly open to anyone from the north who might be listening. But the interview left the questions most ordinary Chechens would have posed unanswered. Dudayev spoke in terms of a centuries-old vendetta which I did not understand at the time. The Chechens I talked to had their minds on the here and now, they wanted stability and prosperity. They thought Dudayev's posturings and pretensions as absurd as everybody else. If the Kremlin had bided its time, kept up the blockade, however imperfect, and let the general stew in his own juice, it is unlikely Dudayev would have lasted more than a year.

The interview also underscored the strange nature of Dudayev's 'dictatorship'. I was cross that my interview was filmed for propaganda purposes. But then my questions were quite tough and were broadcast unedited, unlike the staged press conferences in some of the Central Asian republics where only trusted journalists from the local official news organization got to ask questions with nauseating, toadying obedience. Although my interview did not produce any scoops – the editor on duty at the news agency sighed at having to put out such an uninspiring story so late in the day – it did show Dudayev open to question in his own land. Printed in his own collection of 'government documents, articles and interviews' were questions from a number of Russian reporters that any other president might find embarrassing. This exchange is from 1992:

*Journalist*: Not one state officially recognizes the Republic of Chechnya. This doesn't disturb you?
*Dudayev*: I'm completely calm, you're not mistaken. It wouldn't be worth having a complex over this. Especially not to panic . . .

In the late summer of 1994 I was scrambled from Grozny to Baku, capital of Azerbaijan, to cover a coup attempt in the former Soviet republic, the details of which need not concern us here. On the road at dawn, Chechen troops manned a roadblock on one side of Freedom Square, warming themselves by the oily flames of a burning tyre. This was new. One fighter, the short fat tube of a Mukha, or 'Fly', anti-tank rocket slung across his back, stopped me and asked for i.d. He waved me on sleepily. That summer and the hot autumn that followed, Chechnya was dotted with similar checkpoints, some claiming to support Dudayev, others various incarnations of the anti-Dudayev opposition. My BBC colleague and I were driving in northern Chechnya and crossed a short bridge with a checkpoint at each end of it. One side had a series of concrete blocks and a *shaitan*, the Afghans' name for the devil and the mujaheddin's nickname for the strange, squat-looking Russian gun that sprays out belt-loads of grenades. On the other, fighters in a mix of civilian and military clothing had assault rifles and a sandbag arrangement. Both sides looked relaxed.

'I wonder if they're different factions?' I asked my colleague, as we slowed into the first chicane on the bridge and flashed our press cards.

'Don't be ridiculous.'

I wound down the window quickly and asked those manning the first checkpoint who they answered to.

'*Za Dudayeva!*' they shouted.

Over the river, at the next checkpoint, about 30 yards away, we asked the same question.

'*Za oppozitsiyu!*'

My colleague turned the jeep round and drove back and forth over the bridge to knock off a quick radio feature.

Dudayev's grip on Chechnya was now measured in a war of checkpoints which were moved about the territory in a complicated game of chess played simultaneously against his diverse Chechen opponents. Beslan Gantemirov was the twenty-something policeman who helped form Dudayev's National Guard in 1991. Made mayor of Grozny until 1993, he withdrew to the town of Urus-Martan south of Grozny after breaking with Dudayev. He brought with him several hundred loyal 'troops' and a motley array of weapons, including an old truck-mounted rocket. Over the Sunzha Range, about an hour's drive northwest of Grozny, another ex-policeman, Umar Avturkhanov, held court in a two-storey administrative building with bare walls and cracked paint in the town of Znamenskoye. Both men lacked charisma and were completely without inspiration as to what a future Chechnya without Dudayev might look like. They had both been bought by the Kremlin. Avturkhanov's 'Provisional Council', a Russian puppet government, was pointedly paying out pensions and salaries with bundles of cash brought in by shady Russian advisers. They flew in and out of the town in helicopters and did not bother to change out of their Russian army uniforms. The mercenary character of the Provisional Council – Avturkhanov's sorry-looking troops got new Russian uniforms and a regular salary – was its principal weakness. Its forces, when told to attack Grozny later that year, crumbled in a matter of hours.

The Chechens living on the flat plains of the north had a more constrained history than those from the mountainous south, having for nearly three centuries shared the banks of the Terek with the Cossacks and a permanent Russian military presence. Lev Tolstoy, setting the scene on the Terek in his novella *The Cossacks*, wrote: 'On the right bank lie the villages of the pro-Russian but still somewhat restless Tartars; along the left, half a mile back from the river and five or six miles apart from one another, lie the Cossack villages.' They were by force of circumstance more willing to accommodate the *gaiour*, the infidel, but they were unnatural allies.

Confusing everything further was a third unlikely 'warlord', the economist and former speaker of the Russian parliament, Ruslan Khasbulatov. He had been recently released from Lefortovo Prison in Moscow for his part in the armed stand-off between parliament and president in 1993. He had set up headquarters in an identical two-storey administrative building to Avturkhanov's, this time in the village of Tolstoy-Yurt, only 10 kilometres north of Grozny. Elders in *papakhas* and younger supplicants streamed in and out of the building. Khasbulatov was genuinely popular when he first arrived, a Chechen who had made it in the outside world and who had stood up to Yeltsin. He looked like the economist and academic he had started out as, dressed in baggy corduroy trousers and puffing on a pipe as he sheafed through papers in an armchair.

'My mission here is a peacekeeping one,' he explained loftily.

'So why do you have a tank outside?'

'It's a peacekeeping tank,' he snapped.

Khasbulatov was as much a political enemy of Yeltsin as Dudayev, but in this instance, Yeltsin's enemy was his enemy and the slippery parliamentarian manoeuvred himself into alliance with Avturkhanov's Provisional Council. Khasbulatov's claim to the status of peaceful intermediary was further undermined by the company he kept. Ruslan Labazanov was a convicted murderer in his twenties and had been a member of Dudayev's bodyguard in the early days of the republic until the two had fallen out. A walking fantasy from the pages of *Guns and Ammo*, Labazanov confirmed all Russian clichés about the Chechens. Every part of his muscular body strained to carry some kind of weapon in a system of harnesses and webbing that must have taken some time to put on (if he ever took it off): a pistol in a chest holster; a dagger slung horizontally beneath it; another pistol on his waist; pouches of spare ammunition clips; and dinky little *limonki*, 'lemons', the Russian slang for grenades, pinned to his belt. He gestured with an AK47 assault rifle. In one of several minor and isolated skirmishes between Dudayev's fighters and opposition groups, Labazanov and his small band of armed followers were nonetheless quickly expelled from their base in the town of Argun, east of Grozny, by Dudayev's men early in 1994.

Labazanov had then shown up in Tolstoy-Yurt to lend Khasbulatov some muscle. Labazanov's acolytes were equally dressed to kill, with RPGs stacked in the back of Japanese four-wheel drives, identifiable by the gang sticker, 'Big Boss', on the tailgates as they bounced over the potholed roads at top speed, their gun barrels poking out of the windows. All who spent time with Labazanov came away with the feeling that they had spent the day with extras from a post-apocalypse action movie. The sounds of explosions, screams and gunfire would emanate from darkened rooms where his dead-eyed men passed the time watching bleary action videos. By the autumn, Labazanov, his eyes red-hot with what looked like drug use, would pause with only one line: '*Smert Dudayevu!*' 'Death to Dudayev!' He would then stomp off, seething with anger, waving aside any supplementary questions with a shake of his rifle. Here was proof positive of Chechnya's *banditizm*, only this one was indirectly employed by the Kremlin.

There were some strange scenes on the floating lines of checkpoint land. On one of the northern roads, for a diversion my BBC colleague and I pulled up and waved down an armoured personnel carrier to ask which side it was on. The APC was going at full tilt with fighters riding on top, their rifles pointed skywards like the spines on a hedgehog. To our amazement the machine suddenly lurched and then stopped dead in its tracks. '*Za oppozitsiyu!*' they cheered. The driver, his head poked out of the front like a frog's eye, ground the APC into gear and sped off again, its four pairs of rubber wheels humming and throwing up a great cloud of dust as the passengers on top waved their rifles in farewell.

A middle-aged Chechen woman who had been waiting at the roadside for a bus could not contain herself after the APC had vanished. '*Eto vsyo yerundà!*' – 'This is all nonsense!' she shouted testily. 'Under Brezhnev we had sausage on our shelves.' '*Ranshe bylo luchshe!*' she added in a refrain that was repeated the length and breadth of the former Soviet Union. 'It was better before!'

One evening in early autumn, on the crest of the hill between Grozny to the south and overlooking Tolstoy-Yurt to the north, I spotted a couple of self-propelled anti-aircraft guns parked a few hundred yards off the road. A few armed Chechens were lying in their shade, resting on their elbows and throwing an occasional glance through binoculars down at Khasbulatov's headquarters. Off a switchback on the road below lay the burned-out hulk of an armoured vehicle, the result of a scrape earlier that year. As the sun went down, a Czech-built reconnaissance aircraft – Dudayev had 'inherited' dozens of them when the Soviet Union collapsed – flew below the ridge and down towards the town's Khankala Airport. The Chechen fighters were still on my approach. A man in a T-shirt stretched over a powerful torso made a joke and the others laughed obediently. He had a face that gave orders but did not take them. The commander cracked open walnuts with a bayonet. He looked up from the ground where he sat and bid me join him with a mock bow and flourish. On my own, I was a little less cavalier with the questions.

'I was just wondering whose side you were on?'

There was a momentary silence as the commander paused and thought. He then replied with a tough, bearded smile of his own. 'We're opposition.' He looked behind him at the descending jet. 'And that's one of that creep Dudayev's planes.'

The opposition this close to Grozny? Dudayev was in real trouble. These fighters looked serious. This was a scoop! But the commander's guns were turned the wrong way.

'What do *you* think of Dudayev?' he asked me, catching my eye and holding it. I ummed and erred in the broadest of generalities, going back and forth for a chilly half-hour, as the commander flicked his bayonet through the pile of walnuts with precise and evident satisfaction. At last he introduced himself.

'Colonel Iles Arsanukayev. Chief of the Presidential Guard!' and he and his men burst out laughing. Dudayev's bodyguard. Muttering to myself about Chechen machismo, I wondered the whole way back to Grozny what they would have done with me if I'd told them what I really thought of Dudayev.

Moscow's poorly hidden backing of the opposition was made public – to noone's surprise – in August 1994, enabling Russian attack helicopters to be more active against Dudayev's forces, particularly as the opposition, for all their bravado, only ever engaged Dudayev's forces when attacked in small, infrequent skirmishes that autumn. One of Arsanukayev's anti-aircraft guns was now parked permanently in Freedom Square in front of the Presidential Palace. A series of hostage-takings by Chechen gangs in neighbouring republics provided fuel for the Kremlin's propaganda machine. One evening the main television news in Moscow carried a picture of three severed heads lying in Grozny's Freedom Square, the newscaster claiming they were the heads of Russian officials. There were no severed heads on display when I had walked through the square several times that day.

On one of many mad dashes to Grozny from Georgia during that period, I stopped to find a pro-Dudayev camp next to the Rostov-Baku highway had been shot up by Russian attack helicopters. A tracked armoured vehicle had been hit and was still burning. The attack had occurred early in the morning. The red bedding of one of the fighters was still laid out on the top of another armoured vehicle parked under a tree nearby.

'*Oppozitsiya*,' a fighter said angrily. He walked away towards a crowd of onlookers who had gathered to see what had happened. He levelled his machinegun over their heads and fired off a few rounds, shouting at them to get back.

Each opposition attack, usually from the air, pulled Dudayev a little further back from the brink of his own political demise. His naive obstinacy was his strength. The escalation in opposition-led violence promoted him in ordinary Chechens' eyes to a grudging 'least bad'.

During the increase in tension, physical like the build-up to a storm, there was one moment of release. Udugov, on behalf of the Chechen government, invited journalists from Moscow and the region to attend

Chechnya's celebrations on 6 September to mark its fourth anniversary of independence. We were given rooms and board in the hastily refurbished Hotel Kavkaz ('Caucasus'), on the opposite side of Freedom Square from the Presidential Palace. The outside walls were painted a strawberry pink. Workmen were still painting the interior when we checked in. The smiling doorman's RPG-7, with rocket attached and slung over his back, got in everyone's way.

As midday approached on the baking September day, several thousand Chechens gathered in the square. Many of the men wore a jumble of Soviet army surplus. Almost all came with a rifle. Chechen elders in long coats, *papakhas* and prayer caps jogged vigorously behind one another in a wide circle off to one side, chanting the *zikr*, a Sufi prayer of 'remembrance to God'.

One Chechen ambled in on the back of a thin horse, a large black *burka* draped over his shoulders, the very picture of a *dzhigit*. '*Dzhigit* is an untranslatable word,' wrote Baddeley. 'It means one who can perform all sorts of tricks on horseback and is, by implication, a very fine fellow.' The Caucasian *burka* is not to be confused with the Afghan veil. It is a tent-like cloak, a rainproof sheepskin which, Baddeley explained, 'should stand upright of itself after being held up by the neck band and dropped gently to the floor.' He also believed they were used as toboggans, extrapolating this from Strabo's account of mountaineers 'glissading downhill on skins'.

The National Guard and the Presidential Guard turned out in smart dark green tunics, striped breeches and polished jackboots. They clutched their rifles tightly, turned their jaws right to the reviewing stand and goose-stepped past in fairly good order. Dudayev, looking out from behind bodyguards in black berets and dripping in weaponry, had left his *caudillo* outfit at home, opting instead for a perfectly creased doublebreasted suit and one of his trademark fedoras. Following the elite units came some scruffier marching from Chechens in regular combat uniforms. Then came a couple of tanks and anti-aircraft guns whose engines roared, belching diesel fumes as their tracks screeched and clattered across the square.

A short while later, the elite units came round the corner again, having marched round behind the Hotel Kavkaz, the parliament building and back into the square. The audience cheered and the soldiers beamed with modest pride. A fly-past completed the Lilliputian copy of a Soviet May Day parade. A single, ancient snub-nosed MiG streaked in low over the square, its engines drowning out all sound for a moment. Someone in the crowd said Dudayev's son was flying the jet. It turned and came back and proceeded to fly loop-the-loops over the square to more cheers. This was the last time the sound of a jet over Grozny brought joy.

The Chechens' martial national anthem was played over loudspeakers. Dudayev then gave a speech railing against the Kremlin. He urged the Chechens to stand fast for their independence, raising his fists – meticulously, to just the right height – to acknowledge the crowd's approving cheers. But knowing what the crowd in the square was waiting for, he kept his speech short. Almost as soon as he had been whisked away by his bodyguards, hundreds of men in the square raised their guns spontaneously and fired off clip after clip after clip into the hot blue sky. The sound was deafening, exhilarating, the machinegun fire like the drilling of a woodpecker, only a hundred times louder. I retreated into a doorway with a colleague – the bullets had to come down at some point. But the Chechens stood exactly where they were, laughing, smiling and shouting *Marsho!* – the Chechen word for 'freedom' – as the empty brass cartridge cases continued to jump from the breeches of their guns and spin onto the square.

# Freedom or death

Better to die standing than live lying down.

Written on a Chechen
volunteer's rifle strap in 1995

'TASS IS REPORTING that the Chechen opposition are well on
their way to taking the Presidential Palace in Grozny.'

The agency's message from Moscow broke the leisured disor-
der of a cold November morning at home in Tbilisi. The editor's
voice, which echoed down the aged copper wires in tinny beeps
and hisses, the signal struggling to cross steppe and mountain,
fired a starting gun.

I threw notebooks, Swiss army knife, pens, chocolate, torch,
dictionary, shortwave radio, more notebooks, crumpled articles,
lucky hipflask, camera and dusty cartridges of film into a rucksack. I stuffed a few clothes into another bag which could be discarded if I needed to abandon a vehicle or walk out of a problem.
Leads and batteries with laptop: check. Passport, Russian multiple entry visa (printed on mint green paper, the colour code for
correspondents), second passport (in case somebody went off
with the other one), Russian press accreditation and dollars, all
checked, counted, rechecked and recounted about four times in
a ritual to placate the playful demons at checkpoints and border
posts. One piece of paper absent and you would see nothing,
miss everything. I strapped the lot under my shirt in a moneybelt
stained grey with a summer's sweat.

I left Sasha and Matt in the yard with a brusque kiss. They
carried on playing as I sprinted out, banging down fuel canisters

into the back of my BBC colleague's jeep. The petrol sloshed about in a satisfying metallic warp. I switched on the radio, poking the aerial out of the window, which amplified the jeep being revved up as it swerved out of Tbilisi for another breakneck drive over the Georgian Military Highway.

All-Russian Radio: 'The news, on Saturday 26 November. Itar-TASS is reporting opposition forces in Chechnya have attacked the Presidential Palace in the centre of Grozny.'

I relayed this information to my colleague who, in reaction, put his foot on the gas. A red-cheeked Russian border guard at Verkhny Lars disappeared into a cabin with our passports. His post was dwarfed by the steep black sides of the Dariel Gorge, scored with toy trees out of a Japanese print above the white noise of the River Terek as it spewed over the rocks on its way to the Caspian. The guard seemed to take hours. The sun had already gone down behind the mountains.

All-Russian Radio: 'Itar-TASS is reporting opposition forces have stormed the Presidential Palace in the centre of Grozny. The building is on fire.'

The border guard, the fake fur collar of his winter issue jacket set at a jaunty angle, walked out of the cabin with a smile, a stamp in one hand and our passports in the other. '*Shastlivogo puti!*' he said, handing us our passports and touching his forehead. 'Pleasant journey!'

After passing the Russian checkpoint on the Ossetian-Ingush border, we found the Rostov-Baku highway empty. A white fog had rolled in as we reached the wooded turn-off for the town centre, marked by a traffic police watchtower and an electric sign that had once lit up to warn of fog, ice or snow further east along the road to Makhachkala in Daghestan. I wound down a window to see if I could hear any shooting. Mist hung in the trees. Silence.

The jeep slowed along the approach to the southern district of Chernorechye. Past the reservoir and up the hill was the outline of a tank. We drove up to it. It had been abandoned. Its barrel and part of the turret were painted a ghostly white. The whole town seemed asleep as we cruised slowly up Lenin Avenue towards Freedom Square.

The square was empty also, save for the wreck of a light armoured fighting vehicle, the BMP with a small, flat turret and gun used by Russia's airborne forces. Its tracks had snapped. There were no flames or smoke pouring out of the Presidential Palace. A few electric lights burned in some of the windows. We sped over the Sunzha bridge and parked the car near the door. A couple of armed fighters at the entrance confirmed they were *za Dudayev*a. We sprinted up to the offices of Chechen Press.

The information minister, Udugov, a leather jacket over military fatigues and a mink *shapka* on his head, was haranguing a news agency in Moscow by telephone for erroneously reporting an opposition victory in Grozny. 'I tell you, I'm talking to you from the Presidential Palace. The Bee-Bee-Cee has just walked in,' he said with a shrug and a grin in my colleague's direction.

'Everything's calm.'

A Kalashnikov rested on his desk. Even by TASS's low standards, the lies were extraordinary, reinforcing a decades-old Chechen turn of speech, 'lying like the Soviets'.

'Cancel your subscription to TASS!' Udugov had crowed at the Reuters reporter, the only other journalist in the city.

I demanded an interview with Dudayev and Udugov directed me upstairs. I found the bearded vice-president, Zelimkhan Yanderbiyev, also in military fatigues and sweating in a fur hat, working the telephones. Otherwise, the Palace appeared deserted. Yanderbiyev picked up a telephone, said a few words in Chechen and then handed me the receiver.

'President Dudayev here. What can I do for you?' The careful enunciations in Russian, from this fan of Pushkin and Lermontov, were unmistakable.

'Where are you?'

'At home,' he said in an upbeat tone. He had no doubts as to who was behind the attack and vowed to fight. 'If Russia continues on this path, we have no other option – Russia is the aggressor.' I ran back down the damp concrete stairwell to Chechen Press and Udugov got me a line to the agency in Moscow.

The night had obscured the full ferocity of the battle. The next day, the overhead lines of the city's trolleybuses lay in a tangle on the pavements along Victory Avenue. Townspeople began sweeping up the glass from shop windows lying in shiny puddles. Flames jetted from broken gas pipelines, giving off a strange heat in the chill, foggy morning. In the turret of the BMP were the burned remains of a soldier trying to climb out, half of a charred arm reaching up to the sky. A few passers-by stopped to contemplate the torched and melted remains of another soldier near a T72 tank, also with a white barrel, already undergoing repairs by a Chechen fighter. In one corner of the square, a crowd buzzed as it listened to Chechen elders decry Russian imperialism. The white barrels and turrets were the markings daubed on by the opposition forces to ensure they did not fire at each other in Grozny. I found seven such 'peacekeeping tanks' parked outside Khasbulatov's base in Tolstoy-Yurt later that morning.

It was unclear just how many Russian troops were involved in the failed operation to unseat Dudayev. As the Kremlin moved quickly to disown its own soldiers, sent in with the Chechen opposition to take Grozny, there were no reliable figures. Udugov quickly revised down his own claim of 90 Russian prisoners to 58 – there were probably about 20.

In the building belonging to Dudayev's secret police, 'Colonel' Arsanukayev, now in winter uniform with a tall grey *papakha* on his head and a *kinzhal* on his belt, escorted in two of the prisoners to show to journalists who were now trickling into Grozny. He kept a cold eye on twenty-one-year-old Andrey Chazov, a young *tankist* who wore the blackened overalls he was captured in. Chazov said he was assigned from a Moscow regiment for an operation in Chechnya. Next to him, Nikolay Gliminkov, thirty-eight, a tank mechanic from the Volga town of Cheboksary, sat with a bandaged hand and a burned face. An RPG, a rocket-propelled grenade, had hit his tank. He had narrowly escaped the fate of the melted corpses left on Freedom Square. He said he had been paid $625 to take part in the operation. 'For the past two years I have not worked,' he explained, gingerly weighing each word so as to say nothing.

Moscow kept up its own denials. 'Any information about

Russian regular servicemen who allegedly have been taken prisoners of war in Grozny is a malicious slander,' the commander of
the North Caucasian Military District insisted.

The Russian denials energized the sleepless Dudayev. When
he spoke he would clench his fists so tightly that his knuckles
popped and cracked.

'We want an answer – is it your force or not your force? Do
you deny it or not? If they do not deny it, the prisoners will be
dealt with according to international law. If they deny it the
Chechen Republic has the right to treat the prisoners as mer-
cenaries and criminals,' he said, a winter wind blowing through
the windows of his office which had been smashed in the attack.
He wore a cardigan under his suit jacket to keep out the cold. He
threatened to execute the prisoners.

Dudayev's foreign minister, Yusuf Shamsudin, confirmed the
threat. A Chechen from Jordan, Shamsudin was once an official
at the airport in Amman and helped keep up a steady flow of
friendly if guarded correspondence between Dudayev and the
late King Hussein (who employed Jordanian-Chechen bodyguards). On the wall of his office was a poster depicting a bucolic
mountain scene over the words: *Chechenistan – the world's new
tourist paradise*. He spoke no Russian but had a colourful
command of English. 'If they are coming to fight for money,
they are spiders!' he exclaimed. He sported a moustache like
Dudayev's, only silver in colour and a little less meticulous. 'We
have to kill them!'

Chechen fighters held back a crowd several hundred strong
outside the Presidential Palace which had gathered to see the
prisoners put on show two days after the attack. The first snow
of winter started to fall on the square, muffling the shouts and
conversations. The display was cancelled. One of the fighters
trying to hold back the disappointed crowd said, 'If anyone
comes to fight against our state, whether they're Chechen,
Russian or any other nationality, we should deal with them the
Muslim way, under Islamic law. We should shoot them.'

Reporters returned to the DGB building a few days later
with permission to interview a dozen of the prisoners, drawn

from the Russian army's Taman and Kantemirov divisions near Moscow. They were still watched by Chechen guards, but the men, seeing how their commanders had washed their hands of them, were eager to talk. They said they had been promised about $1,500 by the domestic wing of Sergey's KGB successors, the Federal Counter-Intelligence Service, or FSK, to fight in a special mission alongside the armed opposition to Dudayev in Chechnya. They had been told opposition fighters would guide them into Grozny, where they were to position their armour at the Presidential Palace, the Post and Telecommunications centre and other strategic buildings in the city. They were promised air support and told to head for a field on the edge of the city where helicopters would be waiting to evacuate wounded.

Around two hundred Russian soldiers arrived only the day before the planned attack. There was no time to train with opposition fighters. On the day of the attack, faulty radios strangled their communications. Opposition 'forces' ran away as soon as the firing started in Grozny. Commanders of the hopelessly small force had to wrestle with maps in the noisy, cramped metal interiors of their vehicles to try and navigate through the strange city. There was no air support. The white paint on their turrets and barrels made the job of picking them off easier. One of the prisoners, Captain Alexander Tryukov, said that when he had made it to the appointed field to be evacuated, no one was waiting for him. If the attack failed, it turned out, as little thought had been given to their fate as to that of the hundreds of thousands of civilians living in Grozny.

Even after their release had been negotiated over the following days, the prisoners were nervous about going home. I found Major Valery Ivanov, in stained canvas trousers and a padded winter jacket, behind the Presidential Palace helping Chechen fighters with repairs to a captured T72 tank. It was a rare sunny morning in early December, the sky a shock of blue after days of snow and fog. Some of the early snow had begun to melt. Major Ivanov quietly sorted through a toolbox, his hands black with grease.

'Some of us fear the FSK and they're afraid to go home. But I must go home – my family, my parents are waiting for me.'

Dudayev was saved by the attack. Many of those Chechens embittered by his cronyism and misrule now found themselves on the side of the Great Dictator. Umar Hambiev, the chief surgeon and a Chechen at Grozny's military hospital, was one such reluctant supporter. He wore a dirty white labcoat, surgeon's pyjama bottoms and a white cotton headcap. I had come round late one evening to try and establish some reliable casualty figures. He opened the door to an unheated room where the waxen bodies of two peasant women, stiff in winter woollens, awaited identification and collection by their families. A young Russian conscript lay unconscious on a stretcher on the floor along with a dozen other wounded in the failed opposition attack.

'He's Russian,' said the surgeon, standing over the boy, 'but that's all he knows.' The makeshift ward, stuffy and dark for lack of lightbulbs, carried the nauseous, sweet smell of viscous brown iodine used by the surgeons, unemptied bins and uncleaned lavatories. Hambiev had worked flat out since the attack and his face, grey and unshaven, was grateful for the short break in time in which he could order his thoughts. 'Maybe I'm not pleased with this regime,' he said finally, 'but when they kill our people they are a hundred times worse than Dudayev.'

The warplanes started coming.

Watched by Udugov and bodyguards in the Presidential Palace, Dudayev was lecturing a group of journalists about the evils of the Kremlin when some jets screeched low over the building. The anti-aircraft gun in Freedom Square let fly a deep burst of ack-ack. There was a large explosion. We hit the floor, all save Dudayev who sat where he was on a fake leather sofa. There was a crackle of small arms from the square as Chechen fighters fired uselessly into the sky after the jets. Udugov listened to a walkie-talkie and then muttered that a plane had been hit.

'Here you see the situation with your own eyes,' said Dudayev, calmly denouncing the inhabitants of the Kremlin as 'satanists'. 'You hear and have seen the plane go down.' Out of the window there was a thick black column of smoke.

Dudayev left the building, pushed out by his nervous body-guards. I ran down the stairs, not wanting to get stuck in a lift, and out into the square. Chechen fighters, some of them wearing green headbands which declared them *smertniki,* those willing to die in battle, scanned the darkening skies as the sound of the jet engines faded. Women, their faces puffed with tears, jostled in queues to climb onto buses to get out of the city. Children clung to their thick winter coats.

The traders in the central market, who had begun to reopen their businesses after the opposition attack, fled once more. The metal skeletons of the stalls stood abandoned and empty in the mud and wet leaves, except for a few elderly Russian women begging for bread. Large rats rooted brazenly in piles of uncollected rubbish. One Russian journalist based his entire month's reporting in Grozny on his unobtrusive trudges through the snow and slush round the bazaar, returning to Chechen Press each afternoon to send estimates of how many traders were operating on a given day. You could tell the market was open if he came back munching from a plastic bag of provisions.

The Chechens had not downed a jet. The column of black smoke was out at the northern airport of Khankala, where great orange flames leapt from punctured aviation fuel tanks. 'Drive quickly,' urged the head of the airport, who took me on a tour to see the damage, 'they might explode.' The remains of four civilian jet liners, with the dizzying spiral emblem of Chechnya's national airline Stigl on the tailfins, lay smoking with their spines broken on the apron.

Back in Grozny, cars groaned under the weight of families and bedding, sliding on the muddy roads out of Grozny.

As with the Russian captives, the Kremlin at first refused to acknowledge the warplanes as their own. Ella Pamfilova, one of Yeltsin's former ministers and in Grozny a few days later to negotiate the release of the Russian prisoners, rubbished Moscow's silence as the warplanes flew sorties for a fourth day over the city.

'It is clear that these planes are not English or French but Russian.'

At night, the jets continued to fly over the city. They flew high up but the phantom sound of their engines, rising in tone like a metal jug of milk being steam-heated, clawed at your sleep. They left strange lights floating in their wake, dropping spooky tangles of magnesium flares which fell like radioactive snow. Designed to light up a battlefield, they were dropped to grind down the nerves of the city's inhabitants. We would find their elfin parachutes, bright orange, tangled in the trees and the trolleybus lines the next day. I woke up one morning with a start, imagining that a bomb had exploded outside my window. It was only the light of dawn streaming in. I dreamed that I was trying to run out of the second floor of an administrative building but at each of the doors and the windows there were helicopters, like wasps, waiting. I would then be out on the street and the jets would come out of the sky. I would run for a bus shelter and a bomb would drop, clanging onto the roof of the shelter without exploding, dropping onto the pavement beside me, when I would wake up. Whenever I was inside a building, at the first sound of a jet or helicopter I would want to get out. The Chechen fighters later laughed at my discomfort.

The jets attacked a second day and I saw them this time, two MiGs which tipped their wings over the streets and then swerved off in a Vulcan roar towards Khankala. They hit four more liners on the ground. I ran to the PTT to file news of the attack. As I went in, a Chechen woman at the telephone counter was shooing out a crowd of women waiting for a line out of the city.

'Quick,' she said, 'go home!'

The women picked up their bags and I followed them out into the street.

I went to Chechen Press to try and beg a line there. I found a press release; it was a smudged copy of a telegram from Dudayev addressed to another of his unwilling pen-pals, Colonel-General Pyotr Deynekin, commander-in-chief of the Russian air force and Dudayev's old boss.

'I congratulate you, commander-in-chief and the brave

Russian air force, for winning supremacy of the air over the Chechen Republic of Ichkeria,' Dudayev had written. 'We shall meet on the ground!'

A correspondent had crisscrossed the Chechen Press office windows with masking tape. The small concentration of taped diamonds stood out like a rebel schoolboy's red socks among the building's vertical lines of dark, unlit windows.

I sought to find out what plans – if any – were being made for the defence of the city. I was told to look for a Colonel Aslan Maskhadov somewhere in the basement. I made my way through a gaggle of fighters hanging about in a corridor. They carried Kalashnikovs, canvas packs of rockets for their RPGs and knives on their belts. One of them knocked on a door, poked his head round, gargled something in Chechen and then showed me in. Young Chechens in combat fatigues and elders in long coats and *papakhas* sat in a semi-circle in front of the mapped desk of an operations room. At their centre was a quiet man with the jug ears of a bat, wiry grey hair and who wore a combat jacket printed with the thin, pine needle lines of Polish army surplus. On Maskhadov, it looked like a gardening jacket. He looked up awkwardly from a map. He confirmed that he was Colonel Maskhadov and that he was in charge of the Chechen armed forces.

'We've already waited three hundred years for our independence and we're prepared to wait longer,' he mumbled. 'Today we're ready to fight.'

The Colonel's army started to gather in Freedom Square like adrenalin into a cornered animal, occasionally firing their automatics at the passing jets. Some called for a Russian prisoner to be hanged for every Russian sortie over the city. Elders and some of the younger men danced the *zikr* in front of the parliament building. Others shouted what was to become the rallying cry of the war, *'Svoboda, ili smert'!* – 'Freedom or death!' The words were written in ballpoint pen on the green headbands of the *smertniki*.

A *dzhigit* rode into the square cloaked in a black burka edged in pink silk, a white scarf round his unshaven neck and a black sheepskin cap with wild corkscrew curls, a style favoured by Turkmen nomads. The leather harnesses on his chestnut horse were decorated with small silver stars. He held the reins in his left hand and an old carbine in the other. He was a proud sight but untypical. Most turned up in workaday clothes – jeans, a leather jacket, a dark blue parka, a black woollen cap or a bright red scarf. The webbing worn to carry ammunition clips and grenades was stitched at home. When the snow settled, many of the fighters walked round like Hallowe'en figures in bed-linen they had sewn into winter camouflage. They ran in the cheap, zipped plastic boots of the Soviet winter. A lucky few had proper camouflage uniforms or army boots. A well-armed fighter might carry an RPG, spare rockets and an assault rifle but this was rare. Whatever the volume of trade on the Chechen arms bazaar in prewar days, ordinary Chechens had to buy their weapons – often from the Russian military who later cared little that their clients were also picking them up off their dead Russian comrades. Chechen boys, eager to join their older brothers and cousins, started filling vodka bottles with petrol and stuffing rags into the necks to make Molotov cocktails.

The fighters boiled water for tea on a gas flame which was supposed to burn eternally for the dead of the Great Patriotic War at one end of the square. They looked an unpromising army. The flame threw black shadows among the men whose talk bubbled quietly, their breath rising in the cold air like the steam off the water in the billycan. They shifted their weight from foot to foot to keep their circulations going. The barrels of their guns slung over their shoulders followed their movements like thistles bending in the wind. A few young boys darted between them like an excited school of fish to catch the different currents of conversation. With great pride, the boys would open their coats to show Molotov cocktails stuffed in their inside pockets.

My notebooks of this time are full of tough-talk quotes of telegraphic brevity as I struggled to write them down in the dark and without gloves in the December frost. 'We shall raise the green flag of Islam above the Kremlin!' was a popular boast. The shout of '*Allahu akbar!*', Arabic for 'God is greater!', shouted at

Russian jets seemed more for grateful television crews than any indication of warrior spirit. Imran Oysayev, a modest veteran of the Red Army's expedition to Afghanistan, was on guard duty outside Maskhadov's operations room. 'We don't want war, but they're attacking our families, our homes.'

On the Terek, up in the town of Znamenskoye, was yet another opposition leader, Salambek Khadzhiev. He was disarmingly honest about the opposition's disarray. They were divided, squabbling over who had been to blame for the disastrous November attack. Khadzhiev was a Chechen, short with fox eyes, who had also made good in Soviet times, rising to become minister for the chemical industry. Unusually for a Soviet minister at the time, he had openly opposed the Communist hardliners' 1991 coup. He saw no future for Chechen independence and wanted an agreement with wide-ranging autonomy for Chechnya like the one Tatarstan had eventually penned in February 1994.

'Can you live next to Russia and ignore it?' he asked rhetorically. 'We are like Cuba next to America.'

The Kremlin continued to ignore the Chechen historian Avtorkhanov's warning of 1991 against dealing the Chechens ultimatums. Yeltsin now threatened 'direct' Russian intervention if the Chechens failed to disarm. However ugly the Kremlin's handling of Chechnya, Khadzhiev's words in the early days of December rang true. When Grachev denied that the Russian prisoners were his men, the defence minister reasoned that if the army had been involved in the failed opposition attack, 'one paratroop regiment might have solved all questions in two hours.' I thought Grachev's boast to be a reasonable estimate of Maskhadov's forces.

Udugov approached me one afternoon in the offices of Chechen Press and told me to be in the town of Sleptsovsk, in neighbouring Ingushetia, as soon as I could get there. He gave no reason. The second car I waved at on the street stopped. We drove west for an hour and approached the town as two Russian attack helicopters wheeled continuously over the rooves in hypnotic figures of eight. A small crowd gathered outside another squat, two-storey administrative building to watch Russian Alfa troops, wearing the oversized helmets of the special forces, stand guard outside. The defence minister, Grachev, was inside waiting for Dudayev.

I sprinted down the road to the local PTT, my hopes of a line to Moscow concentrated in waves at the repeater dishes strapped to the side of a tall metal aerial. I thrust a handful of roubles across the counter at the operator who freed up a line, I filed the news to Moscow and then sprinted back.

A few minutes later, a convoy of Japanese four-wheel drives careered round the corner, the Chechen national anthem blaring from a car stereo and a Chechen flag flying from the back of the lead vehicle. Dudayev stepped out balletically in plain military fatigues and a forage cap and acknowledged an enthusiastic *Allahu akbar!* from the waiting crowd. The two men talked for over an hour while Dudayev's guards stood with their weapons ready, their feet planted firmly apart next to the Alpha men, green headbands tied round their foreheads. The helicopters continued to circle the town. Grachev was the first to leave. He marched out in tall leather boots, flicked a sour grimace at the crowd and muttered something inaudible under his breath, in stark contrast to the smiles he afforded Dudayev for the Russian television cameras inside the building.

Dudayev followed him out shortly afterwards, an ecstatic smile on his face as he looked out at the small crowd gathered at the foot of the steps up to the building. Someone of rank had finally deigned to meet him. He had agreed magnanimously to release all the Russian prisoners, the first seven to go back to Moscow that night. I shouted from the back of the crowd: 'Will there be war?'

'Why should there be a war?' The crowd cheered. 'The question of independence is a political question, and the question of war or peace is a military one,' he said. 'We have agreed to peacefully decide the military issue, but a political decision has yet to be decided.' Would he meet Yeltsin? 'It may not be my wish, but it is necessary,' he replied.

Udugov offered me a lift back to Grozny in his car and gunned the Zhiguli's engine to keep up with Dudayev's motorcade. Out of a shaky window, the hills were white with snow, reflecting what little light there was up to a grey band of fog in the flat night sky. I wondered if the Russians had considered shooting at the motorcade but then felt buoyed by Dudayev's positive words. I asked Udugov if he thought there would be peace. He projected his deadpan voice into the back of the car.

'There will be war.'

Russian troops and matériel clogged airports and roads around Chechnya's borders. The Russian army did not hide the crates of shells stacked under the canvas-backed Zil transports that thundered along the potholed roads in convoys tens of trucks long. The borders to the republic were sealed. A line of Chechens on a road between the opposition town of Znamenskoye and the Ossetian town of Mozdok to the west, where the bulk of Russian forces were gathering, were told by police they were not allowed to leave the republic. Natural gas piped into Chechnya had dipped to low levels. Russian officials blamed a faulty pipeline.

'It will be wonderful to be independent, but our only chance is if the Russian Federation falls apart,' said Husein Kurbanov, a Chechen builder in Grozny, just turned fifty, who feared a war. He had lost two cousins a few days previously in an air raid on Argun, southeast of Grozny. 'If the Federation doesn't break up, 90 per cent of Chechens will die fighting for their independence and still not achieve it.'

Back at the Operations Room in the Presidential Palace, Colonel Maskhadov estimated that three Russian divisions were poised on Chechnya's borders. He spoke of defences being prepared for Grozny but there was little evidence of this. There was the anti-aircraft gun parked on Freedom Square. An armoured personnel carrier drove in much the same circle as that followed by the military parade at the independence day celebrations in September. A few T72 tanks, some of them captured from the opposition in November, were parked at a base north of the city but were moved around out of sight as Russian jets continued to criss-cross Grozny.

'Our last option,' said Maskhadov, already thinking ahead, 'will be to retreat to the mountains where we have prepared bases with food and matériel – it's the Afghanistan option.'

Yeltsin authorized the use of all available means to put an end to the 'unbridled banditism poisoning the lives of the Chechen people and their neighbours'.

A few days earlier, I had stopped a Chechen woman in her sixties as she made her way through the deserted stalls of the bazaar. She had her hands thrust into the pockets of an old leather coat with large plastic buttons and had wound a thick grey scarf carefully round her neck and tucked it into the collar so as not to let a cubic centimetre of cold air in below. 'Whoever fights the Muslims,' she said, 'never wins.'

In the early 1900s a shy, fastidious Englishman by the name of John Baddeley rode across the remote mountain passes between Chechnya and Georgia, recording the customs and legends of the people he met. Save for the pink shaven face, or perhaps the Winchester repeating rifle strapped to his saddle, he might not have been immediately recognizable as a foreigner to the sharp-eyed mountaineers as he had taken to wearing native dress. His Ossetian *passepartout*, Ourousbi, had suggested he buy the kit in Tbilisi. He had bought: a *cherkeska*, the mountaineer's tunic with *gazirei*, or cartridge pouches, sewn on in lieu of breast pockets; a *beshmet*, or undershirt; a *bashlyk*, a cloak of camel hair; a *burka*; a *papakha* of karakul wool; and to finish off the outfit, a *kinzhal* (to add to the Winchester and the Browning automatic pistol he habitually carried) bought from a smith. Having dumped his tweeds, Baddeley sneaked out through the back of his Tbilisi hotel and mounted his horse, 'transformed as far as possible into a *gorets* if not into a *dzhigit*'.

Baddeley's father, Lieutenant-Colonel Fraser Baddeley, was killed in the Crimean War just after he was born. Having finished school at Wellington, Baddeley met, through his socialite mother, the jovial Count Peter Shuvalov, then the tsar's ambassador to London, who delighted in the anti-Russian nickname he had been given by Britain's jingoistic press, 'Count Shovel-off'. Finding that the young man had nothing to do, Shuvalov invited Baddeley back to St Petersburg. 'My father, who died young, could not of course have known, as he shivered in the trenches before Sevastopol,' Baddeley wrote in the memoirs of his St Petersburg days, *Russia in the Eighties: Sport and Politics*, 'that in the opposite bastions was a Russian guardsman, a little younger than himself, who would in after years befriend his son, invite him to Russia, and, while both lived, treat him with all a father's kindness.'

On his first journey to Russia, the view out of the train window depressed him. 'My spirits sank below zero as we rumbled through the white wilderness under a leaden sky.' He cheered up on arrival, the count yelling at the 'lazy log' to get up at the crack of dawn after a hard night's drinking to go and shoot wolves at his estate north of St Petersburg – hence the 'sport' in the title of his book. Baddeley, wanting to learn Russian, took himself off to a village near Moscow, this time donning a peasant's belted *rubashka*, or long shirt, and heavy boots. A door balanced on a couple of chairs did for a bed. As well as learning his ABV, Baddeley helped the family plough their fields and claims he thrived on a diet consisting of 'bread and butter, potatoes, *shchi* – cabbage soup, and *kasha* – buckwheat porridge, with plenty of good milk'. After a month in the country, Baddeley went to Moscow to call on some of the Count's aristocratic friends and aquaintances. Nobody would receive him, fearing he was an upstart nihilist with revolutionary sympathies. He returned to England and worked for a spell on *The Observer*.

Count Shuvalov, recalled to Russia under a cloud, invited the now Russian-speaking Baddeley back to St Petersburg. He told Baddeley: 'I am leaving England for good this time and I promise that you shall shoot bears and wolves and all sorts of things to your heart's content.' Baddeley demurred. He had no money. The count suggested journalism and Baddeley, armed with a letter from the count promising open doors in Moscow, secured a correspondent's post with *The Standard*.

Baddeley accompanied the count from England back to St Petersburg in 1880, stopping off briefly in Berlin so Shuvalov could talk shop with Bismarck. He gave Baddeley the pencil Bismarck had used during the meeting as a souvenir. In St Petersburg Baddeley busied himself in following the futile tacking of Alexander II against the winds of revolutionary change then blowing in Russia. His scoops are full of the journalist's thrill of the chase: running with a rumour picked up from the milkman that the Empress had died one morning – the milkman was right; getting sensitive news past the censor by sending it in code.

The readers of another empire found particular interest in Russia's move eastwards into Central Asia. 'Indian troops had been brought to Malta by Lord Beaconsfield [Disraeli] in 1878, a theatrical coup avowedly aimed at Russia. That power was now grimly determined to achieve such a position in Asia that, in future, whenever any question arose threatening hostilities between England and herself, Sikh, Pathan and Gurkha would be wanted at home to defend the Indian frontier.' Baddeley, despite entreaties to his protector, was not allowed to travel with Russian troops to witness General Skobelev win the decisive battle for control of Central Asia over the Turkmen tribes at Geok Tepe, now in Turkmenistan, in 1881. And no wonder. 'The unhappy Turkomans lost twenty thousand men in the siege and storming of their wretched fortress, in the subsequent merciless pursuit, and in the orgy of lust and rapine deliberately permitted to the troops for two and seventy hours by their commander-in-chief; for Skobelev, like Yermolov before him in the Caucasus, believed that with Asiatics the only way was to deal them at once a smashing blow.'

Baddeley always found time to shoot with bullets he cast himself, setting out over the snow on thin skis. He bagged: bear, elk, wolf, otter, mink, lynx, fox, capercaillie, partridge, willow and hazel grouse, woodcock, three varieties of snipe, and gluttons, a type of wolverine. But he felt the killing wanton, writing later: 'I was never quite free from reservations and qualms on the score of cruelty, and eventually, after shooting a great deal of game, big and small, I dropped it, on Schouvaloff's death, without regret and even with a sense of relief.'

After Shuvalov's death in 1889 (in his protégé's arms), Baddeley gave up journalism and turned to business. He represented Sheffield's Cammell Laird at the Bogoslovsk iron, copper and gold mines in the Ural Mountains and in 1898 joined a syndicate of friends in St Petersburg anxious to catch the Baku oil rush. He found Grozny, then a second Baku (it was nicknamed in Russian *Neftyanka*, 'Oil Valley') 'remarkable for streets which without exaggeration might be set down as among the worst in the world'. He did not make the syndicate any money but this did not bother Baddeley. He noted with interest how the Chechens in one village used carefully preserved crude from a natural seepage as a cure for rheumatism and tuberculosis. Under the pretext of prospecting for oil and comfortably out of range of post and telegrams, his heart was taken captive by the mountains.

On arrival he was immediately regaled with grisly tales and warnings to be on the watch for Chechen and Ingush bandits. One tall story has a couple of Chechens shooting a Russian officer and his son from behind. When caught and asked why they had done it, they 'said frankly that they had challenged each other as to whether they could hit or not, and, being doubtful, tried!' But however long his time in St Petersburg, Baddeley was quick to find sympathy with the mountaineers. 'Brigandage with them was the very breath of their being,' he wrote, adding: 'Here, again, however, qualification is necessary. The very men who would rob and kill without compunction within sight of Vladikavkaz or Grozny would, if, as well might be the case, they came from the higher and remoter districts, refrain in their homeland from any such crimes.' Staying with the Chechens and Ingush in their mountain villages, Baddeley saw and heard how the 1859 surrender of the mountaineers' Avar leader Imam Shamil, who had led a *ghazavat* for a quarter of a century against the Russians, still rankled with them. Writing in the late 1930s near the end of his life in Oxford, he blamed continuous attempts by the Russians to disarm them for much of the 'discontent and consequent lawlessness of the Ingooshee and the

Tchetchens. So it was then; so it had been ever since the surrender of Shamil in 1859; what it may be under the Bolsheviks I cannot say, but as human nature changes slowly if at all, and Russian officials are said still to be underpaid, I fear that little improvement can have taken place.'

Baddeley's memoirs of the Caucasus, published posthumously, are fascinating, though rambling. His real skill, which he played down, was as a historian, inspired by Imam Shamil's long and desperate stand against incorporation into the Russian Empire. Published in 1908, his *Russian Conquest of the Caucasus* remains the classic work of the region's history, reading like a Buchan thriller, and full of observations on mountain lore that leapt out at me at every turn in the Caucasus. He did not let his years with Shuvalov, or the fact that his history was almost wholly based on Russian official sources, blind him to Russian iniquity, taking a very modern view of empire, decrying its 'civilizing mission' as a figleaf for conquest, commenting on Russia's bloody subjection of the Caucasus: 'Politically, it is difficult to see where justice came in, but in this respect Russia was only doing what England and all other civilised states have done, and still do, wherever they come in contact with savage or semi-savage races. By force or by fraud a portion of the country is taken, and, sooner or later, on one excuse or another, the rest is bound to follow.'

His detailed descriptions of mountain customs were to a purpose. Dismounting for a night at a Chechen or Ingush village, he saw in his hosts' love and care of arms – which, as tradition demanded, they carried on greeting him outside their *aouls*, or villages – a people determined not to be hunted down and enslaved, a determination not blunted even by Stalin.

Shortly after the 1994 independence day celebrations, I stopped the car I was travelling in next to a field where a young Chechen was shooting a Kalashnikov at a tin can for target practice. I asked if I could have a go. The man was reluctant to hand me the weapon, fussing to make sure the safety-catch was working and craning his neck around to make sure I would do no harm to anyone. After I had missed the tin, he whipped the gun back off me and visibly relaxed. After watching Georgian,

Afghan, Russian and other troops loose off rounds under the influence of alcohol or ebullient youth – usually both – with blatant disregard for the consequences, the discipline of the young marksman, who kept shooting and adjusting the sights until the tin went flying, stayed with me long afterwards.

Baddeley never married. Perhaps he was as scrupulous in love as he was with his sources. He described the devotion of Shamil's favourite wife Shuanet, a rich Armenian woman who had been abducted for him by one of Shamil's lieutenants (the *nayib* captured Shuanet on a promise from Shamil that he could be exempted from the Imam's strict no smoking law): 'there is no doubt that she loved Shamil with that whole-hearted, lasting devotion many men think themselves entitled but few inspire.' Nonetheless, the reporter-turned-oilman had a keen eye for domestic details. He noticed the Chechens ate little, eating perhaps twice a day and drinking only water and sour milk. 'I never saw a man who could by the wildest exaggeration be called fat.' In a range of mountains legendary for its strict codes of hospitality, I found the Chechens' widely observed abstention from alcohol also unchanged, a blessing after having to sit through toast after blear-eyed toast in Georgia and elsewhere.

Baddeley also describes with awe the lot of the Chechen woman. 'Muhammad said that women were camels to carry man over the desert of existence; the mountaineers of the Caucasus apparently took this dictum more or less literally and put all heavy burdens on the backs of their womenkind.' The lot of the Chechen woman is unchanged today. Arriving unannounced at a Chechen family's house late at night, you would leave your cares with your mud-caked boots at the doorstep, the crud-covered laces as difficult to untie as the deliberately tangled, taunting stays on a Chechen wedding dress. While the men sat and talked, the women – wife, sisters, daughters – would quietly zip about the house, heating up pans of food they could ill spare with the faintest clatter for a second dinner, and with the guns booming a few miles away, make up a bed with the crispest and whitest of linen. Given my unwashed state, it seemed a crime at times to get in under them. One of the women would hover unobtrusively with a kettle of piping hot water to top up your tea, taken with a large bowl of sweets set down on the table after the meal. Any offers of help to wash up afterwards were met with awkward amazement. The only men I saw carrying water were shaven-headed Russian conscripts, young boys with dirty, scared faces, who had been taken prisoner and, grateful to be fed, appeared unaware of the humiliation that performing women's chores brought them in the eyes of their Chechen captors.

As journalists, we were bad and demanding guests, asking to use a noisy generator when it was unclear whose forces were where, commandeering an entire floor to set up an instant bureau and selfishly typing away instead of talking to our hosts. We were also rude. A colleague and I could not get a satellite telephone to work. The head of the household, scratching his head through a mink *shapka*, looked thoughtfully over the contraption. His breath rose in the weak light of a bare bulb in one of his open-sided outhouses, whitewashed in clay, where we had placed the machine to keep the snow off and which ensured a clear signal. His hovering presence annoyed my colleague as he fiddled unsuccessfully with the machine. The Chechen's request to have a go met with a sharp 'no'. What the hell would this peasant know about a satellite telephone? The Chechen gently persisted and removed a small glass fuse from its side, stuffed a small scrap of copper he found at the back of the outhouse into the tube and popped it back into the machine. The telephone's green lights began winking again.

The locusts did try to pay for their trouble but this was often met with genuine affront and our hands, clutching with hesitation a few grimy dollar bills, were pushed away physically. Whatever their strict laws on hospitality, I hated going away having eaten into a family's supplies – households were often doubled in size with relatives who had fled the assault on Grozny. So I met the head of the household's firm refusal with an even firmer reply, that if I did not pay for my board and lodging, my agency would fire me. This white lie made the transaction almost acceptable, if still uncomfortable.

Baddeley, who coolly mentions elsewhere an American oilman 'murdered by the natives' during his time in the mountains, described the Chechens as

> alert in mind, brave and cruel, treacherous and cunning; yet strange as it may sound, honourable according to their own peculiar code, to a degree little known to more civilised races. Hospitality, as with all mountain tribes, was – and is still – a most sacred duty; and the man who would slay a chance-met traveller without pity or remorse for the sake of a trifling gain, would lay down his life for the very same individual were he to cross his threshold as an unbidden guest. Cattle-lifting, highway robbery, and murder were, in this strange code, counted deeds of honour; they were openly instigated by the village maiden – often, by the way, remarkably pretty – who scorned any pretender having no such claims to her favour; and these, coupled with fighting against any foe, but especially the hated Russians, were the only pursuits deemed worthy of a grown man. Household and agricultural work were left to the women-folk or to slaves, the latter being mostly prisoners of war.

One of the most awkward moments of my day was washing before turning in for the night. One of the women would stand in the yard holding a metal ewer of water, a dish of soap and a fresh towel, watching patiently while you scrubbed your face and hands and brushed your teeth, spitting the paste out onto a pristine concrete drain. In the morning, you would find your boots and laces washed and clean. It was embarrassing to have to leave the house before morning and return again, perhaps to scout out the sound of moving armour, because the women took it upon themselves to clean your boots all over again.

But the women were never servile and spoke for themselves. A few of them fought alongside the men – during the war there was rumoured to exist a group of deadly women snipers called the 'Black Stocking Brigade' – and many times Chechen women said they would fight if it were not for their children. Some waved their fists and shouted at Russian tanks creaking towards Grozny. All showed the same extraordinary courage when they hurriedly packed a few essential belongings into large, checked traders' bags and made their way with their children under shell-fire out of a village, their menfolk either fighting or in hiding to try and evade the Russian authorities' notorious 'filtration camps', where Chechen men are to this day detained without trial and tortured. They are supposedly being 'filtered' to check if they are 'terrorist bandits'. The men's real crime is their Chechen nationality.

In a village near Grozny, still in the hands of the fighters, I was packed off to a neighbouring house with a wood-heated boiler to take a hot shower, picking my way on a wintry, clouded night through glutinous mud in a borrowed pair of galoshes (my boots were being cleaned). They had the pointed toes of oriental slippers. I walked out of the shower, numb with the pleasure of it, and dressed. Asya, the wife, in neat headscarf and apron, bade me sit by an iron range to dry my hair, the kitchen warm with low-voltage light.

'You'll freeze, otherwise.'

We talked, inevitably, of the war but not before she had set down a glass of tea in front of me. In the Murid Wars of the nineteenth century, Chechen men unable to defend their villages would kill their own women and childen rather than surrender them to the violent whim of the Russian army. The sound of guns was not far off from the village that night and the wife teased her husband who, she said, was considering the same course of action.

'The men want us to stay but I want to go back to my relations in Urus-Martan – we have no cellar here, nothing. The men say "Stay in your places" but they just want us to die to make sure we don't go off with anyone else – as if anyone would want me with all these children,' she laughed flirtatiously.

On another occasion I was driving alone and needed to cross the hazy front line to get to a village held by the fighters. I stopped to give a lift to a Chechen woman bundled up in a ball of grey and brown woollens with a large bag of shopping who was heading in the same direction. I was nervous and wanted company. I asked her as she climbed in with a couple of companions if she wasn't afraid. Her brown eyes shone out from under a headscarf printed with flowers and with complete equanimity she replied: 'Allah has written which bullet is for me. Why worry about it until then?'

Baddeley's words may sound old-fashioned but remained accurate in Chechnya: '. . . it was inevitable, in the circumstances, that the division of life's burden amongst them should be, not "Men must work and women must weep" but "Men must fight and women must work" – they had no time for weeping . . .'

# Cossacks and mountaineers

When o'er the Terek, steely-grey,
The Russian drums began to play . . .

Alexander Pushkin, *The Prisoner of the Caucasus*, 1821

A WEAK DECEMBER sun pushed through the kitchen windows on the ground floor of the Frantsuzsky Dom, the Chechen government hotel in Grozny, early on the Sunday morning of 11 December 1994. Needles of snow flecked the air outside. The motherly Russian women who ran the hotel had decided to make their guests breakfast. They did not have to. It was the only hotel functioning in the city (the Hotel Kavkaz had shut again soon after the independence celebrations) and was packed with journalists who paid dollars cash to be able to sleep on the floor with up to ten other guests. The women had simply taken pity on their unwashed and hungry clientele. My stomach was full of fried eggs and fresh bread still baked somewhere in the city. Slurping coffee, I wound the dial of my shortwave radio across the Babel of different stations in search of fresh news.

'KkhhhhhzzhhLebanesepopmusickkkhhhhhkkkkhhhhkkkhh . . . Russia's official news agency, TASS, is reporting that its troops have moved into Chechnya this morning at dawn . . .'

I telephoned the agency to make sure it had picked up the report, ran out onto the street next to the market to stop a car, and drove to the invasion.

At Goragorsk, on top of the Sunzha Range about 40 kilometres northwest of Grozny, we saw an armoured column driving in single file headed in the city's direction. A warplane flew over

the column and headed southeast towards Grozny. Mi24 helicopter gunships, which the Russians nicknamed *Krokodily*, hung
in the air over the column like hornets a little ahead of the
column, the chatter of their engines and blades compounding
the din of the column's metal tracks chewing the road. The concrete blocks of a checkpoint from the autumn were abandoned.
A few villagers stood by the roadside and watched as the column,
with a tank flying a bright red, blue and white Russian pennant,
snaked southwards.

The last vehicle in the column halted and a machinegun swiv-
elled round to aim at a photographer, the Chechen driver and
myself. We had both been filming. We could not reason with a
noisy, lidded armoured vehicle. I thrust both hands high in the
air in what I hoped was an obvious act of surrender. The
photographer and our Chechen driver, whom I had waved
down in the market only that morning, did the same. With the
machinegun quivering in its socket, a lid on top of the vehicle
opened and two Russian soldiers climbed out. They jumped
down onto the road and pointed their assault rifles at us.

One of them led the Chechen away into a ploughed field, on
which the snow had melted, ordering him to put his hands on
his *shapka* and kicking his legs apart as he stood so that he
wobbled unsteadily in a sticky clay furrow. I felt sick. They were
going to shoot him. I did not know his name.

The other soldier walked up to me and gestured to me to
open my camera. He pulled out the cassette of film and thrust it
into his combat jacket. Without a word spoken for virtually the
whole encounter, the two soldiers then climbed back up onto
their vehicle, leaving the Chechen standing alone with his back
to them, his hands still on his head. They slipped back inside,
clunking the lid behind them, sailors on a land-borne subma-
rine. A cloud of black smoke kicked out of the exhaust as they
accelerated to catch up with the rest of the column.

The invasion was on. Yeltsin, humiliated by the failure of the
Chechen opposition's November attack on Grozny that he had
backed, had authorized all means to bring Chechnya back under
Kremlin control and warplanes had for days given the territory's

population sleepless nights. The arrival of ground forces pushed Chechnya to war. A Chechen official purportedly in charge of the republic's civil defence said underground shelters had been made ready and that instructions on what to do if there was an all-out assault on the city had been broadcast on Presidential Television. But there was no sign of any preparations on the part of the Chechen fighters for the defence of the city.

There were no air-raid sirens. The jets flew over the city without warning, low in the daytime and high at night. A gentle rain of yellow flares continued to fall from the sky, flickering in the snow-filled cloud. As the crowd of volunteers in Freedom Square grew, civilians who had wavered over whether to stay or go found themselves trapped. Katya Golsova, a Russian woman in her late sixties, stood at a bus stop with her two grandchildren. She wrung her hands in panic as she spoke, the two children next to her silent, impassive.

'I want to leave, but there aren't any buses.'

The three Russian army groups predicted by Maskhadov, comprising 40,000 troops, started to move towards Grozny from the north, the east and the west.

Dudayev's people appeared confused. Some still wanted negotiations and drove past the invading Russian troops to faltering peace talks in Vladikavkaz. Others, like the 'foreign minister', Shamsudin, ruled them out. 'How can they take place when they send in the army? There will be no negotiations between Chechnya and Russia. We'll fight.' The diplomat now kept a Kalashnikov on his windowsill with a spare clip of ammunition. 'We need tanks and weapons. So we'll take them from the Russians.'

Chechen fighters fought Russian troops north of the city in Dolinsk, 25 kilometres northwest of Grozny, the day after the invasion. I caught up with some of them revving the monstrous engines of three precious T72 tanks in a field. Orange oil flares smeared the night. I shouted at a Chechen in a sheepskin jacket crouched on the back of one of the tanks, hot air pouring out of the grille over the engine. It was hopeless trying to speak over the noise. The Chechen shouted through cupped hands straight into my ear. He turned out to be the commander of the unit.

'We're off to defend our land!' he bawled. 'And thank our Ingush brothers!' he added. The Russian column driving in from the west had been attacked by angry Ingush who set vehicles on fire in the village of Barsuki. A Russian troop train was derailed when the tracks were blown. With a cry of *Allahu akbar!* from the fighters, the tanks tipped forward with a jerk into the field and into the night.

A few minutes after the tanks had left, a heavy, coughing Zil truck drew up on the roadside with a complement of Grad rockets, literally 'hail', loaded in the multiple launcher attached to the back. A bearded Chechen wound down the window and asked some bystanders for the direction in which the tanks had gone. Where had he found this machine? Where had he learned to use it? There was no time to find out. He crunched the gears into reverse, turned and drove off back up the hill towards the Russian invaders.

The first people to be fired on by the Russian army as it crossed the Terek were predominantly Russians and Cossacks. The elderly remnants of a Cossack community lived on the Sunzha Ridge in a small clutch of single-storied *izby* called Pervomayskaya, about ten kilometres northwest of Grozny. Meaning 'the first of May', after the Soviet workers' holiday, the name was pinned to many villages and factories across the old Union. During the Russian Civil War, the Cossacks of the Kuban had fought for General Denikin's White Army but proved skittish allies. Cossack leaders demanded their own independent state and threatened to drive out ethnic Russians as well as the mountaineers. Denikin, out to preserve empire, regarded the Cossacks as renegade Russians. For their alliance with the Whites, which in reality extended only as far as the lands the Cossacks considered their own, both the Don and Kuban Cossacks were either deported or killed under Stalin's directions, and the Chechens, Volga Germans and other nationalities were treated similarly in the 1940s.

Under Yeltsin, there was talk of recreating the Cossacks as a 'military service estate'. The army officers and bureaucrats who had rediscovered their Cossack roots were a bit like the enthusiasts who dress up in English civil war uniforms. The few that remained or who had returned to the Terek, poor Russian peasants in all but name, found themselves once more on the front line of empire, unable, as one journal put it, to 'make up their minds – let alone "prove" – whether they are a race apart from "ordinary" Russians'.

In the summer of 1994, Ataman Giorgy Galkin, the local Cossack chieftain, had invited me to lunch at his modest farmhouse. The entrance was choked with dark green vines. The chieftain's eyes had a Father Christmas twinkle and he ran his fingers continually through a bushy silver moustache. I said he did not look much like a Cossack. He scraped back his chair, led me into his bedroom and opened a tall cupboard. A coat-hanger held a powder blue *cherkeska* and a pair of striped cavalry trousers folded carefully underneath. A pair of black, ill-polished riding boots stood to attention below. A sabre rested in a corner at the back of the cupboard. He smiled and raised his eyebrows in such a way as to say: 'You see? I *am* an Ataman!' His wife, with the quiet energy of a Chechen woman, ferried salads, soup and bread to the table while Galkin dispensed the vodka, chuckling as he did so. Like the Orthodox priest in Grozny, he was careful not to say too much about Dudayev or the Chechens. I subsequently learned that his family and many other Cossacks had faced repeated petty harassment by the Chechens.

'We have lived together with the Chechens. We intermarried for centuries so we practically are Chechens!' In the uncertain months leading up to the war, the merry ataman was critical of Moscow's use of armed proxies to subdue the Chechens, fearing the effect it might have on his own fragile community. He spoke of the need for a 'Scottish' type settlement to meet the Chechens' demands for independence and hoped the tensions would not lead to war.

While the genuine victims of robbery and violent attacks, few local Russians and Cossacks welcomed the armed intervention. Their families and homes were in direct physical danger. While the army bombed and shelled from a safe distance, they had to live among a people angered as hopes of independence came under fire from Russian soldiers.

Elderly Russians, abandoned by younger familes who had left for steppe towns further north, sold their last possessions to buy food and begged for bread in Grozny's market. 'The Russian *babushky* always ask "Give us bread",' harrumphed Zina Kurasava, a forty-year-old geography teacher and a Chechen. Her face was framed in a purple-woollen scarf dappled with melting flakes of snow as she stood in the market. 'We give bread to them – but the Russians don't.'

In Grozny's northern suburb of Katayama, a bus had been towed back to a transport depot. Many of its windows were blown out, the remaining glass in the frames an opaque green mozaic. A woman passenger had been killed when a bomb dropped by a warplane exploded by the roadside. One of the depot managers said both Chechens and Russians were travelling on the bus. Sawdust had been scattered over the seats and the floor to soak up the blood.

Dudayev lived in the suburb with his wife Alla, the daughter of a Russian officer, and their three children. His bodyguards shooed us away from the tall green iron gates around the home. At a base used by Chechen fighters nearby, a young woman in blue overalls and toting a canvas first-aid bag stood near the wreckage of a transport helicopter. 'I live nearby so I ran over to see what I could do after the raid,' said the woman, who introduced herself as Natalya Sholkhalova, a nurse. She said she had a Chechen father and a Russian mother. She urged me to 'write the truth' about Russian-Chechen relations. One of the Chechens pointed at a fellow fighter with cold blue eyes under a black woollen cap. His arms rested on a rifle strapped level across his chest.

'He's Russian!' said one of the Chechen fighters, warming to the nurse's theme.

Sergey Chicherov, twenty-four, said he was a Cossack, not a Russian. He saw nothing strange about fighting against the Russian army. 'If someone comes and attacks your home, are you supposed to just sit and watch?'

The Cossacks along the Terek copied the dress of the mountaineers and strove to emulate and better them in feats of arms and horsemanship, or *dzhigitovka*, so much so that the 1924 *Pocket Oxford Dictionary* describes them as 'Members of a Turkish people subject to Russia and famous as light cavalry'. While their name, *kazak*, 'Cossack' in Russian, is borrowed from the Turkic, meaning 'free man' or 'bandit', the Cossacks were actually a hotchpotch of Slav-speaking brigands, herdsmen, runaway serfs, members of Christian sects fleeing persecution and others who refused to fit into the hierarchy of landowner and serf. They made their homes the dangerous borderlands of the Ukrainian steppe, the Urals and the North Caucasus. They formed small, militarized frontier societies, the *sotnya*, or hundreds, headed up by an *ataman*, or chieftain, who chewed over weightier issues at a regional *krug*, or circle.

Their activities were at first often at odds with the faraway Russian court; they were pirates both on steppe and sea. In 1573 Thomas Banister and Geoffrey Ducket of the Russia Company were attacked by Cossack pirates, 'outlaws or banished men', who made off with their ship and all its cargo which had been bound for Persia. Persian emissaries were still complaining to the Russian court in the eighteenth century that their merchant ships were plagued by Cossack pirates. The bloody rebellions of Stenka Razin and Pugachev – the latter the subject of Pushkin's novel *The Captain's Daughter* – were led by Cossacks.

But the wily bureaucrats in Moscow and St Petersburg, paying lip service to Cossack freedom and culture, moved to assimilate Cossacks into the empire as the rugged guardians of, and often contributors to, its fast expanding borders. Tsars could always dissociate themselves from their more disreputable behaviour while enjoying their services for free. Like the mountaineers, the Cossacks enjoyed a fiercesome reputation, hence the panic in revolutionary crowds in St Petersburg when the cry of 'Cossacks!' went up. They were also the tearaway children of imperial folklore. Maria Dmitryevna, *'le terrible dragon'* in *War and Peace*, waves her finger lovingly at the naughty young Natasha Rostova, calling her 'my Cossack'. Russian parents tell an upset child: 'Pull yourself together Cossack, you're going to be an ataman!'

It was Cossacks who from the time of Peter manned the fortresses of 'the line' in the North Caucasus. The 'line' was drawn between the established empire to the north and the mountain tribes to the south. On the eastern side of the isthmus, the River Terek formed the line, a pale blue band on Soviet maps. To the north of the river is marginal steppeland while to the south, thin brown contour lines tighten briefly on the Sunzha range of hills, relaxing around Grozny before tightening once more a few miles further south in a crescendo of peaks shaded grey to mark the North Caucasus range. The Greben Cossacks lived on the left bank, that is the north side of the Terek, as it flowed eastwards to the Caspian. They manned small forts and villages spaced every twelve miles, each with a watchtower, an alarm bell and a round-the-clock guard on duty. If a Cossack heard two shots being fired, he was being called to arms; four shots warned of a robbery or cattle-rustling; eight shots were a cry for help from a fort under full-blown attack by the Chechens or other tribesmen.

The Cossack wives, some of them Chechens, were expected to work the land like those of the mountaineers on the right bank. Given the nature of the Cossack enterprise, 'recruits' were usually men. 'Wives they must have, and, as a consequence, the capture of women formed a main incitement to their constant raids, a necessary condition, indeed, of their continued existence and prosperity,' Baddeley wrote. 'It follows that those who represent the Cossacks as almost entirely of Slav blood are just as wide of the mark as those who see in them, merely, the descendants of the Khazar and other Turk or Tartar tribes.' Both Baddeley and Tolstoy, the latter in his ethnographically accurate novella *The Cossacks*, tell how Ivan the Terrible granted land to the Cossacks, Old Believers at odds with the Russian Orthodox Church. Their territory started in the ridge (Russian: *greben*) of hills to the north of where the Argun and Sunzha rivers converge, hemmed in to the north again where the Sunzha meets the Terek. The Cossacks who live in this small region are known as

the Greben Cosssacks. Baddeley set down the words of a Greben
song:

'Little Father of us all, Orthodox Tsar,
What will you give and what will you grant us?'
'I will give and grant, little Cossacks mine,
The Terek River that runs so free
From the Greben to the wide blue sea,
To the wide blue sea, to the Caspian.'

The Cossacks preferred to buy their *shashki*, or sabres, *kinzhali*
and even rifles up until the mid-nineteenth century from the
mountain smiths. Their striking dress was lifted wholesale from
the mountaineers. General Velyaminov ordered Cossacks to
keep at least half a *verst* distance from scared peasants as 'the
Cossacks of the Line wear clothes identical to those of the *gortsy*,
[and] peasants are not able to distinguish enemies from
Cossacks.' Baddeley himself observed at the end of the nineteenth century, 'No one but a native of the Caucasus, or one
who had spent many years there, could possibly distinguish the
brigand from the horse patrol set to catch him.' The Cossacks
were products *par excellence* of the shifting, opalescent nature of
the empire, reluctantly serving one master while often in cahoots
with his master's enemy, especially in the avoidance of imperial
customs posts.

If the Cossacks could carry off native dress, Russians could
not. With a brutal ear for the false note, Tolstoy has the young
aristocratic hero in *The Cossacks*, Olenin (a thinly disguied
Tolstoy), try and emulate a mountain 'brave' by wearing a
Circassian coat and red silk *beshmet*: 'He wore Circassian dress
but he did not wear it well: anyone would recognise him at once
for a Russian and not a Tartar brave. It was all right – but it
looked wrong.'

The twenty-two-year-old Tolstoy's drinking, losses at cards,
'actresses' and the rest of his *comme il faut* existence in Moscow
led to some liverish entries in a special diary kept to keep track of
his weaknesses. To try and escape himself, Tolstoy followed his

elder brother Nicholas, an artillery officer, back to the Caucasus with a vague intention of joining the army. The escape route was a well-worn romantic cliché by the time Tolstoy headed south to the mountains in 1851. Russian officers doing battle with native braves and trysts with slim-wasted native women were the staple of coy and violent nineteenth-century Russian thrillers. But there were also tough acts to follow for the future literary general, with Pushkin setting the benchmark for exciting tales of Russia's superfluous men losing themselves in mountain skirmishes.

Pushkin's narrative poem *The Prisoner of the Caucasus* tells the tale of a young Russian soldier captured by Cherkess tribesmen who is shackled in chains in the tribesmen's village. The Cherkess are the 'Circassians' – of a different cultural and language group from that of the Chechens – who fought against Russian domination at the western end of the North Caucasus range. As we have seen, they were deported en masse to Turkey in 1864 with the Abkhaz, a people culturally close to their own. A Cherkess maiden takes pity on the prisoner, feeds him to improve his strength and falls in love with him. The hero turns down the girl's declaration of love – Byronic echoes of *Yevgeny Onegin*. Despite her rejection, the lovelorn girl frees him when the men set off on a raiding party:

> The Russian prisoner hears one day
> A warcry in the hills; 'Away!
> To horse! To horse!' They run, they shout,
> And copper bridles jingle out,
> Black is the cloak, the mail bright-metalled,
> The saddled horses seethe, unsettled,
> The village strains to go out raiding.
> Then, wild sons of war, they run
> In courses from the hills cascading
> To ride the banks of the Kuban
> To strike as only brute force can.

Like Kipling's Raj or Hollywood's depiction of how the west was won, the poems by Pushkin, and later Lermontov, set the romantic tone of empire. Pushkin's maiden guides him to a river, the line dividing 'civilized' empire to the north and the mountain tribes of the south, cast as noble savages whose freedom the young Russian officers sent to fight them by an autocratic tsar can only envy.

The region's hostage-taking became a staple of Russian literary plots, including a story by Tolstoy written for children, *A Prisoner in the Caucasus*, based on his own experience of near-capture at the hands of the Chechens. There is a wonderfully sunny 1960s Soviet film, directed by Leonid Gayday, called *Captive-ess of the Caucasus* − a prim *Carry On* type comedy − which mocks the whole genre. The gawky, bespectacled hero arrives in the mountains on the back of a donkey to collect folk tales for an ethnographic study. A constant victim throughout the film of mountain hospitality, he is told, repeatedly, that it is forbidden − *nelzya!* − to refuse the drink proffered by his numerous hosts. On the road he falls in love with a curvy local girl, a Soviet *sportsmenka* whose hobby is mountaineering − the descendant of Pushkin's Cherkess maiden − whose innocent beauty shines through her 1960s A-line skirt. Swarthy, stereotyped Caucasus types try to steal her off to deliver her to the corrupt local party boss for marriage, in league with the girl's father.

Romantic depictions of the mountaineers die hard. In 1996 the director Sergey Bodrov was told to send the only print of his film *Prisoner of the Caucasus* to the Kremlin cinema so that Yeltsin could watch it. Bodrov's film aimed to show the 'true face' of the unpopular war Yeltsin had started in Chechnya. It was released just weeks before Yeltsin's close run for re-election against his old *alma mater*, the Communist Party. Bodrov got the Russian parts just right: his son played Vanya, a pathetic-looking conscript with shaved head who is captured by Chechen fighters on a dusty mountain road, the double of the conscripts captured in the opposition attack on Grozny; Vanya's mother, like hundreds of other Russian women in real life, tours military camps and headquarters in a desperate search for her missing son. As in the tales of Pushkin and Tolstoy, Vanya and a comrade are tied to the backs of ponies and led to a remote mountain village. The family they are taken to want to ransom them for their own son who they think has been captured by the Russians. The family's daughter (cue Pushkin's Cherkess maiden) warns Vanya he must die in revenge for her brother, who they find out has been killed while trying to escape the Russians.

'I wanted to show something that has not changed for over a hundred years,' Bodrov said after the film's first screening the same year at the cavernous House of Cinematographers in Moscow. 'The Caucasus is the same now as when Tolstoy was writing about it.' Bodrov depicted Chechen fighters as noble savages, who spend their spare time wrestling and drinking vodka like extras in a Russian Forest of Arden. Real Chechen fighters would rest up at home in front of the television (if they had electricity or a generator) with their families. When they drank, most sipped tea. Russian prisoners often proved an embarrassment to the Kremlin in that during the 1994–96 war they regularly claimed better treatment at the hands of their Chechen captors than with their own units.

Bodrov admitted he had not enjoyed filming in Daghestan's mountains. He said one of the local actors, who played a Chechen commander and who doubled as the head of the set's security detail, turned up with an armed gang to demand a bigger fee. 'It's a different century up there,' he said disdainfully. I wondered if Bodrov's scorn had prompted the demand for more money. That and the skewed version of the centuries-old struggle the actor was being asked to play out for this Russian director. The Kremlin returned the film.

The Caucasus proved at first to be no escape for Tolstoy, even a disappointment. His thoughts see-sawed between the lofty and the trivial. His diary entry for 1 July 1851 in the Cossack fort of Stary Yurt: 'In face of everything how strong I appear to myself in this firm conviction that there is nothing to expect here but death . . . Yet at this very moment I am thinking with delight about a saddle I have ordered in which I will ride in Circassian attire, and about how I will flirt with Cossack girls, and feel despair that my left moustache is higher than the right one, and I shall spend two hours arranging it.'

His quivering antennae swept the Greben village of Starogladovskaya, where he was posted as an ensign with the 4th Battery of the 20th Artillery Brigade, soon picking up the Cossacks' preference of the 'enemy' Chechens over their supposed allies, the Russians. 'A Cossack is less inclined to hate the Chechen brave, the *dzhigit*, who may well have killed his brother, than the Russian soldier billeted on him for the defence of his village but who has fouled his cottage by smoking in it. He respects his enemy the hillsman, but despises the soldier, who is in his eyes an alien and an oppressor.'

Tolstoy sketched the Greben Cossacks as a people free of guilt and hypocrisy, living an idyll fresh from the pages of his beloved Rousseau. Tolstoy has Olenin spin in tumults of guilt and lust after 'the firm girlish form under the thin cotton smock' modelled on the Cossack girl Maryanka who, as in the book, spurned the count's advances (he caught the clap off another Cossack girl). Tolstoy knew the Cossacks, could write about them and was remembered by them, but of the mountaineers themselves he had little to say. The Chechens, 'braves', form a continual, brooding presence on the banks of the Terek, like wolves in a forest. Try as he might, the young count failed to banish the romanticism he disliked in the literature of the Caucasus from his own tale.

It is difficult to cut the romance out of the mountains. Alexander Bestuzhev, writing under the name Marlinsky, gained immense popularity in nineteenth-century Russia as the author of novels like *Ammalat-Bek*, a series of contemporary *Flashman*s set in the Caucasus. Derided as pulp fiction by Turgenev and other literary dignatories (Tolstoy raced through them as a boy), they guaranteed high sales of any literary journal that printed them. But Bestuzhev was a character as impossibly romantic as the ones who peopled his stories. Exiled to Siberia as one of the Decembrists, he was transferred to the Caucasus as a soldier when Shamil's predecessor, Gazi-Muhammed, led a *ghazavat* against Russia. The posting

provided useful material for his novels. Bestuzhev made a suici-
dal charge in battle in 1837 in which he was wounded in the
chest. He was under a cloud after his landlady's daughter killed
herself with the pistol he kept under his pillow. But perhaps he
was unable to live with the task he had been charged with,
namely bringing the freedom-loving mountaineers he admired
to submit to the tsar who had exiled him. His body went
missing but rumours went out that Bestuzhev had actually
joined the mountaineers and had taken five native wives. Even
the Ammalat-Bek of Bestuzhev's novel was based on a real
character who escaped house arrest by murdering the Russian
colonel he had befriended, all in the hope of winning the hand
of a mountain princess (he failed).

To pass the time on a hot day in Grozny during a doomed
round of peace talks in the summer of 1995, I chatted with an
American correspondent who had covered the war in Vietnam.
'The problem with this war,' he said, 'is that it's too goddamn
romantic.'

The closest Tolstoy could bring his readers truthfully to the
Chechens was to depict with a pathologist's precision one who
had been shot. In describing the corpse, the muscular arms, the
hollow stomach, the hennaed moustache and finger nails, it was
as if Tolstoy was trying to bring this once living, breathing
human being back to life. In *The Cossacks*, the Chechen
attempts to swim the Terek, a branch tied to his head by way of
disguise, but is shot by the young Cossack hero, a cause for
drunken celebration in the village. The dead Chechen's brother
who comes to ransom the body barely looks at the assembled
Cossacks and Olenin. 'It was plain that this was a brave who
had more than once met the Russians in quite other circumstances, and nothing about them could surprise or even interest
him.' Olenin is unaccountably struck by the waste of the
Chechen's death, his morbid curiosity shamed out of him by
the moody brother puffing at a clay pipe as he squats in the
shade of a tree. He is also sickened at the business-as-usual attitude of the Cossacks.

Tolstoy wrote in his diary on 6 January 1853: 'Stupid people.

All – especially my brother – drink, and it is very unpleasant for me. War is such an unjust and evil thing that those who wage it try to stifle their consciences. Am I doing right? My God, teach me and forgive me if I'm doing wrong.'

# Winter with the wolves

The Moon When the Wolves Run Together

Sioux name for December

TWO DAYS AFTER the invasion began, Russian helicopters fired rockets into Pervomayskaya at nine am in the morning. The villagers, mostly the old, wandered the streets in shock. Four rockets had slammed into the nursery school building. One had punctured a hole in the roof. The other three had landed in the yard. Four warplanes circled high up. An attack helicopter dipped down over the Sunzha Ridge, the flanks of which gleamed in crusted snow. Each time the sound of the helicopters got louder, the villagers would scamper back into their homes, coming back out when the sound had died away again, their faces scanning the horizon for the dark, scorpion forms. An elderly Cossack woman was carried out of her home on a stretcher into the back of a waiting ambulance. She had been injured in the attack. Her neighbour put her hands to the side of her head.

'They're killing peaceful people!'

The nursery school had been empty save for another Cossack woman who had been preparing food in the canteen for the village pensioners. Badly wounded, she had already been moved to a hospital. Pots still simmered on the canteen stove. Plaster and wood splinters boiled in the stew.

The crack-boom of shelling whipped the winter air further up the ridge. Isa Dalkhayev was the Chechen commander in the village. He was young but he moved deliberately, walking in a rhythm of his own and not in reaction to the random sounds of the guns and aircraft. I asked his rank and he ventured 'Lieutenant'. The commander said his men had checked the Russian advance at the village of Keny-Yurt, over the other side of the ridge and down by the Terek. He scanned the ridge with a pair of binoculars. Plumes of grey smoke rose on the ridge, the sound of the explosions catching up later, out of sync.

'They have 60 armoured vehicles, but we're not sending any of our own as we've no air support,' he said.

Volunteer fighters arrived with assault rifles and rocket-propelled grenades, or RPGs. They started to dig slit trenches around the village. In a garage fighters heaved belts of ammunition, slink rolls of copper teeth, onto a mobile anti-aircraft gun. The helicopter engines, continually fading and increasing, had made weather vanes of the ruddy-cheeked Cossack women who came out of their porches when it sounded fair but who went back inside when the nearness of the engines threatened a storm. Leaving the village, I passed an APC dragging an artillery piece towards the ridge and ferrying a group of fighters on top. Dudayev vanished from view, reappearing only to fume at a rare press conference in the basement of the Presidential Palace. His moustache curled above his lip to accent the torrent of abuse hurled at the 'satanists' around Yeltsin. The moustache, now teamed up with a forage cap and camouflage fatigues, gave Dudayev the air of a raffish matinée idol from World War Two.

'It's not merely local military clashes, which are now going on in the outskirts of Grozny, but fierce fighting between a still weak Russian democracy and a new Russian totalitarianism.'

About 30 kilometres on the western road out of Grozny the same afternoon, the tops of the mountains running along the road to the south shone coral pink in the twilight as the foothills and forests darkened below. Their contours were by turns smooth and creased like a badly ironed shirt. On the road, about 500 unarmed Chechens, most of them women, stood with flags and banners. Three hundred metres further on, a large column of Russian armour had halted in the snow.

'We've been standing here since morning – we don't want war,' said one of the protesters, Yakuv Makayev, a Chechen from the nearby village of Dovidenko. The women wore uniform lumpy woollen coats, their heads wrapped in thick brown shawls. A pro-Dudayev vanguard had white headbands tied round their heads and held their palms up in prayer. One woman in combat fatigues held up the Chechen highlanders' Ichkerian flag. Others carried placards:

RUSSIAN SOLDIERS STOP – DON'T SPILL THE BLOOD OF THE
PEOPLE

GRACHEV, COOL YOUR PASSION – DON'T KILL THE FRIENDSHIP
BETWEEN TWO PEOPLES

The crowd talked excitedly, watching the road and the column ahead of them for any signs of movement. Two helicopter gunships floated on either side of the road. Below them, Russian paratroopers paused to draw breath on cigarettes as they attacked the cold earth with trenching tools. We walked up to them, slowly, in the middle of the road and stopped a few metres short of the first trench. Noone was willing to talk. A paratrooper on watch said only, 'We're here under orders', and stared past us with awkward deliberation. Behind him, the fast-dimming outlines of tanks, communication trucks, fuel trucks, generator trucks, trucks carrying shells, APCs and all the metal paraphernalia of a battle group on the march were parked in lines on and off the road for hundreds of yards. Among the trees, their spidery bare branches black against the snow, fires had already been lit for the night. That day Dudayev had promised no quarter to the Russian troops, saying they 'will be attacked from the rear in a traditional tactic of the mountaineers: hit and run, hit and run, which will exhaust them until they, out of fear and terror, give up.' A general, he must have known what a column of armour looked like, how it groaned like a monster, the fabulous noise of all those diesel engines like so many cells, what it could do. At 3.45 pm a tall Russian officer in a black, ribbed tank helmet walked past the sentry and up to the women. He was unaccompanied. Quickly crowded by the women, the officer introduced himself as Major-General Ivan Babichev, the column's commander. He bent his head down to listen to the babble of voices that erupted, a frown etched on his forehead. He told the crowd that he had halted the column. The advance of the western group of forces, he said, would stop indefinitely.

'We don't want to shoot the people,' he said. 'We've saved the lives of our men and your people. That is our achievement today.'

The jets continued to hiss high up like kettles kept hot on a range, dropping flares over Grozny, candelabras on parachutes. The noise of the engines reverberated in the pit of my stomach during the day and played with my sleep, like a cat with a mouse. The next day, an Mi8 transport helicopter, a large red star emblazoned on the side of the fuselage, was parked at a crazy angle in the middle of the main road west of Grozny. Fighters had brought it down by shooting at it with rifles and wounding the pilot. Two crew were said to have been killed. Russian news agencies reported that Chechens had 'literally' torn them to pieces. Chechen fighters hung around the helicopter, looking about them uncertainly. The road sweated with unseasonal rain and was littered by branches and twigs chopped up by the rotor blades. The streets of Grozny were empty again save for a number of volunteer fighters in green headbands who dropped in and out of Freedom Square. A tiny handful were volunteers from outside Chechnya like Sashko. He was a beefy Ukrainian with a pirate's bandanna over his shaved head, extreme anti-Russian ideas and a Kalashnikov with which to try them out. There was no sign of the thousands of Afghan mujaheddin the Kremlin said now swarmed the republic.

I left the square to take the temperature in the bazaar. The only splash of colour in the brackish snow were the clean red and white oblong cartons of cigarettes peeping out from traders' bags.

'I'm afraid but I'm not going to leave,' said Olga Butrinova, a

Russian *pensionerka*. Walking slowly through the market, she did not seem to have anywhere in particular to go to even if she had wanted to leave. 'We will stay together with the Chechens.'

A United Nations advertisement to promote awareness of the hell refugees go through to become pariahs in another country shows armed men, explosions and aircraft descending out of the blue on a western suburban street. The idea is to put you in the refugee's shoes. But it doesn't happen like that. First of all, armed men have hung around this town for years and nothing has happened to you. It's not comfortable. But you make do. There are unexplained gunshots at night but they are always a block away and anyway, mafiosi who live by the gun die by the gun. You yourself have a gun – just in case, you would never use it but it is something a cousin in the militia gave you. But you keep it quiet from the neighbours all the same and stow it under a bed. The town's central heating system breaks down but there is still gas in the pipes so you heat your home with the kitchen stove. Bread is scarce but you couldn't afford it anyway. If you're old, you live like a stray dog, reliant on handouts from stricken consciences or what you find in a pile of garbage. The warplanes are unpleasant but they are meant to scare. They won't really bomb flats and houses – perhaps the Presidential Palace and good riddance – but not my home. And so on, while the sound of real battle approaches until suddenly – and you don't know quite how this has happened – you find it has overtaken you and you are in the middle of it.

Dudayev pulled out of 'negotiations' with the Kremlin for good. In another apocalyptic television address, he declared, 'It's a war for life or death.' Of the invaders, he said: 'The soil must burn under their feet.' Chechen fighters were doing what they could with assault rifles, grenades, shotguns and Molotov cocktails back in Pervomayskaya. Shamil Aslambekov, a thirty-five-year-old Chechen farmworker with a full moustache, sat with other volunteers in the low room of a farmhouse airmail blue with cigarette smoke. A red square, a Persian carpet, was nailed to one of the whitewashed walls. The men were still, squatting on their haunches, doped by a hot stove. They talked in low voices. The single rounds of sniper fire – *chik-kack!* – sounded gently in the street outside. 'My family is in the mountains and I'll wait here with my gun,' Aslambekov said simply. 'What else is there to do? Our morale is strong – it must be with what we're fighting with.' The men complained that the flares made night operations difficult. 'Allah will help us,' said Usman Dauyev, a young volunteer. 'Now every Chechen is a soldier.' A shell crashed loudly nearby. The men looked up. 'They're probing to try and find us,' he said. 'They don't know where we are.'

In less than a day, the battle had already overtaken the residents of Pervomayskaya. An old man on horseback led a flock of sheep out of the village while a group of fighters ran to dodge the snipers. Some of them slipped on ice melting in the street. 'Many people have lost the rooves of their houses since yesterday,' Aslambekov said. The war lapped at the edges of Grozny. The doctor in charge of the Republic Hospital, Hadzhi Bakharchiyev, said he had enough supplies for up to a hundred wounded for a week. 'We have everything for seven days. We sleep here. But that's it. We have no more stocks. We haven't received anything since November.' That day he had treated a woman who had been brought in with rocket shrapnel in her back.

More and more windows on the roads out of the city were criss-crossed with tape. Makeshift barriers were made ready to block the northern road. A field gun was fixed in position in the road's central reservation. A slim volunteer laid out his coat on slush ice next to the road, took off his boots, curled knitted white socks under him and knelt to pray to Mecca. He carried a hunting knife on his belt. The word *Ghazavat* was written on his green headband.

'I am praying to Allah to show us the truth and to bring us help for freedom, independence,' he said, after he put his boots back on. He watched approvingly as I scrawled down his name in my notebook: Gaziyev, Ibragim, twenty-eight. 'Never in Chechnya will we give up our weapons. The war hasn't started yet against Russia. It'll start very soon.' Darkness had fallen. I stopped to try and locate the orange and white flashes of explosions near the Mayakovsky settlement, drab sets of five-storey *Khrushchevki* built for oil workers on the northern edge of Grozny. Dashes of tracer fire scored livid red lines across the suburbs in short, angry half-lives. Russian women shouted at each other in the street, running to find shelter. As the sound of a tank and an APC died away, both vehicles heading towards the city centre, I heard an old woman hiss at her daughter to be quiet. The daughter fretted about a son she had sent to Krasnodar. 'I can't leave, there's no way out of the city. I can't telephone to tell them how I am.' They held onto each other in the street, the night black and cold, the taut line of the daughter clinging onto the sagging line of her mother, herself leaning on a walking stick. There was a deep burst of machinegun fire from one of the balconies. 'What's he firing for?' the mother cursed. 'He'll draw fire on himself.' Chechen men suddenly appeared on the street from behind the shrubs and balconies across the road. A couple of flares streamed in – an attempt to place a large gun which had been firing on and off nearby. It was impossible to tell who was firing what. One young fighter carried a shotgun. Another a hunting rifle. They paused for a moment on the road with Rusumbek Aliev, who could not stop moving, springing up and down on his knees as if treading grapes. He reached into a thick, rough-cut sheepskin coat which stretched down to his knees to pull out a pistol of World War Two vintage. He shook it in the air in front of me. He said he was sixty and told of how he had been pushed into a cattletruck by NKVD troops in 1944 and sent to the icy steppes of Kazakhstan.

'We'll fight to the last drop of our blood!' Unable to stay still any longer, he raised his pistol in the air and ran off into the night.

 About fifty women and children spent that night beneath a grain elevator at the collective farm of Artemovsky Elevator, a couple of kilometres further west of Pervomayskaya. They had followed a black rubber grain belt below ground into a cramped tunnel. As I waited for my eyes to adjust to the pitch dark, the candles and kerosene lamps placed along the belt at intervals lit slivers of pale faces. The belt also served as one long bed. Cold water dripped off the ceiling. The air was stale. Every few yards, a cluster of children, tired, stretching and flopping, some crying, hung on one of the women, cramped in thick woollen coats and blankets. 'I've been here all night,' said a Chechen woman wearing a sky-blue headscarf. It had been her third night in the tunnel. The previous night two of the men had been killed when a rocket landed near the mosque. She held the youngest of seven children in her arms, a baby of a few months. Despite the poor light, I could see her eyes were red with exhaustion. 'I have no relatives in the mountains. We have no place to go. We have a few loaves of bread, but that's all.'

At the farm next day there was no shelling or small arms fire. The inhabitants talked outside in small groups, enjoying the lull in the fighting. Luiza Musayeva's nose twitched as she breathed in the grey winter air on a mud track near the farm buildings, the first time she had done so in four days. The seven-year-old girl moved between the barns and the silos like a colt, stretching her limbs just for the sake of it. Her face glowed with a little colour. She had just eaten bread washed down with hot tea. It was all her family had.

'I don't want to go back to the shelter,' she said, standing next to her two elder sisters, Khava and Khayda. 'We're cold.' School had not reopened since the Chechen opposition's botched attack on Grozny the previous month. Luiza's brown eyes leapt from beneath the woollen scarf tied round her head. 'I want to be at home but I'm afraid of the aeroplanes.' She led me over to the family home and showed me a hole in the ceiling where a rocket had hit. She stomped and crunched over broken glass in small red boots. Bled of any colour in the mud, snow, slush and fog, they stood out like Dorothy's ruby slippers in *The Wizard of Oz*.

Several rooves were smashed in the settlement, home to about fifty families. One kitchen was a jumble of pots and crumpled timber. The villagers said five of their neighbours had been killed and five injured since the invasion. Guns still sounded occasionally in the distance.

Back in Pervomayskaya, Lieutenant Dalkhayev said the area was quiet after his men, with a few of their precious tanks, had repulsed a Russian push towards the village the previous night. 'They are around two to three kilometres from here, can't you hear them?' The sound of a grumbling Jabberwocky, though distant, rode down on the winter wind. The shy commander made a comment. 'It's not the Russians who're fighting – they don't want this war either – but their government.' On the road out of the village, a group of fighters stood round a fire to warm up. A plastic drinks crate full of Molotov cocktails and cardboard boxes containing outsized green cans in the shape of round tuna tins, anti-tank mines, was jammed in the mud. A measured defiance had replaced the volunteer bravado of the beginning of the month. 'We're ready to stop fighting if the Russians do,' said a volunteer, in his thirties. 'But we won't join the Federation.' Another fighter, balancing a Kalashnikov on his shoulder, did not hold out any hopes of a settlement. 'We hear so many lies on Russian television, how can we believe anything they say? I distrust Yeltsin absolutely.'

The silhouette of a wolf with two slanted triangular eyes rests beneath a full moon on the Ichkerian flag, coloured lincoln green and bordered at the bottom by red and white stripes. I assumed the flag was a Ruritanian emblem of Dudayev's invention. But the wolf was also worn on the fighters' berets and the Chechens took a deep pride in their 'state' symbol. On the road one day, a Chechen driver rewound the cassette on his scratchy tape player to pump out for a fifth time the Europop band Ace of Bass's song 'All that she wants, is another baby . . .' The song was universally popular among the Chechens we drove with at that time. I asked him, a touch fed up, why this was so. 'Well, the words,' he said, grinning guiltily, 'sound like "Chechen wolf".' He jiggled his shoulders and sang something in Chechen to the music.

Baddeley left a few clues to the Vainakh peoples' pride in wolves. Mountaineers propitiated a wolf god called Toutir, asking him not to attack their flocks. Baddeley noted a ceremony at New Year's Eve in which Ossetians wound a switch of willow round a column by the hearth which would tie up the wolves' jaws for the coming year. 'Clean Monday' was a Lenten fast which was called 'the holding of Toutir's mouth' and corresponded with the April feast of St George, the patron saint of cattle, horses and wolves across Eastern Europe. Baddeley overheard an Ingush roguishly put down his peoples' provenance to a woman raped by a wolf. Wolves' teeth were valuable amulets to ward off malign spirits. In the mountain aoul of Ghimree, in neighbouring Daghestan, Baddeley writes that the muezzin's call to prayer had 'something, indeed to my ears, of the howl of the wolf in it'.

The Chechens' identification with wolves can have only demonized them further in the eyes of the Russians, brought up on tales of wicked, slavering wolves lurking hungrily in their dark, northern forests like the 'evil Chechen' creeping along the banks of the Terek in Lermontov's *Cossack Lullaby*. Sasha and Matt liked to watch the Soviet cartoon equivalent of Bugs Bunny, a series called *Nu pokadi*, in which a loutish, unshaven wolf in a vest with a cigarette hanging out of his mouth chases after an innocent-looking hare. The details in the cartoon are priceless, from the wolf as a drunken Russian muzhik to the dried fish hanging out on the washing lines in the balconies of apartment blocks. The hare always escapes with the wolf growling: '*Nu zayets! Pokadi!*' – 'I'll show you, hare!'

The Chechens' wolf is not the 'devil's hound' of the Inquisition's Malleus Maleficarum, the werewolf, seducer, sorcerer and liar of the western imagination. Ibragim Aliroyev, in *The Language, History and Culture of the Vainakh*, dutifully describes the influence first of Christianity and then Islam among the mountaineers but warms up considerably when he begins to recount older, animistic beliefs. 'The Vainakh mullahs had to fight long with the folk medicine men,' he wrote. Vainakh shamans were said to cure illness by placing a scrap of paper carrying holy sayings in a cup of water to drink. There were gods of thunder and lightning, the sky, sun and moon (who also symbolized man and woman respectively), bread and wheat, water, war and paradise. There were abundant folk beliefs linked to animals: that the sound of dogs fighting in the night signals the death of a man; a cat that starts to lick herself means guests will soon arrive; a cat that leaves a home takes with her the happiness of the household.

When Imam Shamil was near the end of the *ghazavat* he led against Russia, the most honoured guest at his table was a black and white cat presented to him by a Russian deserter. 'For this animal Shamil had a great affection,' wrote Baddeley, 'and, when at Veden, he never dined without his four-footed friend nor began his own meal until he had prepared hers. The table was small and low, and pussy and her master sat on the floor on opposite sides.' The cat apparently died of grief when the Imam retreated to a nearby forest when Vedeno was besieged by Russian troops. A trusted lieutenant buried the cat with honour, making a funeral oration over her resting place, but the cat's death spooked Shamil, who is supposed to have said: 'Now it will go badly with me.'

The wolf, in Chechen *borz*, is the Chechen's prized totem. Aliroyev explains: 'The wolf is the most poetic beast in the understanding of the mountaineers . . . the lion and the eagle represent strength but eventually weaken while the wolf becomes stronger than he [Chechen/wolf] is himself; bravery, audacity, cunning replace the lack of strength. In the dead of night he ambles round the herd on the outskirts of the aoul from where death threatens any minute. If caught in a hopeless situation, the wolf dies in silence, he shows no fear or pain. These properties characterize the real hero of mountaineer beliefs.'

A wolf is said to howl every time a Chechen is born. A wolf's tendon was thought to have magical powers, enabling its owner to unmask a thief. Chechens are said never to curse a wolf for attacking a flock. A Chechen legend recounts how a wolf approached a slave watching over some sheep and asked him for one of the flock. The slave said he would have to ask his master. 'Put on me all the sins the master would commit by deceiving a guest by telling him he has fed his horse while leaving it unfed if I touch even just one sheep while you go and ask,' said the wolf. The master told his slave to return to the wolf and give him three sheep. The wolf, waiting by the flock, had kept his word. But the slave hid two of the sheep for himself and gave the wolf only one sheep. The wolf, on departing, cried out: 'Let the two sheep be man's debt to me. For all time, man will be my debtor.'

The wolf in Chechen cosmogony mirrors that of the first peoples of North America. George Catlin lived and travelled among the Plains Indians in the 1830s. In his Letter No.30 from the mouth of the Teton River, Upper Missouri, he describes a sojourn there while he painted the portrait of Wolf On The Hill, a Cheyenne chief in the Rocky Mountains. 'These people [the Cheyenne] are the most desperate set of horsemen, and warriors also, having carried on almost unceasing wars with the Pawnees and Blackfeet . . .' He observed how Plains Indians wore the skins of wolves when they hunted buffalo. 'While the herd of buffaloes are together, they seem to have little dread of the wolf, and allow them to come in close company with them. The Indian has taken advantage of this fact, and often places himself under the skin of this animal, and crawls for half a mile or more on his hands and knees, until he approaches within a few rods of the unsuspecting group, and easily shoots down the fattest of the throng.'

Catlin predicted the Cheyenne's alcoholic nemesis, writing that 'they easily acquire a taste, that to be catered for, where whiskey is sold at sixteen dollars a gallon, soon impoverishes them, and must soon strip the skin from the last buffalo's back that lives in their country, to be dressed by their squaws and vended to the Traders for a pint of diluted alcohol.' In the early nineteenth century, before Islam took a strong hold in the mountains, the Chechens were also in danger of succumbing to the bottle, wine – the syrupy Caucasian *chikhir* – and vodka having inevitably followed the Cossacks and Russian soldiers south. Imam Shamil, when a boy, was desperately ashamed of the drunkenness of his father. The young ascetic tried to make his father stop drinking, persuading him to swear on the Koran on seven different occasions, but in vain. Exasperated, the pious fourteen-year-old threatened to stab himself to death in front of his father if he refused to give up the wicked habit. Shamil's father is said to have sobered up. Shamil later had himself flogged publicly for having once tasted wine. After subduing the mountaineer village of Akusha in Daghestan in 1819, General Alexey Yermolov, praised his foe, 'but dissoluteness has already made its appearance in the wake of strong drink.' The Plains Indians' identification with the wolf – indeed, their conscious debt to the wolf for tried and tested hunting information and techniques – sits closely with the Chechens, down to the wolf tooth amulet. 'The Indian did not think of the wolf as a warrior in the same sense as he thought of himself as a warrior, but he respected the wolf's stamina and stoicism and he encouraged these qualities in himself and others.'

There was something inherently wolf-like in the way small bands of Chechen fighters loped through Grozny, the 'leader' of any such group being difficult to identify. When Russian forces supposedly 'held' Grozny from early 1995, wild gunfire would break out as soon as the sun went down as flocks of nervous conscripts shot at anything that moved in case it was a Chechen fighter. A group of two or three Chechens would have weapons hidden in the city and would slope in at night and fire them at Russian posts, moving from time to time to shoot from different positions to inflate their strength in the terrified conscripts' imaginations. They would then cache the weapons and slink off before dawn. When two or three wolves howl, they each do so at a different pitch, the harmonics producing a sound that makes the listener believe there is a pack up to two dozen strong.

'What is the force that moves nations?' Tolstoy demands to know in *War and Peace*. For a split moment, the fate of Grozny – the volunteer fighters, the *babushki* with nowhere to go, sleep-deprived surgeons,

1. Lev Tolstoy served as an artillery officer during the Russian wars of conquest in the Caucasus to escape boredom and gambling debts; the experience haunted him in old age

2. Mikhail Lermontov was sent to serve in the Caucasus as a punishment for duelling in St Petersburg; he was killed in another duel at the age of 26. On hearing the news, Nicholas I is said to have remarked: 'A dog's death for a dog'

3. Imam Shamil, the Avar warrior and Imam of Chechnya and Daghestan, led Russian troops a merry dance for more than a quarter of a century; he surrendered outside the Daghestan hill village of Gunib in 1859. His *ghazavat*, or 'Holy War', against the Russian Empire foundered on the mountaineers' disunity in the face of a Russian force three times larger than the one now deployed in Chechnya

4. Cruelty was the cornerstone of the Russian commander General Alexey Yermolov's Caucasus policy in the early nineteenth century. He declared: 'I desire that the terror of my name should guard our frontiers more potently than chains of fortresses'

5. John Baddeley, a British reporter-turned-oilman, rode through the Caucasus Mountains in the early 1900s. His history of the Russian conquest and observations on mountaineer culture are unsurpassed to this day

6. As a young Chechen the future Soviet general
Dzhokhar Dudayev gave 'Ossetian' as his nationality on his
application papers to win a place as a trainee Soviet pilot at
the Tambov air school. Here he is pictured in his cadet's
uniform with his mother in 1963. They had returned to
Chechnya from exile in Kazakhstan only six years earlier

7. A Chechen fighter watches rebel television pictures of Dudayev in April 1996,
the day after the Chechen president was killed when a Russian missile locked on to
the signal of his satellite telephone

8. Eduard Shevardnadze, once Mikhail Gorbachev's smiling Soviet foreign minister and now Georgia's head of state, pictured here at a banquet hosted by the Patriarch of Georgia's Orthodox Church in 1994. The war-torn republic's constant power cuts meant the candles were not entirely for show

9. Georgia's Stalin Party brings its campaign to the streets of Tbilisi during the presidential election in autumn 1995. The 'Red Monarch', born in December 1879 in the Georgian town of Gori, still enjoys considerable respect in the republic

10. General Aslan Maskhadov (*right*), the quiet Chechen, won the 1994–6 war in Chechnya against impossible odds but lost the territory's peace. Elected Chechnya's president in 1997 (a result that was recognized by Moscow), he was driven once more into hiding to command fighters against Russian forces which re-entered Chechnya in 1999

11. A young *dzhigit*, or Chechen horseman, ambles past a Russian soldier who has taken cover in a ditch, shortly after Russian troops invaded Chechnya in December 1994

12. A swimmer plunges into the Black Sea at a bomb-damaged resort in Georgia's breakaway republic of Abkhazia. The subtropical territory's political status remains in limbo

13. Chechen men perform the *zikr*, an energetic Sufi prayer, in the mountain village of Itum-Kale in August 1995. The Chechens' secretive Sufi brotherhoods have helped preserve Chechen culture in times of adversity

14. Prisoners of the Caucasus: Russian POWs, captured after the Russian-backed Chechen opposition's failed assault on Grozny in November 1994. Russian prisoners were later exchanged for Chechen men held in the notorious 'filtration' camps in Chechnya's silent war of the missing

15. Last rites: Chechen relatives perform the ritual washing before burial of a Chechen civilian killed by Russian shelling in the village of Pervomayskaya, December 1994

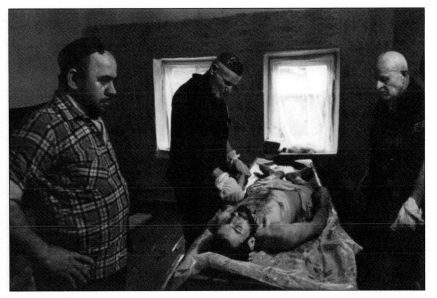

16. Civilians salvage what they can from Grozny in February 1995, days after the Russian storming of the city. In the background is the shrapnel-scarred Hotel Kavkaz, scene of ebullient Independence Day celebrations the previous September

17. Chechen fighters pause after prayer near the town of Goragorsk to watch the sky for approaching Russian warplanes in December 1994

cigarette-sellers and the tens of thousands of Russian soldiers surrounding them – hung on Yeltsin's nose. He had disappeared since early December for what Russians were told was minor nose surgery. Yeltsin was known to succumb to black depression. On the eve of a war, had he lost his nerve like Stalin, who sat in an armchair at his dacha and stared into space as German panzers approached Minsk in July 1941? (Stalin is supposed to have blurted out at his surprised inner coterie: 'Lenin left us a great inheritance and we, his heirs, have fucked it all up!').

For a strange instant, like the last wobble of a spinning top that momentarily rights itself before it falls, the fighting stopped. Yeltsin had vanished. Confusion reigned. 'General Winter', usually the Russian army's ally, kept their aircraft out of the skies and bogged down all three columns. In the course of one day, 17 December, Yeltsin's deputy prime minister threatened a missile strike against Grozny if Chechen forces failed to agree to disarm by midnight the same day; the Chechens said they had pulled back some of their forces as a goodwill gesture 'in the anticipation of a similar move by Moscow'; television pictures showed Major-General Babichev, the commander of the western column, hugging elderly Chechen women demonstrators west of the city. 'Tanks can't advance on people,' the major-general told the women in a surprising break with military logic. 'Our military regulations say we can only fulfil legal orders. Can an order be legal if you have to crush people?' He urged the women not to 'let your sons and husbands shoot at these soldiers. They are people just like you.'

I caught up with the column the day afer the missile strike failed to materialize. The women stood fast. One of their banners had expropriated a Soviet slogan which cheered up many a collective farm gate – *Miru mir!* – 'Peace to the world!' Fresh snow covered tank tracks on the road. The battle group had pulled back half a mile, the hard outlines of the trucks and armour disappearing in a sea of white. Small needles of snow fell, the cold snatching at your neck through a maladjusted scarf. The snow in the fields and the surrounding hills smothered the sound of revving tank engines and muffled the soldiers' chatter. Clouds of snow had grounded the helicopters. The soldiers on sentry duty creaked through the snow in *valenki*, large felt boots, screwing their eyes up against the cold white flakes. They were willing to talk. 'We stopped when we saw the people with banners. It was clear they didn't want us,' said a moustachioed lieutenant-colonel. A grey *shapka* jammed on his head, he was lean and fit for his years. 'I was in Abkhazia where they offered us bread and salt – here we weren't so we stopped.'

Major-General Babichev had been summoned to explain himself in the Terek town of Mozdok, now a town of pea-green canvas pitched for the Russian command, where soldier ants squelched through the mud with orders and counter-orders, buzzed about by helicopters, dun dragonflies, which constantly wobbled in and out of the base. The colonel did not know what headquarters had said to his commander. But he was quite clear about what the halt meant. 'A mutiny? You could call it that.'

We were not allowed to amble too far down the column but the relief at not having to fight appeared genuine. Viktor, a lieutenant, was quite happy to stay where he was. 'I personally have no interest in being here – I don't see it's in Russia's interest either if these people don't want us. I don't think letting Chechnya go will cause Russia to break up – we're not murderers after all.' His tank helmet gave his head the shape of an octopus. He shuffled his feet inside a pair of *valenki* to keep warm. 'If we get the order to move forward, none of us will go – we all prepared our letters of resignation two days ago. If we send tanks against civilians, it'll be just like the Soviet Union – what if they did the same to my mother in Belarus?'

Overnight in Moscow to pick up dollars. My editor took my socks home to wash. I dumped my bag in my room, a small pigeon's loft overlooking the Kutuzovsky Boulevard in one of the towers of the Ukraine Hotel, a vast palace of Stalinist gothic. I stared out of the window at the sea of red tail lights as the cars crawled home at the end of the working day. The telephone rang.

'Reception here. Would you like a woman?'
'— No.'
'Maybe later?'
I put the telephone down and switched on the television to watch the news. The pictures showed long lines of black metal rhombuses on tracks driven on roads thickening with white snow and grey ice. They also showed men with white faces in grey *shapki* holding black rifles. Grey-white cars slipped on the roads, heaving under the weight of women, children and belongings leaving Grozny. The flickering pictures, supposedly in colour, showed a war in black and white. I had passed a similar column of troops on the way to the airport. The pictures were not of poor quality. There was virtually no colour. The first pictures of women with suitcases and children abandoning a city under air attack, that is, the first pictures of modern warfare, were from the Basque region. On the afternoon of 26 April 1937, *der totale Krieg* – in which no distinction is made between soldier or civilian – was tested out on the small Basque town of Guernica. It was a Monday, market day. The Condor Legion flying for General Franco – pilots loaned from Hitler – was commanded by Lieutenant Colonel Wolfram von Richthofen, the Red Baron's cousin. The pilots attached sirens to the undercarriages of their Stuka dive-bombers so that they screamed as they fell on their targets. They also attached whistles to the fins of the bombs, both noises intended to shatter 'enemy' morale. Colonel von Richthofen reported back to Berlin that the operation was the 'greatest success'. Picasso painted Guernica in shades of black, white and grey.

The fog lifted. Shelling and bombing recommenced. Vice-president Yanderbiyev had appealed to Chechens in a television address to have courage and stay calm. 'Thanks to the will of Allah, the evil hanging over our people will pass by.' The telegrams he and Dudayev sent to Yeltsin requesting a meeting at state level, in Moscow or the Middle Eastern state of his choice, went unheeded. They in turn had turned down the offer of a helicopter ride to meet the Federal Counter-Intelligence Service at their tented base in Mozdok. Yanderbiyev's stance had not changed. 'Russia must quickly withdraw its forces, apologize and recognize independence.' Moscow closed Russia's borders with Georgia and Azerbaijan indefinitely. Airports across the North Caucasus were shut.

The anti-aircraft gun in Freedom Square fell silent as the Chechens' ammunition had run out. Volunteers stacked sandbags in the ground-floor windows of the Presidential Palace to protect Colonel Maskhadov's Operations Room. Artillery was audible to the north of the centre of the city. Ahead of New Year, a group of fighters was busy in the next square standing a large *yelka*, a dark green Christmas tree, on an empty plinth where a statue of Lenin had once stood. The Chechens' Presidential Television channel repeated a short educational video for the population on how to load, fire and target a rocket-propelled grenade. A fighter drew the rough outline of a tank in one of my notebooks. There is a large black dot where the turret joins the chassis, the point the grenadier must hit to knock out the tank at a range of 20 metres. On the northern outskirts of the city, black crows pecked at piles of uncollected rubbish which had begun to disappear under a fresh layer of snow. Men walked in and out of the tall green gates which shut in their homes, guns in their hands. On open ground next to the road was a widely spaced cluster of black patches in the snow where a salvo of Grad rockets had exploded. Near them, a group of about twenty fighters shouldering assault rifles and anti-tank rounds leaned out of the back of an open truck on a snow-covered road. A small poster of Dudayev in his generalissimo outfit was taped up on the cab's windshield. Most wore the Chechen volunteers' standard issue winter camouflage, white bedsheets turned into flapping ponchos. Morale was high. 'I have just one grenade,' said one of them, 'which I'm saving for the Spetsnaz.' We heard a jet scrape above the low metal clouds. The fighters dismounted in response. One said they had lost three of their men in fighting around Petropavlovskaya, a settlement a few kilometres north of Grozny on the River Sunzha. Standing on the road and passing round a pack of cigarettes, they said Russian tanks and heavy armour had massed there.

Another truck passed ferrying more volunteers and towing a
field gun covered with branches.

I went back to the collective farm at Artemovsky Elevator to
find out what Luiza Musayeva and her sisters were up to. The
road there was virtually empty. Heavy guns fired every few
minutes but it was impossible to tell where they were or what
they were hitting in the confusion of sound that rumbled over
Chechnya. It was midwinter and the light had all but gone for
the day. There were no lights in the windows of the houses at the
settlement. Many of the families had left, save for a few men who
had stayed to look after the animals. A group of them, in sheepskin coats, stood by the Musayevs' home. They said a tank round
had hit the house the day before. Luiza and four of her brothers
and sisters were killed. They said Luiza's parents had left to search
for somewhere to bury the children as the shelling had stopped
them from digging graves in the village. Bloodstains and a girl's
hairband lay in the snow.

The crowd of reporters staying in the French House
were headed for sleep after a night of writing, talking
and filing on empty stomachs and frayed tempers when
we heard explosions in the north of the city. Russian jets dropped
large bombs on the Lenin oil refinery on the outskirts of the city
just after midnight. A group of us drove there in the dark and found
a giddy nightwatchman at the refinery who opened a wire gate to
let us in. A fire still burned in one part of it, lighting up the dented
tangle of pipes and the sides of the tattered cracking towers, but the
darkness made it difficult to gauge the extent of the damage.

Standing on the embankment, we heard the sound of jets
again, unseen in the dark. Somewhere to the south, the horizon
lit up in three quick flashes, orange tongues of flame, which spat
from the earth and disappeared, followed by the roll of deep
explosions. I headed for the Second City Hospital, hoping to
find out from any wounded brought in where the warplanes had
struck. The doctors were coping with casualties from shelling in
Pervomayskaya. They were short on blood. Red Cross supplies

were not getting through. There was no electricity and the ward was lit with candles. Ahmed, a six-year-old boy, had bandaged legs. His face was grey, scared. Zaryema, nine, had shrapnel in her legs. Zelimkhan, four, had a shrapnel wound in his left arm. All were quiet. Their mother was crying. After hiding in a cellar for four days, she had ventured above ground to prepare food for her family. She said she heard shooting in the street outside when a shell exploded, injuring her kids. 'I don't know where my husband is,' she said, the tears streaming down her face. Her body heaved with exhaustion and fear. One of the explosions I had seen from the refinery had struck close to where the anti-aircraft gun was often positioned, only 500 yards from the Presidential Palace. The explosion had scooped out a crater two metres deep and three metres across. A metal hurricane had bent and snapped tree trunks like so many twigs, flinging branches across Lenin Avenue and down towards a disused cinema. A middle-aged man in a respectable-looking winter coat lay dead, flat on his back on the pavement just before the bridge over the river. His eyes were wide open in shock. The kiosks looked like so many shoeboxes which had been picked up, crushed and thrown back down again. A woman in her thirties shouted at the driver of a car who stopped nearby. 'Turn off the lights! Turn off the lights!' she shouted hysterically at the driver. She spoke in a quavering voice, both terrified and ecstatic. 'When I heard the planes I hid in the car and took cover,' she said, sick in the knowledge now of how useless the car would have been if the bomb had come down any closer.

A cloud of blue flame poured from a severed gas pipe. The explosion had blown in a Russian *pensionerka's* windows in a nearby apartment building. The old woman was speechless, arranging and rearranging the curtains over the empty windows. I sprinted a diagonal path across Freedom Square back to the hotel to file. A few fighters loitered in the dark marble doorway of the Presidential Palace. There was a *spetsliniya* to a Grozny operator in a small ground-floor room at the hotel, bare except for a telephone with no dial which was placed on an empty desk. I picked up the receiver and it started to ring. And ring. And ring. Noone answered. It was about two in the morning. I let the telephone ring, willing a line to Moscow.

'*Allo! Allo!' Allo!*'

'*Allo! Allo!*'

'Er, Moscow, 2-4-3, 5-1-5-3. *Srochno!* It's urgent!' There was a pause as the adrenalin coursed through my body in waves. Not to file was not to exist. The risks, the absences from my family, the merciless probing of grief-stricken men and women – the whole wild gamble – rested on a telephone line and ten minutes – even five minutes – to the news agency.

'The war's started, hasn't it?' the operator said balefully.

'I don't know.' Of course the war had started.

'Please, Moscow 2-4-3, 5-1-5-3. It's really very urgent.'

'I should go home.'

'Please.'

A deadpan, sleepy duty editor answered in Moscow, quickly took my copy and then hung up.

In the city's Mikrorayon district, a residential suburb of drab apartment blocks, the morning showed where the jets had hit the top of a building on Kirov Avenue. The ceiling was open to the elements. What was left of the top floor was piled with fallen masonry and bent girders. Noone knew if the apartment had been abandoned or not. Trolleybus lines jerked in a metallic whinny as cars drove over them. The snow had been scorched off the ground, leaving black earth. All the windows on the side of the building were blown out. Residents left in the district made the glass on the pavement crack and tinkle as they walked about, talking to one another angrily.

'Just before the bombing I heard Yeltsin's appeal to the Chechen people. He said "We're fighting bandits, not peaceful people",' said an elderly tractor mechanic.

'They're only killing civilians – Yeltsin, *spasibo!*' He turned dramatically away from me to underline his disgust. Gas, electricity and water to the district had been cut. An eighteen-year-old girl wandered about searching for something, dazed. 'I think father is dead.'

Yeltsin remained AWOL but senior Kremlin officials assured a suspicious Russian public that everything was being done to prevent civilian casualties and the President's absence was even cited to explain away the Russian army's slow advance on Grozny. They accused Chechen fighters of blowing up buildings like the one in the Mikrorayon district in Grozny to 'fake' Russian air attacks. Bad weather, not Kremlin squeamishness, had halted the advance. Snow and fog hampered air support for the ground troops in much the same way as had helped finish off Germany's Sixth Army at Stalingrad a little further north. Resignations and firings among the Kremlin's brass hats showed the armed forces in further disarray before Chechnya's ragged volunteers. The Deputy Commander-in-Chief of the Russian Army, Colonel-General Eduard Vorobyov, resigned rather than accept the mission to command the Russian campaign in Chechnya. Towards the middle of the morning, the sky cleared. Back in the centre of Grozny, there came as if out of nowhere an overpowering wave of sound. The thunder and crash of an explosion was doubled by a roar of engines as a jet streaked over the tops of the low apartment blocks after dropping its bombs. The lines and fins under the grey fuselage were crisp as they flashed past overhead.

People in winter coats ran along Victory Avenue. They waved their hands at cars and trucks in the hope of transport out of the city. They ran jerkily as they slipped on the ice, snow and soapy shards of broken glass on the pavements and in the road. Cars skidded and wobbled in panic. Women and children seated on mattresses and sacks in the backs of trailers pulled by tractors headed out of Grozny. The sound of jet engines crescendoed back. I ran to a door into one of the yellow-bricked *Khrushchevki* but it was locked. I banged on the door but noone answered. Corroded steel grilles on the windows fanned out in the rays of a setting sun. I crouched by a wall as the jets screamed overhead once more. A door opened into the street and a Russian man laughed. He was drunk. A truck and three cars were on fire in

Red Front Street. A pair of charred hands gripped a steering wheel. Three men lay dead in the snow in front of the Oil Institute building. One had been decapitated. A group of Chechen men prayed over another, palms held up. There was a large patch of red slush in the snow from where two men had lifted an injured woman.

Fighters had started to repair power and telephone lines near Freedom Square as I looked for a way to get out of the city. A photographer colleague had found a bus driver willing to take us to Khasavyurt, a small town in Daghestan, just east of Chechnya on the Rostov–Baku highway. Through the bus windows, Grozny was in flames, people ran and gesticulated, volunteers with guns looked up at the sky unsure of what to do. One of the correspondents, someone I hardly knew, clutched onto my arm and sobbed. A numbness set in. In Khasavyurt a television producer was editing footage of a British journalist weeping over a rolled-up carpet. In the morning bombing raids the American photographer Cynthia Elbaum had been killed while taking pictures of the aftermath of the bombing in the Mikrorayon district. The jets had flown over and bombed the district again. Her remains were wrapped in the carpet. She was one of a group who had shared Room 14 in the French House, cooking a roast chicken for us one evening in the small kitchen.*

The next day, 23 December, people clogged the roads south and east of Grozny. Women pushed or pulled small carts like toy prams, or small sledges loaded with blankets, jars, a metal churn. They bumped in places over tiles and smashed bricks. Thick black smoke hung over the city. Jets and helicopter gunships dimmed the skies. The sound of shells and rockets drummed closer to the city's northern edge. I

---

* Much was made of her 'inexperience' by journalist veterans who commented after her death. There is no school for war. You must go and weigh your risks with the best of them and in this, Elbaum, working with the most experienced photographers of the day, was utterly professional. Her death at the age of twenty-eight was completely random.

stopped at a Muslim cemetery on the way into the city on the Rostov-Baku highway on the eastern side. A group of some thirty men had gathered to bury a victim from the previous day's bombing, twenty-three-year-old Ruslan Pashayev. He had been driving past the cinema on Lenin Avenue. The men had finished digging the grave, a black oblong in the snow, but they constantly turned their heads to the sky to search out the jets. When the sound of jet engines approached, everyone involuntarily stopped what they were doing, not wanting to speak or move until the machine had flown past. The group awkwardly lifted Pashayev's body, wrapped in a white sheet and parcelled up in a kelim, off a hospital stretcher and lowered him into the ground.

'We don't understand it, we just don't understand,' said Beysultan Isayev, one of the mourners. He wore the thick sheepskin coat and grey lambskin cap of a Chechen elder. A cloudy silver beard grew to his chest and his eyes were water blue. 'I fought for Russia against the Germans. I'm an invalid,' he said. He took off his right glove to show three fingers missing. 'And now they're taking away our lives.' A jet flew low overhead, dropping a bomb that exploded with a flash and a crack on the top of a bluff a few hundred metres away on the other side of the road. Not far from Freedom Square, the Ivanov family was huddled in a ground floor flat, among thousands of Russians now trapped in the city. The flat belonged to Chechens who had given them the keys when they left for the countryside. It was safer than their own flat on the fifth floor and led down to a cold cellar, empty save for now useless heating pipes and a couple of wooden benches.

'It's barbarism – it's barbaric, what they are doing,' said Sergey. His voice was slurred, his breath thick with vodka. 'This kind of bombing would never have been done by a clever man, never, killing civilians.' His sons, aged eighteen and eleven, did not speak. His wife was about to boil over, angry at her bosky husband.

'I'm sick of talking about the situation, I'm so nervous,' she said. Sergey smiled sheepishly.

'She hasn't been able to sleep for three nights.'

At the military hospital in Grozny, orderlies rushed to pump air into a blue-faced young boy cut down by the previous day's bombing near the Red Hammer Factory. A power cut had stopped his ventilator. Alexander Gorachenko, a young Russian engineer with slate-blue eyes, lay in one of the wards. Bandages covered the stump where his right arm had been ripped off when he had been standing next to the Oil Institute building. The Chechen doctor left in charge of the hospital's intensive care unit had been on duty for two days. He waved a list of 31 admissions in his care – Chechens, Russians and Ingush. He said eight dead had also been brought to the hospital in the last twenty-four hours. 'We have no heat, many of the windows have been smashed and we cannot use our equipment – it's very primitive.' Jet engines vibrated through the roof for an instant. 'Everything runs on electricity,' he said frustratedly. No medicines were getting through. 'We have no water.' Grozny's inhabitants now boiled snow.

I went to the bazaar. The tables were empty squares of white snow. A few women in bulky overcoats stood in the dirty ice trading boxes of tea, chocolate and cigarettes. 'Of course we're afraid,' said one of the women, a Chechen, 'but what else can we do?' Back at the French House, Cynthia's body waited in a coffin hastily knocked together by her Chechen translator. The wood was carefully covered on the outside with clean white cotton. Fresh snow lay white and undisturbed on the road outside the hotel as many of the city's inhabitants had either fled or were shivering in cellars. Snow lay in steep piles on even the narrowest branches of the trees; the city was momentarily hushed and quiet. The Chechen translator, a volunteer fighter in winter whites and a fur *shapka* and some of Cynthia's colleagues lifted the coffin into the back of a bread delivery van, driven by a cameraman for one of the news agencies. I sat in the passenger seat and we drove out of the city to the satellite dish in Khasavyurt. The cameraman stopped the van on the outskirts of the city to take some wide shots. The inky smoke from the fires left by the jets and scattered about in the December wind grew blacker as the light faded over the city. Further along the road out east, a large white wolf lay on the ground, its head perked up as it watched the passing traffic, immobile. I have never before and never since seen such a large, proud wolf. The animal, in the same posture as the black wolf on the Chechen flag and three times the size of a timber wolf, had been sculpted out of ice.

I woke early the next morning to accompany Cynthia's body from Khasavyurt to Makhachkala, Daghestan's regional capital on the Caspian coast, and from there by plane to Moscow. Her coffin had been moved from the morgue in Khasavyurt to the back of a beaten-up ambulance and jammed in on top of an old mattress. A Russian medical official complained that the coffin, fashioned in such extraordinary circumstances, was not hermetically sealed and would therefore not be allowed onto an aeroplane.

A *feldsher*, a medical orderly in a white coat, sat in the front with the driver while I sat as best as I could in the back, my legs hunched up like a praying mantis's so as not to rest them on the coffin. The road was virtually empty. Though the van was bitterly cold, numbing my fingers and toes, I watched the fields and hillsides quilted in snow pass by in a sleepy haze. The white of the countryside and Arctic grey of the sky was broken by a small dot of black where the two met. As the van got nearer, the dot grew into a *dzhigit*, a mountaineer in a burka whose horse trotted in nervous starts beside the road before he reined it round and headed back into the hills.

# A warning from history

*. . . one cannot preclude the possibility that some form of
equally baneful neo-Stalinism could be restored. This is not a
prophecy, merely a warning from history.*

Dmitry Volkogonov, 1988

THE ROAD CROSSING to Georgia remained closed so I had to
make my way home via Moscow. The airport was swallowed in a flurry of snow. The Georgian passengers popped
open *shampanskoye* as we took off to celebrate the arrival of jet
fuel in Tbilisi the absence of which had threatened to strand our
aircraft in Georgia and us in Russia. Most of the lights were out
in the Georgian capital. There were two hours of Christmas to
spare. The family were starting to clear away the debris of a
fancy-dress party from the dining-room table. As there was no
power in the courtyard, Rachel had had to cook the Christmas
piglet in a hotel oven down the road. The boys' cheeks and noses
were smeared with face paints to look like cats and noblemen. I
had bought Christmas presents in Moscow that morning as the
shops had not yet closed for the Russian New Year. But I had
come home late and emotionally empty-handed. The stove
blazed, the candles and storm lanterns glowed and the boys
smiled but I failed to return any of this precious warmth.

Useless at home, I drove east shortly after Christmas from
Tbilisi for a couple of hours to the Georgian village of Dzirkoki.
The rooves in the village shone weakly in the sun. Woodsmoke
curled from the chimneys. Snow covered the tops of the mountains to the north, over which lay the smoke and fires of Grozny.
A group of about a hundred villagers, many of them unshaven as
kerosene to heat hot water was forbiddingly expensive, had

159

gathered round a small plinth covered in plastic sheeting. One of the men, in the military tunic and cavalry boots of a Bolshevik, stood up from a rickety table, walked over and pulled off the plastic to unveil a bust of Stalin, cast in polished tin with fat moustaches and a crooked smile, a demonic garden gnome.

Another stood up and introduced himself as Shalva Elikashvili, worker and builder.

'The French were only able to keep the Commune for 70 days – we kept socialism for 70 years!'

Applause.

'Without socialism, humanity can't exist! If we still had Stalin's discipline, everything would be better!'

More applause.

Another man then stood up – Soso Songolashvili, collective farm manager.

'The intellectuals are trying to destroy his personality but we, the Georgian people, know Stalin for his role in the war, what he did for humanity, what he did for the poor. For us he lost his wife, he refused to exchange his son with a German prisoner of war. Stalin could have provided kerosene!'

Applause.

A small girl standing near the table watched bewitched as Songolashvili moved his hands and arms in the exaggerated manner of a *tamada*.

'A small boy from Georgia became a world-famous figure. He ruled the Soviet Union for 30 years. During that time, the Russia he created was strong. We live on the foundations built by Stalin!'

More applause.

Nostalgia for the Unbending Commander in creaking, shambolic Georgia came out in kitsch. Bottles of 'Stalin' vodka, with portraits of the Red Monarch on the labels, competed with bottles of 'Shevardnadze' vodka in town kiosks. One kiosk sold a Stalin horoscope with the Great Helmsman's smiling face surrounded by a halo of stars.

I later interviewed Levan Demetradze, the director of Tbilisi's No. 1 wine factory, who went to Moscow in 1979 to save Stalin's wine cellar for posterity. It had been moved from Stalin's Kuntsevo dacha outside Moscow to the wine factory's Moscow office on his death in 1953. 'They were mostly Russians at the Moscow offices who didn't care about the collection. I thought it was important to preserve Georgia's heritage.' The dictator of the proletariat kept a well-stocked cellar to fuel the all-night bacchanals dreaded by his Kremlin courtiers. Rubbing off the black grime and cobwebs from the bottles had revealed Henessey cognac from 1929, a 1924 Chartreuse, malt whisky and a bottle of Booth's High and Dry gin. Demetradze said Stalin himself drank modest amounts of Georgian wine from his home town of Gori, 60 kilometres west of Tbilisi, which was shipped up to the Kremlin in clay *kvevri*. (Stalin made his Georgian wine merchant a lieutenant-general during World War Two and the Georgian chef who cooked his *shashlyk* a major-general.) When Demetradze mentioned the collection of 350 bottles to the Sotheby's people at a Berlin trade fair, he said representatives from the auction house beat him back to Tbilisi. Demetradze took a patriotic stand. 'They wanted to buy, but we didn't want to sell.'

There were parades twice a year in Gori: one to mark Stalin's birthday on 21 December 1879 (born on the cusp, he is usually marked down as an unforgiving Capricorn); the other to mark the day he died after a stroke on 5 March 1953. The townspeople still reserve the first toast for their famous son. There in March 1996, I witnessed a hundred Georgians turn out to mourn the Soviet icon's death and warm their bones on the first day of spring. A portrait of Stalin, with a black ribbon placed at the top and flanked by two blood-red Soviet flags, stood in the entrance to a small cabin which his hagiographers claimed was his ever-so-'umble childhood home and well in keeping with his Uriah Heepish personal mythology. Built over the cabin to protect it was a garage forecourt roof in the guise of a Neo-classical temple. Stalin's death mask was on loan from the next-door Stalin Museum for an exhibition on totalitarianism in Vienna.

Aliko Lurmanishvili, First Secretary of the Gori branch of the United Communist Party of Georgia (one of four), began a long and solemn speech beside the portrait. The previous year, Georgia's Stalin Party, another of the four, had endorsed Shevardnadze over his Communist rival in the country's 1995 presidential elections.

'Today is a day of mourning,' he said. 'The people don't want capitalism – they remember what Stalin built!' Standing in attendance was Stalin's sixty-nine-year-old cousin, Maria Dzhugashvili, who met him in 1947. She worked in Soviet air intelligence during the war and asked permission to return to Gori to see her mother, the only surviving member of her family. Uncle Joe summoned her.

'He was in uniform, he was so strong.' She clenched her fists at the memory and smiled beatifically. 'He was simple and he liked simple working people.'

At the end of Lurmanishvili's speech, a moustachioed Georgian pensioner carefully picked up the portrait and slowly marched with it over his chest, out of Stalin Avenue and into Stalin Square. From a distance the elderly mourners in suits and black dresses looked like an Easter procession in an Italian village. They stopped to place a dusting of spring flowers at the foot of a tall statue of Stalin. Sculpted in a windswept greatcoat, he stared stonily past a large billboard advertising *Coca Cola* on the roof of Gori's empty general store.

Stalin himself showed nostalgia for Georgia only late in life, limiting demonstrations of his nationality to conversations in Georgian with his NKVD chief, the serial paedophile Lavrenty Beria, to further unnerve his quaking Politburo. It was tempting at times to see Stalin and Beria as a weird sort of revenge against the empire. But Georgia suffered like anywhere else. Dozens of local 'anti-Soviet elements' were arrested when the Immortal Genius took his holidays, surrounded by thousands of NKVD troops, on the Black Sea coast.

I invited myself to tea with Nino Ramishvili, eighty-six, the head of the Georgian State Dance Company for half a century. I had watched her one morning preparing another generation of dancers in the troupe's unheated theatre in Tbilisi. Ramishvili shouted impatiently at the men who leapt and landed 'bang!' on their knees in a celebrated Georgian sword dance as they hurled blades into the stage. She wore the carefully arranged turban of a prima ballerina above a nose as sharp as a *kinzhal*. Her apartment was airy and light, the elegant wooden furniture carefully spaced on a gleaming parquet floor. A small card table groaned with pastries, bottles of Georgian wine, gilt-edged wine glasses and delicate china cups.

Stalin was a regular at the Bolshoy Theatre in Moscow and the young Ramishvili, then one of the Soviet Union's foremost ballerinas, caught the dictator's eye. He demanded an audience after one of her performances. The year was 1937, the start of the terror. When she repeated her name at their introduction, there was a mental shuffling in Comrade-Card-Index's head.

'Ramishvili, eh? That's a Menshevik name. All such people should be arrested.' The young ballerina froze. 'Whether it was a joke or not, Stalin's word was already law.'

Stalin was apparently enjoying a joke, since Ramishvili continued to dance and avoided both the camps and the firing squad. But there were moments. Beria had started to drop by the Bolshoy and made his intentions clear to the beautiful young woman. Beria usually left it to his chief bodyguard, the Georgian Colonel Nadoraya, to procure women and under-age girls; 'the slightest resistance would bring tragic consequences for both the girl and her family.'

Ramishvili tried to brush Beria off, underlining her marriage to another famous dancer of that time, Idiko Sukhishvili. Beria did not consider a husband much of an obstacle and sure enough, the NKVD came banging on the door of Sukhishvili's Moscow hotel room. A short while before, Stalin had come backstage after one of his performances to congratulate Ramishvili's husband and asked the dancer what he would like as a gift. Sukhishvili had wisely asked for a signed portrait of Stalin. The dancer pulled the portrait off the wall and waved it at the NKVD agents like a crucifix against a vampire. Beria backed off.

As in 1991, many of the Russian Empire's subjects saw the weakening centre in 1917 as a chance to escape and it was from this point that Stalin's vendetta against the *Kistebi*, the Georgian for Chechens, can be said to have begun. Najmuddin Samursky, first secretary of neighbouring Daghestan's Communist Party, wrote in 1935: 'The October Revolution was understood by the people of Daghestan first and foremost as one of national liberation from under the yoke of Russian rule.' For one of the Communist leaders charged with bringing the North Caucasus under Bolshevik rule during the Russian Civil War, this sentence was remarkably honest, especially at a time when Stalin was sharpening his knife for the coming purges to remove the 'clerical, feudal counter-revolutionaries and bourgeois nationalists', in short, all those who wanted out of the Bolshevik empire. Samursky, a Lezghin from Daghestan, was liquidated in 1937.

On 11 May 1918 a committee of mountain peoples declared outright independence for a new North Caucasus Mountain Republic which comprised much of Chechnya, Daghestan and parts of modern-day Ingushetia and Ossetia. Unrest and war meant that the borders were hazy but the new state won recognition the following month from the Central Powers – Germany, Austria-Hungary and Turkey. The declaration sparked armed incidents between the mountaineers and the Cossacks and the North Caucasus was soon engulfed in civil war. The towns and villages in Chechnya and Daghestan were a complex and terrifying patchwork of hesitant alliances. No prisoners were taken in the fighting. General Denikin's White Army sided with the Cossacks against the mountaineers who were thrown together by circumstances with the Reds. The mountaineers then switched and deployed their forces against the Reds when promises of autonomy and independence were reneged on whenever the Bolsheviks thought expedient. English and Turkish army officers confused the already complicated battleground further by seeking to influence the outcome with arms and bullion.

Officials from the North Caucasus Mountain Republic slipped out through Georgia to Paris in 1919 to try and secure recognition from the Allies. There must have been some head-scratching from Wilson, Lloyd George and Clemenceau as they crawled over maps at the Paris Peace Conference, for they were presented with similar demands for the same territory by Terek Cossacks, while the overriding Allied aim was to keep the creak-ing Russian Empire from falling apart.

Driven out of its 'capital' of Vladikavkaz by Bolshevik forces, the republic moved east to the Daghestan town of Temir Khan Shura, now Buynaksk, where its main threat was once more General Denikin, supported by land-hungry Cossacks. With defections inside the Mountain Republic's ranks, the republic was snuffed out, with Temir Khan Shura falling to the Whites in May 1919.

During this time Uzun Haji, an elderly sheikh, never for a moment lost sight of the opportunity revolution and civil war brought the mountaineers. He was a Chechen spiritual leader who had spent fifteen years in Siberian exile before the Revolu-tion for fighting Russian rule in the Caucasus. He sided with the Bolsheviks to defeat the Whites and the Cossacks and then turned on the Reds when his North Caucasus Emirate, a theo-cratic state in the Ichkerian mountains of upper Chechnya, was under threat.

An Avar Bolshevik has a vivid description of Uzun Haji's fighters as they entered Temir Khan Shura for the first time in January 1918 (and Marie Bennigsen Broxup writes in her account of Uzun Haji's *ghazavat*, '. . . the rebels fought to the last – there were no survivors to write their memoirs . . .'): 'They were dressed in rags with white bandages on their heads, horse-men, infantry, old and young, armed with rifles, flintlock guns or simply sticks; some fired by fanaticism, others with indifferent and tired eyes; they felt victorious.' Discipline in this bloody theatre was strong. All the turbaned fighters expropriated from the population was some wooden fencing to burn against the January cold.

The Chechnya and Daghestan that Baddeley had ridden through less than two decades earlier was only then recovering from Imam Shamil's *ghazavat* of 1832–59 against the empire and a further mountain uprising which coincided with Russia's war against Turkey in 1877–78. Baddeley deduced from Shuvalov's trips to the Caucasus that the 'empty' villages in this crowded territory which the count described to him were the result of the menfolk hiding themselves in fear of further Russian reprisals.

Uzun Haji died aged ninety in March 1920 but an assembly called the following August by Najmuddin Gotsinsky, an Avar sheikh who was elected Imam of Chechnya and Daghestan in 1917, called for the creation of a 'Shariat Army of the Mountain Peoples'. Villages provided fighters which reported to a high command via a local commander called a 'centurion'. Fighters provided their own weapons but were fed and billeted by the local population. Soviet sources estimated Gotsinsky's forces at about 3,000, against the 40,000 troops of the 9th and 11th Red Armies sent to smash the emirate.

Soviet commanders ill-versed in both mountain warfare and the history of the region found themselves trounced repeatedly by the mountaineers' hit-and-run tactics. About 700 Red Army soldiers and 24 field guns were sent to take the mountain town of Arakan, 120 kilometres southeast of Grozny, in October 1920. After shelling Arakan for ten days, the troops marched into the gorge leading up to the town. The mountaineers sealed off both ends of the gorge and slaughtered the entire detachment, capturing all their weaponry.

The following month the Soviets sent another 700 men against the emirate, the 1st Model Revolutionary Discipline Rifle Regiment, this time by way of the Chechen hill town of Vedeno, about 40 kilometres southeast of Grozny. The unit took hostages and looted its way into the Daghestan mountains in pursuit of the rebels. One part of the regiment chased the mountaineers to a higher village, found themselves encircled and were all killed to a man. The remaining force was surrounded in the town of Botlikh to the south. The regiment's commander pleaded for safe passage to Chechnya in exchange for their weapons. No sooner had they surrendered their arms than the rebels executed all officers and political commissars. The other ranks were stripped naked and left to freeze to death on the mountainside. Red Army soldiers were also besieged for two months in the hill towns of Khunzakh and Gunib. Succumbing to typhoid and hunger, they were reduced to eating their horses until First Secretary Samursky appealed to Gotsinsky's men: 'If you have honour, if you are indeed the sons of Shamil as you claim, if you want to show yourselves to be eagles of the mountain, send us some food and then we will see who will win.' Shot at as they approached, the fighters left food below the Red fort at Gunib, a few kilometres south of Arakan, the town way up in the sharp, rocky fastnesses of the Caucasus Mountains which had been the scene of Shamil's last stand in 1859.

The Red Army finally bettered the rebels in May 1921 but at a cost of 5,000 men. While the conflict raged in the mountains, the People's Commissar for Nationalities, Joseph Stalin, met a congress of mountain peoples in Vladikavkaz. He bought the Bolsheviks some time by appearing to concede to the mountaineers' demands, granting them a 'Soviet Mountain Republic', exacting a promise from them in return to recognize Soviet power.

The People's Commissar used all the requisite Leninist turns of phrase to keep the empire's many nationalities under the Soviet flag. In 1913 he droned in *Marxism and the National and Colonial Question*: 'A nation is not merely a historical category, but a historical category belonging to a definite epoch, the epoch of rising capitalism.' With a phenomenal memory, parroting Leninism came to Stalin as easily as reciting the liturgies he had learned as a young Georgian Orthodox seminarian in Tbilisi. As the Party's expert on the empire's nationality 'problem', he thought like the tsars. During Volkogonov's surreptitious journey through the Party archives in the 1980s, the army historian found among the triangles, circles and wolves doodled in red pencil in the margins of Stalin's notes a ruler seeking comparison with Ivan the Terrible. 'The conquest of the Tatar Khanate of Kazan, the attainment of a way out to the Baltic and the creation of a ruthless cohort, the *oprichniki*, made Ivan even more appealing in Stalin's eyes.' Stalin checked on Sergey Eisenstein personally when the film director made *Ivan the Terrible*. In his cant about the 'fusion of nations', Stalin declared his aim to preserve and enlarge the empire. But in his pursuit of empire, the Chechens dogged him at every turn, with his security *apparat* locked in an almost permanent blood feud with the mountaineers.

In 1929 the North Caucasus was chosen as the first area for complete collectivization of the region's agriculture, with the richer peasantry, the kulaks, to be deported to Siberia. The Chechens immediately rose against the order. Official buildings were occupied, archives were burned, a petrol refinery siezed and Party officials arrested. Chechen leaders demanded an immediate end to collectivization and arrests, ordered the replacement of Bolshevik officials by Chechen nationals, courts to follow Sharia law and all future decisions in the autonomous republic to be taken by the mountaineers themselves. One morning before dawn, a 150-strong detachment of OGPU troops, the precursor to the NKVD and KGB, surrounded the house of one of the Chechen leaders in the town of Shali, 20 kilometres southeast of the Chechen capital. The leader, Shita Istamulov, and his brother opened fire on the Soviet unit. About a hundred Chechen horsemen galloped to the brothers' aid and cut the detachment to pieces. Istamulov called a *ghazavat* against the Soviets and was joined by mountaineers in Daghestan and elsewhere in the North Caucasus.

In December of that year, the Soviets, intent on crushing the insurgency, sent in four infantry divisions, three artillery divisions, two border guard regiments and three squadrons of OGPU troops. The rebels were destroyed in the town of Goiti but those in Shali, including Istamulov, escaped to the mountains. Soviet forces incurred heavy losses. In the spring of 1930, Stalin, 'dizzy with success', slowed down collectivization which was now deemed premature for the North Caucasus. Stalin blamed the haste on 'leftist deviators' and Red troops were withdrawn from Chechnya. Istamulov came down from the mountians to become head of an agricultural cooperative in Shali.

The regional OGPU boss invited Istamulov to collect an official amnesty paper from Moscow. While handing the document to the Chechen leader, the official emptied a Mauser pistol into him. Istamulov managed to stab the official to death before he himself perished. His brother organized a group which specialized in tracking and assassinating OGPU officials to avenge his death up until 1935.

Guerrilla warfare echoed across the mountains and valleys. The guerrillas often bought their weapons from corrupt OGPU officials, in the same way that many fighters sourced their own weaponry from Russian forces in Yeltsin's war.

Chechen and Ingush officials working in the Soviet administration, facing threats from their own people, took the mountaineers' frustrations to Sergo Ordzhonikidze, Stalin's henchman in the Caucasus, who was taking the waters in Pyatigorsk in the spring of 1935. At the meeting Ordzhonikidze noticed that none of the Chechens carried a *kinzhal* and was told they had been banned from doing so by the NKVD, the new acronym for OGPU. 'A Chechen without a dagger,' said Ordzhonikidze angrily, 'is like a European without a necktie.' He arranged to have the ban lifted and to release saddle horses from the collective farms for the mountaineers' full self-expression. In 1936 the atmosphere calmed with the promulgation of a revised Soviet constitution which created a Chechen-Ingush Autonomous Soviet Socialist Republic.

Stalin had bought himself some more time while he turned his attentions to first starving the Ukrainians into submission and then liquidating the last of the old Bolsheviks, along with their wives and children. Ordzhonikidze's meagre protection of the Chechens and Ingush, some of them Civil War comrades, did not last for long. Though no stranger to the Party's pitiless methods, he started to rebuke Stalin for the mad, distorting mirrors of the purges. In return Stalin flourished in front of him NKVD reports on his old comrade which cast doubt on his loyalty. To try and blood him, Stalin demanded that he denounce many senior Soviet industrial managers for 'sabotage' at the Seventeenth Party Congress. Another Politburo member, Molotov, announced in February 1937 that he was standing in for Ordzhonikidze at the Congress and read out to the delegates a fantastic report on 'The Lessons of sabotage, diversions and espionage by Japanese-German-Trotskyite agents'. Ordzhonikidze had shot himself the previous week. Like a mafia don, Stalin arrived at Ordzhonikidze's Moscow apartment in person and ordered that the suicide be described as a heart attack. A suicide note left the building in one of the pockets of Stalin's khaki tunic.

Stalin's terror machine ground into gear in the Caucasus with a 'General Operation for the Removal of Anti-Soviet Elements' executed on the night of 31 July 1937 in Chechnya-Ingushetia. Avtorkhanov estimates that 14,000 Chechens and Ingush were arrested, with troika summary courts despatching some to the Gulags, others to the NKVD's 'relay chamber' in Grozny, so-called because the condemned were told they were in a holding area awaiting deportation to Siberia. 'The relay chamber was made of reinforced concrete and hermetically sealed from the outside world. Revolving firing positions were fitted into the walls and ceiling from the exterior. The bodies were carried off in lorries under cover of darkness, and taken to a mass grave in a forest at the foot of the Goryachevodskaya mountain.' When one junior NKVD officer asked how he could carry out an order with no evidence, his senior is said to have replied: 'We can always find evidence provided he wears a Caucasian hat!'

The result was predictable. With nothing to lose, thousands of Chechens and Ingush fled to the mountains to join guerrilla units still in existence. The leaders of such bands were a new generation educated, like Avtorkhanov, in the Soviet system. One of them, Hassan Israilov, went to secondary school in Rostov, was a member of the Komsomol and then joined the Party. A regional reporter for an agricultural journal, he won notoriety in a series of articles describing what he termed the 'plundering of Chechnya' by Soviet officials. He served three years of a ten-year prison sentence but the young Komsomolets persisted in warning the Soviets that their policies threatened more uprisings in Chechnya. When a new regional Party boss invited Israilov to petition for reinstatement to the Party in 1940, he received the following letter: 'For twenty years now, the

Soviet authorities have been fighting my people, aiming to destroy them group by group: first the kulaks, then the mullahs and the "bandits", then the bourgeois-nationalists. I am sure now that the real object of this war is the annihilation of our nation as a whole. That is why I have decided to assume the leadership of my people in their struggle for liberation.'

Israilov took command of the Provisional Popular Revolutionary Government of Chechnya-Ingushetia in February 1940, promising to fight like the Finns who 'are proving that this great empire built on slavery is devoid of strength when faced with a small freedom-loving nation.' Avtorkhanov gives few further details on the guerrilla leader whose forces fought on until 1942, obliterated by the Soviet aircraft diverted from the German front to bomb and strafe Chechen villages in the spring of that year.

Chechen and Ingush guerrillas had the support of the population, Mao's 'sea of the people' so essential to the existence of darting guerrilla fish like Israilov. So Stalin, with the vision of the central planner, ordered that this sea be drained. He deported the entire Chechen and Ingush population to Kazakhstan in the harsh February of 1944.

The previous few weeks, Red Army and NKVD units spread out across the mountains in Chechnya. In the squares and other prominent places, placards proclaimed: 'WE WILL HELP THE RED ARMY UNITS, HERE TO MANOEUVRE IN MOUNTAIN CONDITIONS'. No one believed the story of 'mountain manoeuvres', supposedly to prepare for the Red Army's glorious advance into the Carpathian Mountains on the way to Berlin. More and more units began to arrive.

On 22 February 1944, a group of soldiers wheeling a heavy machinegun asked for directions to the Stalin Collective Farm in the village of Alkhazurovo. This was repeated in villages across Chechnya. At the entrance, armed soldiers gathered for a *prazdnik*, a celebration to mark Red Army Day, gathering round bonfires there and in other settlements. The Chechens noticed with alarm that none of the soldiers drank. In the early hours of Wednesday 23 February, red and white signal flares were shot into the pre-dawn sky. In the mountainous regions, soldiers went from house to house, firing into the air and banging on doors, giving families minutes to throw on some clothes. After they had been assembled, the Chechens were then told to wait in the snow until dawn. The NKVD officers mounted Georgian horses and drove the inhabitants of the villages down through the snow, like cattle, to collection points where trucks waited to drive them to a railhead in Grozny.

In the larger towns the men were called out and told to hand in guns and knives. One Chechen pensioner recalls throwing his toy pistol onto a weapons pile. The men made to wait in line at the Stalin Collective watched as one of the NKVD officers caught up with a straggler who had emerged from one of the farm buildings, shooting him point-blank in the head. Two Chechens in uniform, Sergeant-Major Betigov and Lieutenant Nukayev, stood apart from the line-up. They were back from the front on leave, the lieutenant on sick leave after losing an eye. The head of the NKVD unit, Major Reshetnikov, drew his sabre and put the point against Betigov's chest, ordering the men into the line-up. 'You are all bandits, enemies of the Soviet state!'

Lieutenant Nukayev demurred, saying the major had no right to speak to an officer and an invalid, who had shed his blood for the Soviet Union, in such a manner. Major Reshetnikov bawled at the Chechen officer: 'Even if you were a general, if you're a Chechen, you're an enemy of the Soviet state!'

Stalin ordered the deportation on the grounds that the Chechens and Ingush had collaborated with the invading German army. The Wehrmacht struck south to try and capture the oilfields and refineries in Chechnya but, caught in the Stalingrad meatgrinder, never made it onto Chechen territory. The Chechen mountain guerrillas still operating in the mountains, after hearing about the activities of the *Sonderkommando* in Ukraine, had sworn to treat the Germans as they had the Soviets. Their 'treachery' was an invention by Stalin and his minions in agitprop. The accusation against the Chechens as traitors hurts to this day, the slur still believed by many Russians. Chechens volunteered to fight Hitler as they had done to fight the Kaiser, forming the Dikaya Diviziya, the 'wild division', which ambitious Russian aristocrats queued up to serve in during World War One. A Chechen teacher, M. Munayev, remembers that when in exile in Kazakhstan after he had been deported, he asked the local Party chief if he could resume his profession and give classes. The *chinovnik* put him in his place: 'Who do you think you are? Do you think they'll trust a bandit and a traitor like you? We, veterans of the civil war, old Communists, we spilt our blood for the Soviet state, and you, you! You're a bandit and a traitor and we will put you in a deep mine, on hard labour that finishes you. That is your place!'

The label of 'bandit', liberally fixed on the Chechens by both Yeltsin and his successor Putin, was hardly appropriate coming from Stalin, who in pre-revolutionary times had himself been an accomplished bankrobber, making off with 300,000 roubles in one hold-up alone from a Cossack detachment transporting cash to Tbilisi. In Party history the robberies were accounted for as 'expropriations'.

In the towns on the day of the deportations, doors were rattled and shots fired as thousands of frightened families were pushed into groups ready for transport as the morning wore on. Many men were executed immediately. Kh. Muradov, twelve years old at the time, remembers he was with his fifteen-year-old brother at his aunt's house in Novy Atagi to collect a bag of maize flour to bring back 20 kilometres north to Grozny. When they were rounded up, his brother took the flour while Muradov grabbed a small bag which contained photographs of his mother and father. Rain was falling with the snow. Before the boy was put on a truck, an NKVD officer grabbed the bag, emptied it onto the ground and stamped the portraits into the mud. The open-backed trucks were brand-new, five-ton Studebakers, sent to the Soviet Union by the United States under the lend-lease act, the same trucks as those used in the gold mines in the forced labour camps in Kolyma.

On the same day the Chechens were moved from the trucks

and onto cattle wagons, about 30 families to each car. The train transports travelled for 15–17 days eastwards across the steppe. In the corners of some wagons, the men made makeshift lavatories with what they could. The clatter of the wheels on the tracks beat out a steady, *Ku-da ve-zut? Ku-da ve-zut?* – 'where are they taking us?' Every so often the train would stop. The sides of the tall, rough-hewn wagons were hauled back, shaking snow off onto the track and letting out the stink of disease and human waste. The view the mountaineers glimpsed was a flat, empty desert of snow, flattened further by the low winter sky. The bodies of those who had died of typhus, now raging in the boxcars, were taken out and left on the steppe. Many Chechens' memory of this journey is laden with guilt as burying one's relatives, before sundown the same day as Islamic custom decrees, is a sacred duty not lightly given up. Chechens shouted at groups of people outside other wagons at the halts in the hope of hearing news of family they had been separated from. Driving snow would start to fill the insides of the wagons and the doors were heaved shut. 'All the time, the snow fell,' Muradov recounts. 'We travelled for a long time like this. Steppe, then stop, and they opened the doors. We quickly took out the corpses and buried them, if we had time, but if we didn't, we just left them.' Muradov and his brother eventually found their mother Ata in Dzhambul in June of that year, sick with fever. They buried her three months later.

On arrival at their destinations in the Central Asian republics of Kazakhstan, Kyrgyzstan and Uzbekistan, the Chechens were dumped by the side of the tracks on the open steppe or near collective farms. When the deaths from hunger, cold and typhus are added up during the period of the transportations and in the lean months that followed, it is clear that about half the 425,000 Chechens deported to Central Asia lost their lives that year. Robert Conquest, the historian of Soviet terror, writes that as the deportations lacked 'the spectacular horrors of the Nazi gas chambers', they have failed to catch the west's imagination. 'But there are other ways of destroying a nation. To remove it, in circumstances of "misery and suffering" from its homeland, and scatter it widely over an alien territory, with a minimum of economic resources, deprived of civil rights, of cultural opportunities and of education in its own tongue is, even leaving aside the high incidence of actual deaths, a sign that the aim can hardly be other than the extinction of a nation, as a nation.'

After the deportations, the Chechens disappeared down an Orwellian chute, a 'non-people'. A short article appeared in *Izvestiya* on 26 June 1946 declaring that the Chechen-Ingush Autonomous Soviet Socialist Republic had been abolished as the Chechens, along with the Crimean Tatars, 'at the instigation of German agents . . . engaged in armed struggle against units of the Red Army.' On other deported peoples, like the Balkars further to the west of the Chechens in the North Caucasus range, there was no information at all.

After Khrushchev's secret speech in 1956 denouncing Stalin's cult of personality, the Chechens miraculously reappeared and were allowed back to Chechnya in 1957 in much straitened circumstances (Soviet historians backpedalled wildly, in one instance dressing up the deportations as an effort to save the Chechens from German death squads).

Almost all who survived the deportations returned, hitching or faredodging thousands of kilometres back to Chechnya if necessary. The Chechens and Ingush had met kindness as well as cruelty in exile. Ordinary Russians, Kazakhs, Koreans, Germans and Uzbeks, hungry as they were, shared their food and their backbreaking work on the ice-bound collectives with these enemies of the people. The Chechens blew carefully on their history and traditions in exile as on embers in a clay pot, ready to rekindle their lives in the mountains. Solzhenitsyn describes in *The Gulag Archipelago* how Chechen families kept their girls and some of their boys back from hated Soviet schools.

On 23 February 1995 I found a group of Chechen families living in railway carriages on disused sidings in neighbouring Ingushetia. They had fled the fighting in Grozny. The windows of the cramped green carriages were wet with condensation as harassed women draped laundry about the small confined space, heated with small kerosene stoves. Block-loaves of brown bread lay wrapped in dishcloths on the small sidetables below the windows. There were few men around. Ragged children watched the women with wide eyes or skipped over the small peninsulas of grit snow lying between the tracks. In Moscow, Grachev, without a hint of irony, was telling veterans on Red Army Day, once again a dubious cause for celebration, that the operation to take Grozny was 'no worse than any which was conducted in Afghanistan'.

Asyet Murtalaziyeva was helping to look after a large gaggle of children in her carriage. One of them was an orphan and she did not know who his parents were. She had been trapped in a basement near the Minutka roundabout in central Grozny during the storming of the city. When Murtalaziyeva and her children ran out of water, they walked out of the city on foot.

She was eight years old when Red Army troops came to deport her. Her father was called out to a meeting by the NKVD and never returned. The children in the railway carriage stopped what they were doing and listened with rapt attention when she started speaking.

'They put us in trucks and herded us into freight wagons in Grozny. They treated us like cattle. I can't remember how many aunts, uncles and other relatives died on the journey from cold and hunger. Today is a day of mourning.'

Murtalaziyeva was reluctant to equate her tough circumstances with the boxcar she had been deported in five decades previously. But the memory of the deportations was never far from the surface as the war escalated. After the invasion in December 1994, Yeltsin had publicly to dismiss fears of a new deportation as 'malicious rumours', promising at the same time, in a message broadcast to the Chechens, to make sure Chechnya 'will once again become a fully-fledged region of the Russian Federation.'

The previous month two brothers in their thirties, now fighters, had invited me to their home in a village in the foothills of the Caucasus Mountains not far from Grozny. The snow on the fields and gardens compounded the quiet in the village. Their family and neighbours had fled to villages higher up in the mountains.

On the upper floor of the substantial house, one of them pulled a bundle of oilcloths out from under a bed. He pealed the cloths back to reveal a World War Two machinegun with a flat ammunition pan over a corroded barrel. 'My grandfather fought the Germans with it – with a little attention, I should be able to get it working. They think we can't hide, but we're not scared – we'll fight.'

His brother went to the window to check noone was looking in, even though we were on an upper floor. He then crouched down and from a low cupboard in a side wall pulled out a pile of large, flat cards with black and white photographs pasted to them. They were subtitled: 'Liquidation – Staro-Cheber-luyevsky District 1944'. The pictures showed NKVD troops posing with heavy machineguns; NKVD troops in front of a shelled house, their arms around each others' shoulders, their uniforms black against the snow; pictures of 'reactionary' imams. One card held photographs showing dramatic mountain land-scapes like the black and white Alpine plates Baddeley took during his excursions four decades earlier, only in between the pillows of snow were long lines of people.

The first brother said he had taken them from the KGB head-quarters in Grozny in August 1991 and had hidden them for safekeeping. He covered them with a blanket and placed them carefully back in the cupboard. Guns the brothers could find anywhere, but Chechnya's history was fragile and prone to disap-pearing.

# Jesuits of war

Those who are afraid of wolves don't walk in the forest.

Russian proverb

A WOMAN WALKED hurriedly across Mayakovsky Street in central Grozny, throwing bird-like glances in all directions. She clutched the hand of a small child, yanking her like a sledge across the road's oily black surface. There was some shelling and small arms fire, sporadic, which stopped my breath as it beat the January air. I could see no Russian soldiers, only a couple of Chechen volunteers. The bangs and cracks had a poltergeist quality.

A few yards further on at the start of Staropromyslovskoye Avenue, the road north out of the city, a Russian light armoured vehicle stood parked by the side of the road, burned soot-black, the turret and gun lurched over to one side. A bent metal lampost had fallen across it. The steel doors at the back of the vehicle were open. I tried to imagine the teenage conscripts cramped inside who had tried to escape after either an RPG or a Molotov cocktail had set their steel coffin on fire. Below the doors lay a corpse with a bloody rag stuffed over what was left of the soldier's mutilated head. His trousers were ripped where dogs had torn through and eaten chunks of flesh off his legs. Beside him were empty ammunition crates ransacked by the fighters, the clean pine naked against the charred grit, twigs and the dull brass cartridge casings which littered the area below the door of the broken vehicle. Every few yards were more burned-out light armoured fighting vehicles, BMPs, and around them, or in them, burned bodies which gave themselves away through a boot or a piece of exposed flesh.

Air and artillery bombardment had preceded the column into the city, part of a force thousands strong, many times larger than the couple of hundred Russian soldiers sent in with the Chechen opposition to take Grozny in November 1994. And this time the humiliation for the Kremlin was many times more. Maskhadov's lightly armed fighters had approached the avenue as if it were a mountain gorge, the buildings lining the route a concrete forest. The fighters waited until the cramped metal boxes had almost got to the centre of the city and then fired their rocket-propelled grenades, following with textbook accuracy the instructions broadcast on Dudayev's Presidential Television station. Armoured vehicles at the front and back were hit to trap the rest of the column. Many of the bodies were hacked with knives. The historian Volkogonov, then head of a presidential commission on POWs, said later that around a hundred bodies retrieved were mutilated beyond recognition. Like the Red Army columns sent to quell the mountaineers in the Civil War, the soldiers from the 131st Motorized Infantry Brigade, from the steppe town of Maikop in southern Russia, were cut to pieces.

Hundreds of bodies were never even retrieved. A fighter emerged from the doorway of a low building opposite the first BMP. He walked over and looked at the wet, tangled carnage around him which had begun to smell. 'Their corpses lie for eighteen kilometres,' he said with disgust. He said he and some others had begun to store Russian corpses in a warehouse opposite to try and cut the risk of epidemics in the city. 'As you can see, the Russians don't control the city.'

A few days later, a Russian soldier in filthy tank overalls, greasy hair and a dirty bandage round his thumb turned up at the house where I was based temporarily in the Ingush capital of Nazran. His escort was a skinny, ageing Russian hippy with long grey hair clinched in a headband. The hippy had hung about the Presidential Palace in December, preaching peace and asking to meet with Chechen officials. The soldier and the hippy asked to make a telephone call on a photographer's satellite telephone, the hippy adding a request for cash for the soldier's journey home. They were a dubious pair.

The soldier introduced himself as Lieutenant-Colonel Yury Klaptsev, of the 131st Motorized Infantry Brigade. He said he had arrived in Mozdok with the Maikop Brigade on 11 December, the day of the invasion, soon afterwards joining the northern column trying to take the Sunzha Ridge and Pervomayskaya. His unit lost a tank and five trucks in the fighting. On the morning of 31 December, he was ordered to lead 25 armoured vehicles carrying 200 men to Grozny's northern suburbs. There he received instructions to secure the Presidential Palace, the television centre and the railway station.

'The orders were very unclear, there was no planning. Several times our commander went to a radio car where he screamed for orders, but no clear answer came from headquarters.'

At 1400 the same day, Klaptsev's unit made it to the railway station. At around 1600 he lost his first armoured vehicle, knocked out with a rocket-propelled grenade. 'There were many bodies, many wounded, I don't know how many men we lost. We battled practically all night, we lost practically everything except for three BMPs and a tank. There were snipers.' He paused, struggling to find the right words. 'How can I describe when a rocket hits your vehicle, when a tank round lands three yards from you?'

The officer ordered what was left of his unit to try and punch through the encirclement. All lights on the vehicles were extinguished and about 30 Russian soldiers squashed inside or clung to the tops of the vehicles, ready to escape. 'We made it to the suburbs when the tank at the head of the column was knocked out. My own armoured car was hit – everyone inside was burned.' Klaptsev survived as he had been riding on top.

Fighters appeared out of the dark and took the colonel and about seventy survivors prisoner. 'I thought I'd be shot. The fighters said they'd execute me.' He was taken back into the centre and to the Presidential Palace where he was immediately interrogated by Maskhadov for one and a half hours – 'He was very polite.' Klaptsev was then put in the basement of the Presidential Palace with the Chechen commanders and the other Russian prisoners. He said he was sometimes kicked or punched when he was moved around the building. Russian artillery and aircraft continued to shell and bomb. 'The walls and the ceilings shook all day, all night.'

After two days, Maskhadov sent Klaptsev to negotiate a ceasefire with the Russian command in order to collect the dead. The thirty-nine-year-old colonel, with a wife and daughter, did not think of running away. 'It would have brought consequences for the rest of the prisoners,' he said. He delivered the ceasefire proposal in a Grozny suburb to Major-General Ivan Babichev, the commander of the western column who only a few days before had said that tanks could not advance on people. Klaptsev brought back Babichev's answer to Maskhadov:

'"Lay down your arms and surrender or face the consequences."'

Maskhadov released Klaptsev with some of the wounded, with the instruction to tell the world what he had seen. The colonel thought the real reason behind his release was that the Chechens in the bunker were running out of food.

I dialled a number for the colonel in our room in Nazran. Someone answered at the other end.

'Don't worry,' the officer said, calming the person on the other end of the line. Klaptsev's face shadowed.

'Don't cry, Papa, pull yourself together. I'll be home in three or four days.'

The southern route into Grozny, past the reservoir at Chernorechye, was still open. Women in headscarves queued by a frozen hole in the reservoir to pull up buckets of water. A few traded cigarettes and chocolate by the side of the road, flapping their hands in the January cold. Lada Zhigulis beetled in with fighters, bread and ammunition. Trucks ferried men in from the villages. One of them leant over the back and shouted, 'Our morale is one hundred thousand per cent!', to which the rest of his companions cheered:

'*Allahu akbar!*'

A small group of Chechen fighters rested in the courtyard of a low house on Saykhanov Street, sitting on the front step of a porch, pausing to look up at the sky every now and then at the sound of an approaching jet fighter. Some ran their hands through prayer beads. An uneven layer of ice crusted the front yard. A tall iron gate leaked light through holes punched by shrapnel. One of the Chechens, Senior Lieutenant Aslambek Chatuyev, had returned from Moscow to fight. He was slim, pale, with the beginnings of a black beard. He wore a black woollen ski cap and a black denim jacket over a thick sweater. He had bandaged together three ammunition clips underneath his assault rifle to allow him to reload in a hurry.

'The T80 and T82 tanks are difficult to hit with RPGs but there is a weak point at the back,' he said of the newer Russian models. 'We waited in the houses for the column to come past and then came out behind them.' He said he saw three Russian soldiers shot trying to give themselves up.

'Many in the columns were drunk. Some of the prisoners we took stank of drink, they had bottles of vodka.' A Chechen struggled through the gate with a heavy machinegun he had wrenched off a disabled tank. 'We're psychologically prepared for this,' said the commander, who was in his twenties. 'When a football team plays on its own ground, it usually wins. This has been the same story for 300 years, we've always had trouble with the Russians.' He, like so many other volunteers, said he was not fighting for Dudayev but to protect his home. Maskhadov had been promoted recently to the rank of general. The lieutenant did not take this as a sign of vanity on the part of the mumbling commander-in-chief. 'The most notable person in the government is Aslan Maskhadov.'

At the end of Saykhanov Street, at the Minutka roundabout at the top of Lenin Avenue, fighters were gathered below some of the buildings. A few civilians with small bags walked slowly and carefully away from the city centre along the avenue. The road was covered in shattered glass and masonry save for where a bridge crossed it. Several apartments were on fire, a soup of grey smoke pouring upwards to thicken the black pall over Grozny.

On one of the corners of the Minutka roundabout, women, children and the elderly – Russians and Chechens – were sheltering in a basement amid a jumble of old sewing machines which belonged to a collective upstairs. They stared at the yellow light of a single kerosene lamp, wrapped in coats as the basement was unheated. Russian pensioners remembered a trick from World War Two in which the wax which had melted from a candle was carefully prised off the surface and kneaded back round a thread from a blanket to make a replacement candle. Husbands, brothers or sisters who ventured out of the basements to look for bread and water sometimes failed to return, victims of the fighting above ground. A direct hit from a bomb would instantly entomb the occupants of the shelter.

'What can we do?' said a Chechen woman who had been sheltering with her two small daughters for nearly a month. 'We've had no gas, no electricity, no water for four days. We have nowhere to go, no money to leave.'

On the road above them, a group of fighters had gathered in a rough circle and were dancing in a furious rhythm, slapping their legs and clapping their hands to a balalaika that was strummed violently by one of their number. Others chewed bread or knelt on their jackets to pray. One of the characters who had turned up in traditional dress in Freedom Square the previous month reappeared in a toffee-coloured *cherkeska,* a *kinzhal* at his belt, and knelt on his burka to pray in the road, a sheet of orange flame singeing the air above him from a punctured gas pipeline.

Their armour useless, Russian forces began the next day to bomb, rocket and shell the city – indiscriminately – into submission. The volunteers stopped dancing at Minutka. They stood in small groups at the edges of walls next to buildings. Shells fizzed in with great claps, smashing black holes into the sides of the apartment blocks from which steel-grey smoke gushed out.

Helicopter gunships combed the northern edge of Grozny,

floating in and out of the black twisters pouring out of the refinery, firing thousands of cannon shells in short, humming bursts. The sound of impacts was heard every few seconds, fired from guns the fighters said were 12 kilometres north. Among the shrapnel littering the streets were tiny darts with metal flights from cluster bombs dropped by the jets. The bombs explode above the ground and the flights are cast to make the darts spin into their victims and cause massive internal injuries. On the approach to Minutka, Saykhanov Street now bristled with the empty nose-cones of Grad rockets that had lodged in the tarmac. Bent steel girders which swam in a lake of broken glass were all that remained of a bus station. The low houses had geometric holes knocked in the rooves, the tiles were smashed on the street and in the courtyards. There was no target, no logic, save only to exact vengeance for the Russian army's failure to capture Grozny on New Year's Eve.

Zulaya Bersanova rested with her scratch platoon down by the side of one of the buildings near the Minutka roundabout after heavy combat near the railway station. She had wound a red woollen scarf over her green headband to keep warm. The thirty-year-old Chechen woman had left her five children with their grandmother. Her husband was fighting in another district. She said they were under threat from small groups of Russian snipers left in the cellars around the market area. 'It quietens down a bit at night but it's heavy in the day. But we got no sleep last night so we drink tea to stay awake.'

Her unit, sipping tea from thermos flasks, had lost the spring in them that they had had a couple of days previously. 'The bombing has been heavy,' she said, the words understating her exhausted face, 'but our morale is stronger than ever.'

I travelled from an outlying village into the city during the day. I performed an obsessive-compulsive ritual each morning: always do up the left flap of the flak jacket before the right one; carry a bag full of lucky charms (first aid kit, a Swiss army pen-knife and a hip flask); salute single magpies. A relative of mine claims that you can drive away the bad luck of the 'one for sorrow' magpie by making as if to tip your hat to the bird. So I tried to hide my last foible by scratching my head in a saluting kind of way, all the time looking round in the hope of seeing 'two for joy'. The Chechen and Ingush drivers quickly saw through this and teased me about my superstition as each black and white bird – Chechnya is full of single magpies – swerved drunkenly off a telegraph pole and flapped down into a field, each one heralding my imminent death. Stepping on a manhole cover was a presentiment of standing on a mine so I avoided those. Sasha and Matt still tease me for my least explainable mental tic – refusing to shave after midday (local time).

On the journey in, I would urge the Chechen or Ingush driver to move slowly into the smoking city, absorbing every detail, sound, moving person in the misguided belief that I was picking the safest possible way in and out of Grozny under the random bombardment. It is difficult to decipher some of my notebooks from that time. The hasty scrawl indicates someone who never wanted to stand or crouch and talk in one place for too long. The men who drove us did so to feed their families but the money we paid in no way made up for the risks they took. In all the time I worked in Chechnya, I was abandoned by a driver only once.*

At night I stayed with a Chechen family in Alkhan-Yurt, a village just south of the Chernorechye reservoir, near Grozny's southern suburbs. When night fell, there were continual flashes on the horizon to the north and a relentless tinnitus of shelling.

One evening word went round the village that Dudayev was to make an address on the Presidential Television channel at seven pm. My hosts had a generator so most of the village menfolk gathered at our house, leaving a large shoal of muddy shoes and galoshes outside the door for the unfortunate women of the household to clean. There was a steady gargling in

---

* One Chechen driver waited for a day under bombardment in Grozny and stuck by his car and a *Liberation* correspondent's possessions after being overrun by Russian troops while the journalist was elsewhere. The driver found the correspondent two days later to return his satellite telephone and apologized for Russian soldiers having taken two Snickers bars from his bags. (Carlotta Gall and Thomas de Waal, *Chechnya: A Small Victorious War*, London 1997).

Chechen as the head of the household tuned the set. At seven pm Dudayev appeared in military uniform, a badge depicting a Chechen wolf pinned to his forage cap. The grainy black and white picture made it difficult at first to see whether the general's grey, sallow face was live or a still. He leaned forward across a table, mouthing silently for a few seconds, and then looked down at a sheet of paper to read. The head of the household fiddled with the tuning button again but no sound came. Dudayev stopped reading after the technical hitch became apparent in the makeshift studio from where they were broadcasting. I imagined Udugov muttering quietly under his breath. A piece of paper was then held up to the camera. The handwritten note in Russian read:

> RISE CHECHNYA
>
> RISE FOR THE GHAZAVAT

Chechen commentary popped and boiled among the men crowding the room. Another piece of paper was held up to the camera:

> FREE CHECHENS!
>
> Today the hungry dogs are surrounding our rich land.
> At this time not one Chechen has the right to stay at home!
> Before us stands a choice – a free Chechnya or a Chechnya that is not free.
> A Chechen without freedom is not a Chechen.
> Either we die or we're victorious.
> Allahu akbar!

In early January, after Russia's Orthodox Christmas, there was talk of a ceasefire to clear the city of the large number of corpses. Late one morning, there was no sound of shelling from the top of Lenin Avenue. A

Chechen fighter, whom I recognized as one of Dudayev's body-guards, lumbered up with RPG rockets strapped to his back, holding a Kalashnikov. He had lost weight and looked tired. He confirmed that talks were underway.

Maskhadov, who knew intimately the mindset of his Russian foe, gives an account of what was happening at this point in his short memoir *Honour is Dearer than Life,* written in the form of an interview. 'This was an ugly, uncivilised war in all categories. Russian generals in many instances conducted themselves in an appalling manner. Their conduct did not bring honour to the Russian army.' Maskhadov joined the Soviet army in 1969. He entered the elite Kalinin artillery school in 1981, and gained a colonel's stars, the command of an artillery regiment in Hungary and later a division in Lithuania during the Soviet crackdown in Vilnius in January 1991. Dudayev's rise to the rank of general in the Soviet air force is the most well known Chechen example of loyal imperial foot soldier turned separatist fighter but Maskhadov was the most accomplished, and for the Kremlin the most dangerous.

'My first disillusionment,' he writes,

> came in January 1995 when the Presidential Palace in Grozny was surrounded. Then all the roads, all the approaches to the Palace from the side of the Railway Station, from the side of the Oil Institute, from the side of the Sunzha River, were filled with the corpses of Russian soldiers. We did not leave our own wounded and killed behind. The corpses had already been lying for two to three weeks. They were rotting, being eaten by cats and dogs. I personally communicated with Babichev and [Lev] Rokhlin [the overall Russian commander], and proposed to halt military action, ideally for a day, to collect the corpses. They didn't agree to this, thinking that it would somehow be to our advantage. They wanted to capture the Presidential Palace at any price, as if it were some kind of sporting contest.

General Babichev, the commander of the Western group of forces, had apparently got over his squeamishness of the previous month. Maskhadov says that Dudayev had agreed with the Russian prime minister, Viktor Chernomyrdin, to a 48-hour ceasefire to collect the bodies. Maskhadov somehow found his way to a line to speak to Babichev who told him, amid the fighting, he would ring back in half an hour.

He then rang me back exactly on time and said in the serious voice of a television newscaster: 'The conditions are as follows. Put up a white flag on the Presidential Palace, strip to the waist, carry no weapons and come out in groups of 10, with your hands up, onto Rosa Luxemburg Street . . .' I listened to this rubbish, like the ravings of a lunatic, with great difficulty and with the utmost politeness told him where to go in time-honoured Russian fashion. It seems that Babichev was none too pleased with my answer as the Presidential Palace was then subjected to an intense barrage. Under this heavy fire and continuous shooting round the clock, one must stop to remember that fighting against the Russian army were a thousand men. For instance, the Presidential Palace had no more than 30–40 men defending it. The Council building 30, the Hotel Kavkaz 20, the museum 30 men. I'm not going to lie in front of my comrades. How much noise, how much spirit, how many bombs, shells, mortar shells and rockets were spent? The mind cannot comprehend it. This was most probably the most concentrated barrage per square metre in the whole history of humanity.

At about the time Maskhadov was communicating with General Babichev, I hitched a lift with a fighter taking an UAZ jeep to the Presidential Palace. The jeep seemed to move interminably slowly, drifting along the road, slowing down to drive round piles of rubble. Groups of fighters in fives jogged back and forth. Their white sheets flashed in the spaces between the buildings. Flames and smoke poured out of some of the apartments, their cracked windows forming hundreds of empy black eyes. The jeep stopped in Freedom Square near the parliament building, next to the Hotel Kavkaz. Nothing moved on the square, empty except for a few strands of trolleybus wire and the torched shell of a Lada Zhiguli flat on its axles. I got out and lay flat on my stomach. The square's surface was covered by a layer of black grit evenly distributed by high explosive. An exchange of small arms fire echoed nearby. The jeep hadn't moved off. A colleague fumbled with the door. I got up in the large, empty space and ran back to the jeep to open the door. A couple of fighters looked out from where one of the walls of the parliament building had been blown away and beckoned us inside, moving their hands in a gesture of urgency. There was no ceasefire.

Some of the fighters kept to a central corridor blackened by fire, lit only by the winter light coming through the open wall at the end. We were hustled to the back of the building, where many of the walls were blown away and burned the same black, and shown down some steps into a cellar which had part of its roof missing. The fighters were subdued, tired. I began to jabber about being trapped. An American colleague told me gently to pull myself together and start working. I opened my notebook and talked to a boy, Ruslan Muloyev, who stood among the fighters. He said he was fifteen. He looked younger.

'I'm fighting for the fatherland,' the boy said gravely. He had no weapon. When I turned to him, he had been trying to beg a grenade from a fighter in a fedora with an RPG slung over his neck.

The fighter, Khanpasha Turlayev, said he had hit two tanks at the railway station. He said the Russians were still there and that sharpshooters had crept up through the market. Fighters were going from room to room to try and find them. I asked him what the fighters would do with Muloyev who was still waiting next to him expectantly. 'We'll give him a gun.' The boy's eyes widened and Turlayev, only 22 himself, began taking him over the slim RPG in a fatherly manner, showing him which part did what.

A Zhiguli whined into a side entrance by the building, clearing it as quickly as possible to avoid the sharpshooters who were sniping into the windows and entrances. A couple of volunteers in green headbands got out. One of them started to unload bricks of fresh bread. The other set about repairing a tyre which had punctured on the way down Lenin Avenue. *Oskolki.* Shrapnel. There were already several patches on the inner tube. When the tyre had been repaired, we took the place of the bread and squeezed in next to some fighters wanting a lift out, my face pressed up against the back window. When we were settled, the car swerved out of the building, across the bridge and back up Lenin Avenue. The tyres held for the short journey back to Minutka.

The iron clouds and flashes over Grozny drifted south the same month towards the smaller towns and villages as Russian forces moved to encircle the city. In Alkhan-Yurt, Goy-Chu and other villages just south of the city, trailers were loaded up with blankets, food, cattle, furniture, women and children to take them to relatives' houses higher up in the mountains. Tired women and overdressed children, by turns too hot and too cold, their noses running, peered through the steamed up windows of ancient red or sky-blue buses with snout bonnets. Their interiors smelled of filled nappies. The passengers' limbs were crushed by traders' bags dense with food and clothes. A few of the children cried in discomfort but I rarely saw parents lose their patience or their tempers on these epic voyages. Many of the men – young and old – stayed to feed the animals, prepared to defend the villages and even commuted to the war raging a few miles north in the city. The buses would often depart in the icy dusk to evade the eyes of the Russian pilots. An order from Yeltsin, announced on state television, to halt the aerial bombardment of Chechnya had either never made it to the airbases, was being wilfully disobeyed or was simply another Kremlin lie. The Chechens knew enough to expect the worst.

The Russian onslaught saw few Chechen voices raised against Dudayev or Maskhadov's volunteers at this time but many felt the *ghazavat* to be a ceaseless heaving of Sisyphus's rock to the top of a mountain, condemned to roll back in defeat each time.

'Is there any difference between those Russian pigs and the hulks who scream *Allahu akbar*?', asked one young Chechen who refused to fight as he watched the burning city from his home a few miles south. A group of neighbours gathered around him and chatted in agreement.

Suspicion and distrust stalked the villages, the wattle fences and surrounding fields frosted in snow. In the village of Goy-Chu, southwest of Grozny, one group of men in fur hats hushed their talk, fingers to lips, when another group in fur hats passed by on a muddy street. Vakha Soslambekov, the fifty-five-year-old head of the village volunteer force, who took his orders from Maskhadov, said there were Chechen 'elements' still loyal to Moscow.

'They help with communications, agitation. Before, they were the heads of the administrations. Why do they lie to the Chechens?' Soslambekov asked rhetorically. 'Because there are 150 million Russians and only one million Chechens. They think Russia is big and they believe Grachev's threat to take Grozny in two hours. We believe in Allah so nothing is terrifying for us. But for them, titles and their lives are more valuable. They've sold their nation.' He said 70 per cent of the village had gone to fight in the city. 'We're handing out weapons to people and we're looking for people to fight.'

Soslambekov, wearing a heavy sweater, had taken me off the street and had seated himself behind a desk in the cold, bare room of the village clubhouse. I sat on a wooden bench against the wall. We were joined by a fighter whose slim chest bulged with ammunition clips and grenades, an angular child's life vest. He was on a recruitment drive.

'Today I found a hundred men and armed them,' he said, adding that the weapons came from a carefully hidden store. 'The men are grouped in a number of about 15 to 20,' he continued. 'We make sure there are a few with some military experience among them, and one of them acts like a platoon commander. But we don't have ranks. We're all civilians.'

The air war was stepped up in the countryside. In Urus-Martan, a town 20 kilometres southwest of Grozny and where opposition to Dudayev had been strong before the war, Russian jets bombed the mosque, killing nine people and wounding several others. The hospital in Urus-Martan comprised lines of oblong grey blankets on metal beds lit by dim, custard-coloured bulbs. The doctors were frantic. They had fewer and fewer medicines and noone inside the building could rule out that a bomb might fall from the sky and hit them too.

A sturdy Chechen woman lay in one of the beds, dressed in a cotton print frock and a headscarf. She was crying. A bomb had taken her arm and her ten-year-old son. The stump where her left arm had been looked hideously unnatural on this strong woman. 'We'd watched Yeltsin on television saying there would be no more bombing, and then three hours later they hit our house. There may have been a few opposition people in Urus-Martan, but most of us didn't care either way. We're just common people. Now everyone is against the Russians.'

Russian wounded also occupied some of the beds. One of them, Pavel Sapunov, was a pasty-faced paratrooper from Stavropol. The nineteen-year-old, his thin chest bare under a blanket, had been hit in the leg by a rifle bullet. 'On the 30th [December], they dropped us off in the mountains by helicopter,' he said, his voice flat. 'We had no tents, no food. They said we'd only be there for two or three days. Only the officers knew what we were supposed to be doing. One of them was killed. We were given amphetamines to stay awake. It was very cold. We only had our sleeping bags. We had no training in mountain warfare.' He swallowed. 'They sent us to our deaths.'

Sapunov and about 36 other paratroopers were discovered in the woods above the village of Goy-Chu by two Chechen woodcutters. Fearing they would betray their position, the Russians took the two woodcutters hostage. Their disappearance was soon noticed, and the volunteer Zelimikhan Amadov led an armed search party of 17 men into the hills. Stocky, tall and with a thick black beard, Amadov was an experienced tracker who hunted bears and wolves. He came across the footprints of the paratroopers in the snow. Two of the search party, who went ahead after the tracks, were fired at.

'Thanks to Allah, none of us was injured.'

The paratroopers had posted a couple of sharpshooters in the trees. The search party fanned out and fired back, killing two of the paratroopers and wounding Sapunov and another soldier. 'They gave themselves up as they didn't know the territory.' He added with a proud grin: 'They didn't know how many men we had first of all, and secondly, they're terrified of Chechens.' The search party also came away with RPGs, 'Mukha' (fly) anti-tank rockets, flamethrowers and ammunition. Amadov was hoping there might be other units in the hills. 'We'll find them. We need the weapons.' The prisoners were then marched off to Grozny.

Russian paratroopers did not live up to defence minister Grachev's boast that with them he could take Grozny in two hours. In his book Maskhadov recalls how in the January fighting around Grozny, his volunteer forces trapped a unit of paratroopers on the twelfth floor of a block of flats near the city centre. The Chechen fighters were below on the eleventh floor. Their commander called on the paratroopers to surrender. The Russian captain bawled back that it was the Chechens who should surrender, claiming all the surrounding buildings were held by Russian forces. The Chechen commander shouted back: 'Fine, listen up and you'll receive some fresh information at first hand.' He then went to the north side of the building and cried out of the window, *'Allahu akbar!'* and like an echo, fighters in a building opposite cried, *'Allahu akbar!'* The commander repeated the performance on the other three sides of the building.

The paratroopers agreed to surrender their weapons if they could be guaranteed safe passage out. After an uneasy night, Maskhadov went to meet General Babichev on the third floor of the building in the expectation of negotiating the paratroopers' release. 'On that day we could not agree on anything, the meeting ended with no results and we parted coldly. I pointed my finger upwards as if to ask him:

'"And what to do with them?"

'Babichev simply waved his hand, as if to say, "Do what you want".'

'We took those paratroopers and their captain out of the building, after they had put down their weapons, and let them go, as we had promised, even though Babichev was completely uninterested in their fate. Babichev's conduct amazed me, not least because he came to Chechnya as some kind of peacekeeper. People put a human shield up in front of him. Women, children, elders surrounded him, pleading with him not to kill and he made a promise to them all. At the beginning he showed himself to be an honourable officer,' Maskhadov said in his memoir. 'Sooner or later he will be cursed by the Russians themselves because the Russian people are endowed with goodness and nobility of soul.'

Earlier in the day, helicopters with loudspeakers had clattered over Goy-Chu and demanded the villagers hand over the lost paratroopers, threatening to bomb them and four other villages if they failed to comply by the following midnight. They also dropped leaflets on the village. Soslambekov, the village commander, gave one to me, an A5 sheet of cheap paper, printed in Russian and bordered in black (see opposite).

Following Russian orders to stay at home had deadly consequences. Jets attacked the mountain villages up the jade-green River Argun, villages where fighters were sending their women and children to safety. By the side of the narrow mountain roads, cars and tractors were hidden under branches or hay. In Gukhoy, 40 kilometres south of Grozny and 7,000 feet up, a jet had circled and then rocketed a remote farmhouse near the village in mid-January.

I went to see the farmhouse set among bare rocks and moor, the mountain peaks forming an upturned adze near the border with Georgia. I was met by the head of the household, Lechi Sadayev. He held two spent rocket casings which he had extracted from his home. Fifteen members of his family, includ-

---

ULTIMATUM

## THE COMMAND OF THE UNITED
## GROUP OF RUSSIAN FORCES
## IN THE CHECHEN REPUBLIC

The Command of the united group of Russian forces demands that all armed groups opposing Russian forces in the Chechen Republic quickly end their rebellion!

Any provocation aimed at Russian forces will be quickly crushed with the full force of Russian weapons!

Persons caught carrying weapons will be destroyed!

To avoid this pointless bloodshed we demand that all armed groups end their struggle, put down their weapons and surrender to Russian forces!

All responsibility for the blood of Russian servicemen and the peaceful population of Chechnya rests on those who do not put down their weapons!

The local inhabitants must stay in their usual places of abode and cooperate in restoring constitutional law, order and peace.

## THE COMMAND OF THE UNITED GROUP
## OF RUSSIAN FORCES IN THE CHECHEN
## REPUBLIC

---

ing relatives who had fled Grozny, were in the house at the time of the attack. Bedding was ripped, the stove smashed and hard mud and straw from the roof were strewn everywhere. The rooms smelled of cordite. Sadayev's two-week-old daughter had been taken to a hospital in Shatoy further down the mountain. The Sadayevs had not got round to naming their new arrival. The doctor in Shatoy, whose candle-lit hospital was admitting five times the usual number of patients, told me later that evening the little girl had died. The war had moved to the countryside.

'Of course there will be a partisan war. It's very simple – either we die fighting, or, as you can see,' said Sadayev, pointing to the hole in his roof, 'we die anyway.'

Some of the Chechen men had gained valuable experience as conscripts in the Soviet army. But the rambling barracks life, big guns and long-range bombers that Dudayev once commanded were a different order of battle from the Molotov cocktails, shotguns and automatic rifles which were what most fighters possessed under Maskhadov's command.

Maskhadov's determination to sit out the bombardment in the basement of the Presidential Palace, only abandoning the building on 19 January 1995, appeared a brave but senseless stand for a guerrilla army which rarely runs to holding cities. The fighting in Grozny did, however, have a certain logic to it. The Chechens melted in and out of the ugly concrete jungle as if in a Chechen forest. The Russian army lost thousands of men in the assault on the city, dealing a blow to Russian military morale which never recovered. The guerrillas captured a considerable amount of weapons and ammunition. And the occupying forces only ever gained control of the ruins that were left them by day, and tenuously even then.

I caught up with Maskhadov in late February 1995 at his temporary headquarters, the two-storey post and telecommunications building in the town of Shali near the mountains. His forces had been pushed south out of Grozny and Argun. Tired fighters hung around outside. One lolled in a chair, a rifle on his knees, to oversee a couple of Russian boy soldiers hauling water from a nearby stream. Maskhadov was back from the village of Samashki, west of Grozny, after another futile effort to strike a ceasefire with the Russians. He said he had been fired on by Russian helicopters when he turned up at a rendezvous designated by Russian commanders to parley. 'The head doesn't know what the hands are doing. What kind of government is this? How can this war end? We know how to keep our word – they do not,' he snapped. 'I think we've probably had enough talks.'

Maskhadov had grown into his command. The mumbling had gone. His steel-grey hair had thinned. He had swapped the Polish combat jacket for a new one of grey displaced pattern material like those worn by Russia's interior ministry troops.

Shelling rattled the windows of the office where he spoke. A television played footage of the January bombardment behind him, now so much muzak. 'Every fifty years. Every fifty years,' Maskhadov repeated, the muscles in his wiry frame stiffening.

Maskhadov was born in 1951 in the Kazakh village of Shakai, of a deported Chechen family, and grew up with tales of *ghazavats* waged against the Russian *giaour*. 'We've taught ourselves how to fight against cluster bombs and all their other horrific weapons,' he said. 'A storm?' he asked impatiently, when questioned about the barrage now coming down on Shali. 'We're prepared for storms, bombardment, anything. The mountains have always helped us through difficult times.'

From the lessons learned in Cuba's Sierra Maestra and set down in his manual *Guerrilla Warfare*, Ernesto 'Che' Guevara wrote that the guerrilla fighter is '"the Jesuit of warfare". By this is indicated a quality of secretiveness, of treachery, of surprise that is obviously an element of guerrilla warfare.'

The Chechen fighters fulfilled – and still do – virtually all the criteria that Guevara laid down for a successful guerrilla war save for the *guerrillero's* Maoist theories on the peasantry as a revolutionary force. Guevara, like Dudayev, held the hit and run tactic as central to the ultimate aim of any warfare: to annihilate the enemy. In his manual Guevara urges the guerrilla band to come away from a raid with enemy guns and ammunition (in Shali, Maskhadov was being truthful in dismissing Russian reports that weapons were being smuggled to him from Azerbaijan. 'We have enough – when we need weapons, we capture them from Russia. We don't get weapons from Azerbaijan, Turkey or anywhere else'); never to allow the enemy to sleep; to explain the struggle to the local population, who must provide food, shelter and keep their mouths shut; not to fear enemy aviation or guns which make a frightening noise but are wasted against the guerrilla; to treat a prisoner well (Guevara advised: 'If he has not been a notorious criminal, he should be set free after receiving a lecture'); to be fit for long marches over rough terrain; and to be strong in the face of harsh repression by the enemy against the civilian population.

That February, Grachev claimed the Chechens no longer had the forces or matériel to carry out 'large-scale actions' and that the fighters were reduced to groups of 10–15 strong. But the fighters had always moved in similar numbers, in exactly the platoon-sized units being formed in the village of Goy-Chu and recommended by Dr Guevara. The only modern piece of equipment Guevara would have been impressed by was the RPG7, the Soviet-designed rocket-propelled grenade. Lighter than the bazookas of his day, it has a light wooden stock which rests on the shoulder, a green, bulbous metal rocket loaded at the front and a flared metal trumpet at the back to let out backblast.

The Chechens' hit and run tactics were tried and tested in their raiding days more than a century before Guevara wrote his manual. In a detailed memo General Yermolov's chief of staff, General Velyaminov, wrote after their campaigns against the Chechens in 1828:

> Armed force is the chief means of bridling the peoples of the Caucasus. The only question is how to employ it in order to attain this end? The Caucasus may be likened to a mighty fortress, marvellously strong by nature, artificially protected by military works, and defended by a numerous garrison. Only thoughtless men would attempt to escalade such a stronghold. A wise commander would see the necessity of having recourse to the military art, would lay his parallels; advance by sap and mine, and so master the place.

Velyaminov described the first obstacle to Russian forces as Chechen horse flesh: Chechens were 'born on horseback' and were used to riding long distances. Mercedes cars have for the most part replaced the Kabarda thoroughbreds in the Chechens' affections but I remember the magical sight of a boy of about ten cantering down the main street between the low houses of the mountain village of Galashki at dusk with all the grace of a young centaur. Horses remain a trusted means of transport. The Chechens' Kavkaz-Tsentr information service reported in June 2000 that Chechnya's most famous field commander, Shamil

Basayev, was rocketed by a helicopter gunship while on horse-back: 'The Chechen general's horse was killed by shellfire from under him. Shamil Basayev was not injured because of Allah's will . . . In a telephone conversation with our correspondent, Shamil Basayev said that he felt in excellent shape, but he was sorry for his lost horse.'

The Chechens' horses, Velyaminov wrote, were not 'pampered in stables' and the ones picked out for a raid – never younger than eight summers – were carefully fattened and then slimmed again in a process which took several weeks, enabling the animals to cover a hundred miles in a day.

Velyaminov also noted the dumping of all domestic labour on the women as another significant military advantage. 'The Cossack . . . is an agriculturalist as well as a soldier. Being very often withdrawn from his occupations by field work at home, he cannot use either his horse or his arms with the same skill as the mountaineer . . .' In the nineteenth century Chechen raiders moved in on their target weeks in advance, gathering information from spies, careful not to let on what they were about. Only the leader would know the time, place and tactics for the attack. They travelled light, taking food and fodder *en route* from a trusted *kunak*, a person of sworn friendship with duties to the other. The attack itself rarely lasted more than two hours, and the loot was whisked away on horses which neither Cossack nor Russian steeds could match in stamina. There was more to it than booty. Not to raid, Velyaminov noted, would make a Chechen the 'laughing-stock and an object of contempt even for the women, not one of whom would join her fate to his.' In a back-handed compliment to Chechen and Ingush democracy – and also an indication of the autocratic system he served – Velyaminov wrote: 'Finally, it must be admitted that the anarchy prevailing amongst the natives, so fatal in all other respects, has one serious advantage in their raiding warfare, namely, that any man endowed by Nature with the necessary qualities finds the road open to fame and leadership.'

One night back in Alkhan-Yurt, some of the villagers reluctantly detailed for me the orders Maskhadov had given them in case Russian forces attacked the village. The men said they posted guards at night, who were commanded to fire a set number of shots to signal an attack. Others patrolled the countryside around the village. A trained engineer had constructed tank traps on the edge of the village. Another Chechen had mined the bridge into the village and had instructions to blow it as soon as the Russians advanced. 'Everyone knows how to fight the Russian army because we all served in it,' said one of the men. Another, who had spent his conscript years as a forward air controller, said simply: 'If they come, we'll be ready.'

None of the men looked like *guerrilleros*. They did not camp out in the woods but stayed at home and – power permitting – watched television. Their designated tasks were limited to their village. It was canny of Maskhadov to issue a limited set of commands to Chechnya's quarrelsome villages and *teips*, or clans, the lowest common denominator being a desire to defend their property. As the majority of fighters said, they were battling to protect their homes, not Dudayev.

Alkhan-Yurt's neighbourhood watch was effective. Coming back to the village one day in January 1995, I watched a Russian army truck driven by a Chechen fighter, limping along the highway near the village. Its front tyres and its windscreen had been shot out. The truck belonged to Russian soldiers who had been looting flats in Grozny. They had filled the canvas-covered back with fridges, televisions, childrens' clothes still in their packaging and boxes of women's shoes, but the soldiers had taken a wrong turning when they tried to find their way back to their unit. Their vehicle and an APC were stopped and quickly disarmed by Chechen fighters on the road. To celebrate, Chechen fighters on either side of the Rostov-Baku highway fired long volleys into the air (Guevara would have disapproved of the waste of ammunition) and hollered an inevitable *Allahu akbar!*

'Every house, every tree is like a fortress for us,' one of the villagers in Alkhan-Yurt explained. 'We'll fight in the villages, and when they take the villages, we'll go to the hills. When they take the hills, we'll go to the mountains where they'll never follow us.'

Guevara's Jesuitical stealth goes to the heart of the Chechens' flexible organization and communications. Many of them belong to Sufi orders which profess a careful hierarchy, secrecy and discipline among their adherents. The chanting and dancing of the spiritual *zikr* (a modest form of the Sufi whirling of dervishes) which I saw on Freedom Square at the many funerals that followed and at times of celebration came from the Qadirya Sufi order founded in Baghdad in the twelfth century. Chants focus on the proximity of death:

> Hard is the road you must travel,
> Your last hour is imminent,
> As long as the source of your speech exists,
> Prepare yourself to join your creator.

Sufi orders such as the Qadirya formed a strong backbone to the Chechens' struggle against both Tsarist and Soviet rule. *Taqiya*, the Sufi adept's ability to dissemble and hide his or her religious faith if threatened without it being a sin, made the brotherhoods almost impenetrable to the KGB. The brotherhoods' strict discipline – a Sufi saying describes a disciple as 'a cadaver in the hands of an embalmer' – served well in times of war and in setting down the rules of engagement for the *ghazavat*. The historian Alexandre Bennigsen compared the brotherhoods in discipline and ruthlessness to the Bolsheviks. The Tsarist authorities banned the *zikr* following outbreaks of violent unrest in Chechnya after Imam Shamil's defeat in 1859. The Sufi leader Kunta Haji, who brought the Qadirya movement to Chechnya, died in a Russian jail and thousands of *zikrist* Chechens fled their homes in 1865 for the Ottoman Empire. A Russian official commented at the time: 'The *zikrist* movement disappeared as rapidly as it appeared.' But in its place, another Sufi order, the Naqshibandiya, taught a silent *zikr*. Uzun Haji, who led the *ghazavat* against the Red Army in 1920, was a Naqshibandiya sheikh: 'The Daghestani-Chechen revolt was a widespread popular mass movement, resembling a peasant war, but the guerrilla fighters displayed an efficiency that only a brotherhood leadership comparable to that of Shamil's fighters, with their spirit of total dedication and iron will, could ensure.'

Stalin's push to liquidate the 'feudal clerics' saw many imams deported to the camps or executed. But the fluid, secretive nature of the brotherhoods not only survived the purges and deportations, but actually made their adherents stronger; for over a million North Caucasian Muslims in exile, the Sufi orders became a bedrock of nationhood.

Before the 1917 Revolution, Daghestan and Chechnya boasted hundreds of mosques and were famed in the Islamic world for the quality of their teaching at the mountain *medressehs*, or Islamic schools. But Islam came late to the mountains. Imam Shamil had constant battles with the mountaineers in imposing Shariat law over the traditional Adat, or customary mountain law, which went into meticulous detail on how to settle blood feuds. Baddeley weighed carefully the combined influence of Sufism and Islam, declining to characterize it wholly as either 'religious fanaticism', as the Tsarist and later Soviet administrations would describe it, or as simply a national liberation movement got up in religious robes.

The Chechens are devout, not fanatical. I noticed that one of my Chechen drivers wordlessly raised his backside off his seat every time we passed a Muslim cemetery. When I asked him why he did it, he explained, a little embarrassed, that he did it in honour of the dead. The attempts by a small number of conservative fighters to impose Islamic rectitude – taking sticks to the bottles of vodka on sale in a few village shops or dealing out lashes to criminals – were often as embarrassing for the men meting out the punishments as they were costly or painful for the recipients. The public executions after the 1994–96 war, Chechen criminals accused of murder being machinegunned and their deaths broadcast on local television, was not the Chechnya I knew. Udugov, promoted from his position as information minister to Chechnya's vice-premier after the war, announced in 1997 a halt to public executions. But they were symptomatic of a brutalized people. Baddeley, as usual, got the balance right.

The Russians, be it noted, assign religious fanaticism as the primary cause of this and all similar outbreaks [of unrest]; but in truth it was only secondary. It was in the role of invaders, oppressors, conquerors – or, to use the current euphemism, civilisers – that they excited such bitter resentment . . . Zeal for the religion of Muhammad, though mighty the part it played henceforth, but was as air in a blow-pipe feeding a flame that already existed. The *Ghazavat* would never have been preached in the Caucasus had the Russians been peaceful and friendly neighbours.

In February 1995 shells smacked and echoed every few minutes into the thick, sodden wood at the turn-off from the Rostov-Baku highway to Grozny's Chernorechye district, the road I had taken into the city the previous November. Clucking noises issued from a group of middle-aged men and women standing by the roadside, the women's breasts puffed up in scarves folded into large woollen coats. Shopping bags sat obediently at their feet. They wanted to return to their flats in the district further up the road where Chechen fighters and a Cossack were exchanging fire with Russian soldiers, making nonsense of another on-off ceasefire.

'We have not received orders to shoot,' said the commander, 'and neither have we orders not to shoot. We simply answer their fire.'

Back down the road, the group of mostly Russian civilians stood rooted to the ground, the force of the desire to go home cancelled out by the desire to live, a force which pulled back along the road they had come. 'They're firing at everything,' said one of the women, voicing out loud a wish to live over a need to extricate sugar, cooking oil and other valuables from her flat. 'It's too dangerous to go back.'

Lyoma Abzuyev and his wife Bela decided to risk it. I travelled in with the Chechen couple to see their small apartment in a squat cluster of crumbling *Khrushchevki*. The road was scarred with black stars punched by shells and rockets. They wanted to bring out the remainder of their belongings and then leave. Bela was nervous and emotional, trying to fight back the tears as we mounted the empty concrete stairwell to their flat.

Abzuyev searched in his pockets for the keys. He asked Bela if she had them. She rifled through her handbag. They burst out laughing. They had forgotten them. Lyoma broke the door down. The couple found their belongings strewn untidily across the damp flat, signs of a hasty departure a few weeks before. 'There's no end in sight for the war,' said Lyoma. 'They want us to hand in our guns and live as prisoners.' Four of his brothers were missing. His brother-in-law had been killed in a bomb attack. Bela perched on the edge of a cheap sofa dusted in plaster, her chest heaving with sobs.

'We had to bury what we could – arms, legs, whatever was left of them.'

As fighting continued in the south of the city, the road opened to Grozny's inhabitants in the north. On the outskirts of the city, where the Maikop brigade had been slaughtered, Russian soldiers had set up a checkpoint with a shelter contructed out of sandbags and bits of iron roofing. It was furnished with chairs expropriated from abandoned flats nearby. A sign just before the checkpoint ordered: 'Stop! We shoot without warning!'

Dozens of Chechen men waited to pass through the checkpoint. As they walked across, they were stopped and made to stand spreadeagled against the wall while a teenage conscript felt for weapons. 'It's the first time I've raised my hands for anyone,' said sixty-five-year-old Musa Edilov, mortified. He smoothed out his coat and shirt as if brushing off dirt. 'I'm not scared of the Russians,' he shouted so the conscripts could hear, 'just ashamed that I have to enter my own land in such a way. It's like the German occupation.' Edilov harrumphed and cursed, furious that the Russian soldiers ignored him. He swung a tattered canvas rucksack on his back and walked into the city he had left the previous month under shellfire.

Staropromyslovskoye Avenue had been cleaned of the blackened armour and corpses of conscripts. In their place, Russian soldiers wearing balaclavas and mirror-shades rode shotgun on the backs of armoured personnel carriers. The barrels of their automatics swayed skywards as they swerved at high speed round the city, the APCs' knobbly tyres humming as they went and churning up clouds of pale yellow dust. A red triangular warning sign depicting the black silhouette of a tank in the centre was put up on one of the main roads.

Below the cacophony of Russian armour on the streets, stooped Russians and elderly Chechens pushed makeshift carts or wheeled bicycles loaded with cheap carpets, clothes and crockery – anything they could rescue of their pitiful possessions from theft or destruction. Some risked an overnight stay. Others took what they could back to where they had fled from.

'They loot every day – no, make that every hour,' said Supian Magomadov, livid. A history lecturer from what had once been the Chechen State University, he was waiting in line to get through the checkpoint. He said he had watched a group of Russian soldiers leap off an APC in a northern suburb and blow the windows out of a ground floor apartment with a grenade. 'They walked inside and loaded videos, perfumes and other stuff into their APC.' A crowd had gathered round the lecturer, nodding and shouting angrily in agreement.

Looting in the city became so bad that units of grey-uniformed interior ministry troops were tasked with patrolling Grozny to fight the looters in their own army. The deputy head of the Federal Counter-Intelligence Service, the FSK, admitted there were a few cases of looting by Russian troops. He bent the truth by adding: 'But there are also Chechen militants disguised in Russian uniforms who've been looting.'

Chechnya's lawlessness was abetted by the *kontraktniki*, criminals who had been released from Russian prisons in return for fulfilling a 'contract' to serve in Chechnya. Their older faces and malign expressions immediately marked them out from fresh-faced conscripts at checkpoints across the territory. They earned up to four times the monthly salary of a Russian army colonel.

General Yermolov, who took over the command 'of Russia's Caucasian armies in 1816, wrote to Alexander I asking the tsar to put an end to the same practice, by which criminals and political prisoners were sent to serve in the Caucasus. 'Henceforward,' Yermolov wrote, 'officers will no longer see amongst themselves comrades for whom they need to blush . . .'

Whole streets of apartment blocks and houses in the city were roofless. Several floors at a time had collapsed through the large blocks on Lenin Avenue, now crushed like half-burned cardboard boxes. A bath tub sat open to the elements. Radiators dangled in the air on pipes which had saved them from falling with the supporting walls. The frames where windows had once been placed in the façades of buildings formed columns upon rows of empty squares smeared with soot. The sides of five-storied *Khrushchevki* had caved in at drunken angles. Piles of bricks, mortar, timber and pipes were all that was left of some of the smaller houses. A few unexploded rockets remained with their noses jammed in the road. Water-filled craters dotted the roads.

Everything – buildings, armoured vehicles, people – got covered in *gryaz*, mud, of a dense black consistency. A few yellow and black stumps, their limbs torn off in the metal storm, were all that remained of the trees along the River Sunzha. A marble statue of three square-jawed Soviet heroes at the top of Victory Avenue had only a few chunks shot out of it and the men continued to stare purposefully down what was left of the street. The heroes were christened by the shell-shocked inhabitants the *tri duraki*, 'the three idiots'. The heavy traffic of tanks and APCs had cleared the wide avenues of some of the rubble but the streets were deserted by civilian traffic, save for the small home-made carts pushed or pulled by ragged pensioners.

The upper floors of the Presidential Palace were now a ragged amalgam of chipped masonry, a broken tooth left in Freedom Square's blackened jaw. The building was cordoned off with the explanation that it was booby-trapped. There were no taped windows left on the fourth floor offices of Chechen Press. Opposite, the recently refurbished Hotel Kavkaz was roofless. Its stuccoed walls were pocked with bullets and shrapnel dents.

There was a shout from a pile of rubble at the side of the square. A Russian soldier in a black tank helmet popped his head above a large pile of cream rubble, behind which he had parked an armoured vehicle. A red hammer and sickle flew from the aerial. 'Do you want a bullet in your head?' His companions laughed, a hardness in their faces borrowed from later years as they pulled on precious cigarettes. 'Fuck off!'

On Lenin Avenue, the gashed walls of the Church of the Archangel Michael still stood but it had lost its roof. A few bells saved from the steeple were lined down the stairs into a cellar. The ageing Russian community flocked to its wonky gates in the hope of consolation, gossip of the congregation and possibly some food. The church did not have much to spare. A small handwritten notice pinned to the wall next to the gate politely requested donations for restoration. The church's bearded caretaker, Pavel Slavinin, had sheltered in the basement of the neighbouring priest's house during the bombardment. 'At first we could crawl out to a standpipe to fetch water. But when that stopped, we had to ration out the water in the church fire extinguishers.'

Father Alexander, a shiny silver cross on his chest, was one of two priests who disobeyed his bishop's orders to stay in the city, holding services during each day of the fighting. His once sleepy parish now bustled, receiving a flood of Russian soldiers wanting to be christened alongside intercessions for the dead. 'Many Russian soldiers come in and ask if I'll have time to christen them,' he said enthusiastically, 'and I tell them, "Any time! We're always open"!'

For months afterwards, a sudden breeze off the rubble-filled basements would carry the sour-sweet odour of decaying human beings, the city streets long lines of unmarked graves. The corpses of those who died above ground were buried in the empty spaces between the *Khrushchevki*, perhaps below a rusty children's swing. Workers from Russia's emergencies ministry brought in earth-moving equipment to dig out the bodies from the rubble. Sniper fire *chik-kacked* across the city as they worked. A twenty-year-old volunteer working for the ministry said he had helped move 200 bodies from one district. He took off a face mask. 'It's difficult work. I have nightmares – I want to leave here as soon as I can.'

In the north of the city next to the Russian cemetery, littered with spent rocket canisters, about 400 bodies lay unclaimed in three open pits. An elderly woman lay flat on a bloodied stretcher, her cracked spectacles still balanced on her nose. A naked back bore a tattoo in gothic script which read '*Gott mit uns*'. The dead children in the pit looked as if they were asleep.

A woman walked up and down the edge of the pits, a handkerchief over her nose, her cheeks burned by tears, looking down to try and recognize her husband. 'I've been looking for him for four days now – I don't know whether he's dead or alive.' After a short time she shook her head, unable to look in any more. Her teenage son supported her away from the pits. The shoulders of her black dress shook. Two Russian soldiers, curious, walked over to look in.

Nearby, Russians and Chechens queued at an old bottling plant to collect bread and aid they were told would arrive. The morning was unseasonably warm. The road in front of the plant was corrugated with ruts of half-dried mud. An APC pulled up next to the crowd and a middle-aged man with long, unkempt hair, a bushy beard and a paunch under his combat jacket squeezed himself out of the turret and gingerly stepped onto the ground. He had left the top buttons of the jacket undone, revealing a hairy chest in which nestled a large gold cross. On the lapel was pinned a medal for 'exceptional service' to the Russian army. The unkempt soldier was a Russian military chaplain who started to work the crowd, laying hands on a couple of startled women and hugging a tearful old *babushka*.

'You're all my children!' he shouted at the crowd. 'There will be no more war!'

Both Russians and Chechens in the queue looked at the man open-mouthed.

'It's easy for him to say,' said one old woman in the queue, an empty plastic bag on her arm. 'There's no bread. Every day they're letting off the howitzers. *Eto vsyo yerundà!* It's all rubbish!'

'I bless you! I bless you!' the chaplain shouted repeatedly at the men and women in the queue. The tired crowd prickled with hostility and pulled back from his touch as if from an eel.

'Muslims! Christians!' cried the chaplain. 'We're all the same!'

This Rasputin paused in the middle of the crowd, staff in hand, and looked around morosely, discouraged by the lack of adoration he so obviously thought he should arouse. He headed back to his armoured car.

'I serve in the army so that there can be peace,' he said, 'but war is war.'

# A law more inevitable than death

'There is no good news,' the old man began. 'All that is
new is that the hares are all taking counsel to see how they
can drive off the eagles. And the eagles go on killing them
one by one.'

Lev Tolstoy, *Hadji Murat*, 1912

T HE WAR MOVED south in the spring of 1995. The Rostov-
Baku highway served as an informal front line, dividing the
low Sunzha Range and then the flat plains of the north from the
mountainous south. Refugees, civilians and fighters moved
along the road, which curved below Grozny, as best they could.
The Russian army, unable to distinguish one clapped-out Lada
from another, would send out the occasional round after them,
lifting grey cloaks of dirt in a field as they passed, sometimes with
tragic results. Russian armour massed at the northern side of the
road and inched forward to surround some of the villages along
the highway, moving round them like metal phagocytes to
absorb the villages back into the Federation, bombing them
from the air while shelling them and shooting at them with
heavy cannon from a safe distance on the ground. The Russians
rarely engaged in close combat with the Chechen fighters whose
claim on the villages could shift from week to week, day to day
or even hour to hour.

Humanitarian aid was blocked. *'Vot nasha gumanitarnaya
pomoshch!'* angry Chechen villagers would shout in disgust,
holding out handfuls of shrapnel: 'That's our humanitarian aid!'
The phrase formed a favourite chorus in the war's simple
libretto.

At the beginning of March, a column of 50 cars and buses,

stuffed with sacks of flour, suitcases, hot, blear-eyed children and their sweating mothers, lined up at a Russian checkpoint on the western side of Samashky, a village about 30 kilometres due west again of Grozny. The village, after Argun and Shali to the south-east of Grozny, was the next sizeable settlement on the Chechen plain to come into the Russians' sights. It was ground relatively easy to manoeuvre on and located near a railway line.

Children ran about in the surrounding fields while Chechen men leaving the village were frisked by Russian soldiers. The peaks of the mountains were a dazzling, toothpaste white to the south. The Chechen women told the now nauseatingly familiar story. 'I don't know where I'm going to take my kids. I have six of them and no money,' said a forty-year-old woman, standing next to an ancient Zhiguli in the queue; her husband had stayed behind to fight.

Vakha Mirzhoyev was the gruff, bearded Chechen commander overseeing the defence of Samashki and the large village of Achkhoy-Martan 10 kilometres to the south. Russian forces poked and prodded both like a stick in an ants' nest, causing the long lines of refugees to leave. The Chechen commander was pressuring the civilian population – which had more than doubled with long lines of refugees from Grozny and elsewhere – to stay. On ground difficult to defend, Mirzhoyev appeared intent on using his own people, despite any lack of Kremlin scruple when it came to civilian casualties, particularly Chechen ones, to hold the villages.

'We expect an attack any moment,' he said. A Kalashnikov rifle lay on his desk at his Achkhoy-Martan headquarters. 'We expect it and are prepared.' The thirty-six-year-old commander bristled when asked about the overtures Russian forces had made to the village elders, promising an end to the shelling and fair treatment if Mirzhoyev's fighters quit the area. When I began to ask the local inhabitants in Achkhoy-Martan what they thought, a group of fighters pointed me into my car and escorted me out of the town.

A few days later I called on Mirzhoyev in Achkhoy-Martan at the end of Ramadan, on the day of the feast of Eid al-Fitr, which marks the end of 40 days of dawn-to-dusk fasting. 'The bombardment's continuing – the Russians are sending us "gherkins" for our feast.' The previous evening six 'gherkins' (rockets) had hit the town, some landing near a house while the others exploded in a cemetery. 'We're all at our posts and the women are preparing food for the celebrations at home,' he said, a touch defensively.

Mirzhoyev took me to visit a street of low but spacious houses where one of the rockets had landed. His webbing clinked and rustled as he walked. In the front yard of one of the homes, women in fresh dresses busied themselves with basins of food, holding pastried hands askew in welcome. They put on brave faces, as crisp as their headscarves, for the commander who greeted the family with his right hand to his chest, removing his boots at the door. He sat himself on some cushions on the floor inside a large room, his back against a rug on the wall. We talked of the attempts to make peace by the Muslim clerics and the repeated ultimatum from the Russians for his men to leave.

'The spiritual leaders always have a right to try and stop the fighting but by God, there has to be some result. There will only be peace for us when the Russians leave our territory. For 300 years, every 50 years, they destroy our mosques and monuments, they kill our women. It is simply the first time for our generation that we have met the Russians under these conditions.' The commander did not exaggerate: Sheikh Mansur's *ghazavat* against the Tsarist Empire in the eighteenth century; a *ghazavat* fought for much of the nineteenth, under the leadership of Imam Shamil from 1832 to 1859; the *ghazavat* fought in the 1920s, with guerrilla activity almost continuous up until the deportations in 1944; and the return of Russian troops in 1994, 50 years later.

There was no gas or electricity in the home but the woman of the household had cooked a lamb stew on a fire at the back of the house to feed her family and the relatives and friends who, as refugees from Grozny, were guests by force of circumstance. A table was spread with carrot salad, garlicky *chirimsha* fried in oil, a type of spring onion that grew wild and kept many families in vitamins that year, bread, biscuits, bowls of sweets and a colourful cake iced in sugar pinks and blues.

'Our elders taught us how to prepare for the end of Ramadan. It's a difficult time,' she said hesitantly, conscious that the eyes of the commander were on her, 'but in general, I think it's the best Ramadan we've ever had.' She bade me sit and eat, offering to pour out some fruit juice and tea. It was difficult to choose between breaking the rules of hospitality and tucking into valuable provisions in front of this extended, impoverished family. I did my best to compromise with a glass of tea and a couple of sweets, saying I was pressed for time.

Afterwards, Mirzhoyev accompanied me to the town's cemetery, saying a short prayer and running his hands ritually over his beard before he walked through a gate into the fenced-off area. Some of the gravestones, carved in Arabic script, had been smashed by the rockets. In one corner a couple of men were shovelling earth out of a grave, one of six new holes that had been dug in anticipation of a Russian attack. 'They're for civilians and fighters,' Mirzhoyev said in a practical turn of voice.

I wandered over to a Chechen elder who stood as though lost in the cemetery. He gave his name as Magomet Dzhamulayev. He wore a freshly laundered white skullcap. Mirzhoyev watched anxiously to see how the conversation would progress. The other's views were probably opposed to his own but as he was an elder, it would have been awkward for the commander to silence him.

Dzhamulayev talked elliptically. He related how his father had taught him Arabic in secret during Soviet times at the age of seven, so that he could read the Koran. 'Without Islam there is nothing, it is our way of life and guides us along the true path. There are strict rules, no lying or killing. We are taught to be clean. This is a great day for us – it is a difficult time but we will wait to be judged by Allah.' He stopped for a moment but he could not hold himself. His voice wavered and broke. Tears glistened in his eyes. The commander and I looked away in embarrassment. 'I say this with a troubled heart,' Dzhamulayev continued, 'as I cannot understand why this is being done to us.'

Russian forces prepared to take Samashky and the neighbouring villages by force. The day after the end-of-Ramadan feast,
Russian interior ministry soldiers secured a long stretch of the
road between Achkoy-Martan and Samashky, cutting the two
villages off from one another. The road was now lined with tanks
and APCs. Russian soldiers looked over the fields towards the
two villages through binoculars and snipers' scopes. Chechen
fighters had fallen back on Samashky after being attacked by helicopters at midday. A mile from the village, the sound of a Grad
rocket-launcher groaned like a wounded dragon, a low roll of
thunder following seconds later as the long black darts slammed
into Achkhoy-Martan. Four metal dragonflies hovered above the
trees.

Back in Samashky, Chechen fighters were arguing with an
angry crowd of women and elders wanting to leave. 'There can
be no agreement with these people who are burning our land,'
said the local commander, Akhmed Islamov. Tanned and lean,
he was anxious rather than angry. He could feel the sea in which
he swam begin to evaporate. The helicopters buzzed insistently.
'It's because the FSK are working here, they want to clean the
village without war, they're making provocations. Chechnya will
never surrender. Those who don't want to fight are small
people,' he continued angrily. 'We won't put our hands up. We'll
defend this village to the last.'

The sun beat down on tired fighters armed with grenades and
assault rifles who lay incongruously in ditches at the edge of the
road out of the village while the frightened crowd stood above
them on the asphalt.

'How can we stay here?' asked a teacher in her forties. She
cricked her neck about to keep a goose eye on the six daughters
and nieces under her protection. Bulging plastic bags lay at their
feet. All waited in the hope of a truck or a bus that might take
them out. 'We've no money or anything and where the girls will
go to school I don't know but we have to go. We'd leave here
gladly.'

Buses, cars, tractors and trailers started to make their way hesitantly out of Achkhoy-Martan. One bus had hit a mine, killing

nine adults and a child and wounding five others. On the road
between the town and Samashky, Russian soldiers had hastily
established a sandbagged post on a crossroads they had taken
earlier that morning. Remnants of river mist hung in the woods
surrounding them. The soldiers tracked a line of refugee traffic
with long sniper rifles, magnifying hundreds of strained and
frightened faces in their scopes. The cannon on an APC was
trained back on Samashky. Women and kids in bright woollens
stared out from behind truck windscreens. Cattle moved their
heads and stiffened to keep from falling down in the open backs
of the trucks. Buses flew large white flags. The inhabitants could
no longer work in their fields. The strain of living in their cellars
had become too much, whatever Mirzhoyev's command to stand
fast. The checkpoint was a one-way valve, letting people out but
letting noone back in again. The Chechen sea was being drained
once more.

'We haven't been here long, it's still dangerous,' said Kostya,
the young Russian lieutenant in charge of the post. He wore a
green bandanna tied tightly over his head. He was not much
older than the conscripts he commanded. The human current
flowed past as the dam opened and shut with long, worried
minutes as the soldiers scanned the Chechens' papers. 'It'll be
okay till five,' said Kostya, 'and then there'll be more bombing.'

On 10 June 1818 Russian soldiers laid the foundations of a six-bastioned fort near the River Sunzha, a
few kilometres before it meets the Terek. The
Russian commander who had ordered the fort and built others
along the line, General Alexey Yermolov, wrote to Tsar
Alexander I: 'When the fortresses are ready I shall offer the
scoundrels dwelling between the Terek and the Sunzha, and
calling themselves "peaceable", rules of life, and certain obliga-
tions, that will make clear to them that they are subjects of your
majesty, not allies, as they have hitherto dreamed.' The general
named the fort *Grozny*, 'menacing' or 'threatening' in Russian,
and it was soon joined by other military bases along the line with

names such as Fort Storm and Fort Surprise. The 'scoundrels' in question, the Chechens, seeing what was up, sniped at the Russian soldiers as they tried to build them.

Yermolov decided to teach the Tsar's unwilling subjects a lesson near one such fort. His troops pretended to abandon an artillery piece while training the remainder of the detachment's guns on it. The Chechens sloped out from their hiding-places and made to capture the gun as expected. The Russians opened fire with grapeshot. Those that were not hit stood transfixed in shock for a moment but snapped out of it to carry away their dead and wounded. As they did so, the Russians opened fire again. The Russian soldiers counted 200 dead and as many wounded. This was, in essence, the 'Yermolov system', variants of which remain Russian military doctrine to this day.

Yermolov rose quickly up the ranks. He was made a lieutenant-colonel and was awarded the Cross of Saint Vladimir while still a teenager for his part in the battle of Gandzha (where Persian forces sent elephants into battle in present-day Azerbaijan). He was imprisoned and exiled for a short period under Tsar Paul I, accused of being a party to a military conspiracy, gained promotion at the battle of Austerlitz in 1807 and garnered more honours during the Napoleonic invasion and the occupation of Paris in 1814 (where hungry Cossacks added a new word to the French language, shouting impatiently at the French waiters '*bistro!*', 'quickly!'). In 1816 the general took command of the Caucasus, based in Tbilisi.

'Incorruptibly honest, simple, even rude in his habits, and of Spartan hardihood . . . his sword was ever at his side,' wrote Baddeley, 'and in city as in camp he slept wrapped only in his military cloak, and rose with the sun.' He was adored by his soldiers. One night the stocky general was strolling about a camp struck below a Daghestan mountain town he planned to storm the following day. He stopped unseen and overheard a captain run him down in the coarsest language to his fellow officers for being too cautious. The next day, after the town was taken with few losses, Yermolov went up to the captain to congratulate him. 'You, with your company, were the first over the breastworks; I congratulate you on winning the Cross of Saint Vladimir. But have a care, my friend, not to abuse me again as you did last night.' However, Yermolov's arrogance made him many enemies among the influential German party at court. He was said to have boomed at a clutch of generals in the tsar's chambers, 'May I enquire, gentlemen, if anyone amongst you speaks Russian?'

Yermolov's aim to incorporate the Caucasus into the Russian Empire, pushing the Persians and Turks south of the River Aras, was nothing new. What made the 'Yermolov System' different was the general's psychopathic and relentless cruelty to the peoples who got in his way. Yermolov summed up his own policy thus: 'I desire that the terror of my name should guard our frontiers more potently than chains of fortresses, that my word should be for the natives a law more inevitable than death. Condescension in the eyes of the Asiatics is a sign of weakness and out of pure humanity I am inexorably severe. One execution saves hundreds of Russians from destruction, and thousands of Mussulmans from treason.'

Chechen rustlers had made off with Russian horses belonging to Fort Surprise in the summer of 1819. Yermolov's forces traced the horse thieves back to the aoul of Dadi-Yurt on the Terek.

At dawn on 15 September, he ordered General Sisoyev to surround the village with six companies of soldiers, 700 Cossacks and six artillery pieces. The villagers were told they had to leave immediately for the south of the River Sunzha, Sisoyev being ordered to give no quarter in case of a refusal. A refusal was all that was expected. Having had no time to move their families, the Chechens hurriedly set about defending the village of high stone walls. They poured musket fire at point-blank range onto the Russian gunners as they moved their pieces from house to house, blasting holes in the wall. Russian soldiers leapt through the holes, sabres drawn, and in the maze of narrow alleyways and dark rooms, it was kill or be killed. The Chechens slaughtered their wives and children rather than let them fall into the hands of their attackers. The Russians lost so many men that the Cossacks had to dismount and go in after them. The massacre continued for several hours, until only 14 severely wounded Chechen men were left alive. Many of the 140 women and children taken prisoner were wounded. Double their number were killed or were lost in the flames that gutted the houses. Soldiers looted whatever was left. 'The aoul was, in the literal sense of the words,' wrote Baddeley, 'destroyed to its foundations.'

Many such 'lessons' were meted out to the Chechens. Captured Chechen women were raffled off as so many slaves. As the Chechens' anger grew, their popular leaders were picked out and made examples of. Russian sources say in one instance two of them were dealt 2,000 blows in public while a third, Dzhembulat Chechoyev, 'terror of the road and brigand unmatched, passed six times through the ranks, a thousand strong, without medical help, and when, under the last blows, he fell dead, was strung up on a gallows as an example to others.'

Nicholas I's distrust of Yermolov, his enemies at court and his failure to respond in time to renewed Persian and Turkish incursions to the south of the Empire saw the general leave the Caucasus in 1827 in official disgrace. But the swarm of greycoats who had subdued both the Persian provinces in what is today Azerbaijan and Daghestan won him lasting fame while his insouciance at court drew the adoration of Decembrists like Pushkin, who declaimed:

> Bow down thy snowy head, O Caucasus;
> Submit; Yermolov comes!

The Yermolov system, however, brought diminishing returns. The harder Yermolov hit the incensed Chechens the more determined the forest dwellers were to resist. His cruelty toughened them like their own raiding horses for the long *ghazavat* against Russia under Imam Shamil. They had little to lose. 'Tchetchnia,' wrote Baddeley, 'harassed, harried, but never subdued, driven to desperation by Russian encroachments and Yermolov's avowed determination to extinguish its independence, broke out, in 1824, into open hostility.' In July 1825 two thousand Chechen horsemen descended on a small Russian fort of the Line, killing and capturing two thirds of the 184-strong garrison.

Yermolov – 'Yarmul' to the Chechens – left just before his 'system' collapsed entirely, and so the myth of its invincibility went with him intact to his retirement in Orel. 'It is not, in the long run,' Baddeley commented, 'the battles and sieges that signify, but the permanent effect on the human race of the changes they help bring about.' The Chechens now knew they could expect only rank inhumanity from the Empire's generals sent against them.

In early April 1995, Sergey Stepashin, the head of the Federal Counter-Intelligence Service (FSK), declared the war in Chechnya almost over. Dudayev's forces, he said, had 'ceased to exist' and peace would be 'installed' by the end of that month in both Samashky and Achkhoy-Martan. Stepashin was in a hurry to wind up the war in Chechnya ahead of the May celebrations to mark Victory in Europe Day, fifty years since the end of World War Two. Foreign dignatories had been invited to Moscow. The Kremlin did not want the Chechens to spoil the show, with their own troops going home in zinc coffins on a day of supposed Russian might.

For the Kremlin, the fall of Shali, 25 kilometres southeast of Grozny, looked promising. A red, blue and white Russian flag now flew from the top of the town's posts and telecommunications building which up until recently Maskhadov had used as his headquarters. A Russian colonel stood in front of the building among a group of APCs parked outside, a striped matelot shirt showing at the open neck of his combat jacket. A jet streaked overhead. The interior ministry officer said the Russian entry into Shali had persuaded other towns and villages to clear out fighters rather than face assault. 'This is a new step in the war,' he said. His optimistic analysis did little to hide the obvious relief he and his men felt at taking the town without much of a fight. 'We used minimum force to take the town. The initiative is now coming from below, from the people. A few fanatics might carry on but I don't think there will be a large partisan war. People want peace, bread, to earn money,' he said, paraphrasing Lenin's revolutionary slogan. 'This is normal.'

The people's intitiative sat inside Shali's PTT building in the guise of the new mayor, Makhma Basnakayev. At sixty-one, he was a slight man with the face of a thousand Soviet bureaucrats, whose authority and rank would be drawn from the numerous telephones lined up by their desks and not from any personal charisma. A line of elderly supplicants waited patiently outside his door.

'For three and a half years we weren't paid pensions. Schools and hospitals were closed.' This was true but also of many forgotten rotten boroughs in Russia's far-flung empire. Basnakayev claimed to belong to an underground resistance movement to Dudayev which had appeared just as the fighters were preparing to leave for the mountain town of Vedeno. Whatever the townspeople thought about Dudayev, Basnakayev's writ would last only as long as the Russian APCs were parked outside his office. 'We have lived all our lives with the Russians. True, we've had our differences,' he said, no irony intended. 'But you have to look at things objectively – without Russia we cannot live normally and the people understand this. The villagers are against the fighters. It's not on to rocket and bomb civilians, but Dudayev is using them to hide behind.'

On the outskirts of the town, dead cows lay in the fields. A long trench had been dug in one of them by the side of the road to take the bodies of a group of fighters who had been killed in the recent battle for Shali. Chechen men chainsawed wood to line the trench as dictated by tradition. Others wore handkerchieves tied round their faces to unload rotting bodies off the back of a truck. An imam wandered back and forth, planting his booted feet carefully at each step in the long grass, saying prayers over each of the bodies. The men grappled with one large fighter, made heavier by his Russian issue flak jacket, to find identity but the smell in the spring heat was too much. All they managed to find was an amulet, a verse from the Koran carefully folded and wrapped in a green silk triangle.

'They died for nothing,' said one of the Chechen gravediggers bitterly. 'They danced about with their guns but it is we who have to bury them.'

On 10 April 1995 several hundred Chechens, mostly women, gathered on the bright spring grass in front of a brand new mosque in the village of Sernovodsk, about five kilometres west of Samashky. Its straight white walls were like a slab of wedding cake; the schoolroom window frames were painted in Lincoln-green. When the polka-dot and flower-print headscarves focused, the women were distraught, crying, wailing, shouting. Some had their arms round others. Their grief was so strong that some of the women were bent over clutching their fists together and pressing them into their stomachs, unable to breathe. Frightened children stared at their mothers and sisters, women usually so tough in times of adversity. A few old men wandered about or squatted, unable to cope with such an outpouring of misery.

It was difficult to open my notebook that day. From the crazed scenes and pictures that came out of their mouths it was clear Samashky had been the target of a brutal storming by Russian forces four days previously. One elderly woman wore only socks on her feet as she had had no time to find her shoes before fleeing the village the previous day.

A pregnant woman in her forties, Zina Akhmadova, indicated a woman next to her who was too shocked to speak. 'She saw Russians pour petrol over a father and his daughter and set them on fire!' she exclaimed. Akhmadova said five of her seven children were killed in the bombardment that preceded the storm but she could give no more details. She just repeated over and over as she rocked back and forth, 'How can they not be ashamed of themselves?'

An old woman wailed above the others, 'We don't have anything left! We're all dead!'

Zayina Kurbanova had somehow fled the village with her family that day, after the village had been bombarded for 72 hours. 'In our cellar, there were about twenty women and children. We cried at the soldiers not to shoot. They just laughed and shot at us.' She said she had seen a sixteen-year-old boy with his eyes plucked out. My face must have given away my disbelief. 'It was horrible, but I saw it,' she said desperately. The women said Russian soldiers had gone from house to house, throwing grenades into the cellars, that there were bodies lying on the street. Kurbanova said she had seen seven on her street alone.

Helicopters flew over the village towards Samashky, some with Red Cross emblems, landed there and took off again. The Russian interior ministry soldiers blocking the road into the village said the helicopters were collecting the wounded. The women said they were cleaning up the bodies from the streets.

The interior ministry troops blocked the road for several days, parking an APC horizontally across the road. I joined a small group of reporters for a daily vigil at the checkpoint, supposing that the Kremlin would soon want to show off their 'victory'. Young men in grey uniforms joked, smoked, were bored and worked on their suntans. But they were silent, uneasy, when a few more Chechen women and children walked out of Samashky, stooping unaided along the hot empty road.

One woman, in her thirties, looked as if she was about to collapse. 'Bring us medicines! There are wounded lying in their houses! Nobody is helping us. We haven't eaten for three days!' She said her father and her aunt had been killed when a grenade was lobbed into their cellar. They had been sheltering from an air and artillery bombardment. 'They gave us no warning. They just threw the grenade in.' As she stood crying, shaking, the Russian soldiers on the APC froze. They did not try and move us away as more women trickled out, in long skirts, cardigans and thick woollen socks stuffed into rubber galoshes. Some of them carried limp white rags tied to sticks.

Another woman said she had seen two old men approach Russian soldiers for drinking water. 'They fired thirty or forty bullets into them.' Tears coursed down her cheeks. 'You'd think two bullets would have been enough.' The APC moved back a little to allow a truck to drive out carrying fifteen women wounded. No men walked out of the village. A few of the women allowed back into Samashky to bury their dead spoke again of dead in the cellars and in the streets.

A helicopter landed near the checkpoint to stretcher out a Russian soldier. One of the soldiers by the APC walked over, his face rippling with emotion. 'You talk about genocide,' he said, 'but look what's happening to us!' The other soldiers turned their faces away in embarrassment at their comrade's flat note.

A few days later the APC reversed slightly and allowed my car through. In the village a spring breeze carried the smell of ash and burned flesh. From out of the iron gates into the Chechens' homes came the sound of the same crying and plaintive wailing, reaching a crescendo, dying down and taking off again, which twisted and crushed my stomach. The villagers were burying people as quickly as they could to meet the strictures of Islamic belief but bloated bodies still lay abandoned in the streets like lumpy sacks.

Usman Nadirov, eighty years old and wiry in a faded blue cotton overall, looked on, his hands held away from him as if covered with imaginary sewage, while villagers pulled off a sheet of metal that covered the temporary grave where they had put his thirty-five-year-old son Khamzad. The son lay alongside three other bodies. Khamzad's widow ran screaming from the hole. All that remained of her husband was a bloody, charred lump. The men, all elders in skullcaps or trilby hats, lifted the crumbling, blackened bodies onto a line of white sheets to wrap them for burial. It had been unsafe to do so before. 'He was not a fighter,' his father said. 'He had been to Mecca, he was not allowed to hold a gun.'

Some of the men, I was told, went to protest when they saw Russian soldiers load a Chechen household's belongings into an armoured car. 'They were shot down in the yard.' Their corpses were then burned with a flame-thrower.

The villagers said they had heard the Russian soldiers shout, 'Get the cellars! The cellars!' Bekatu Mutiyeva said she and twelve others held their breath when their cellar door was sprayed with automatic weapons fire. When her eighteen-year-old daughter, Khava, crept out to see if the soldiers had gone, she was shot twice in the stomach where she stood on the street. When the soldiers had left, the family ran out to wrap Khava's inert body in a sheet. They left her lying on a bed in the house and hid once more in the cellar. Later they heard a soldier shout, 'A body!', and the room where Khava lay was set on fire. A few charred bed springs and some carbonized bones were all that was left in the room. The roof was now open to the sky.

The villagers collected handfuls of used syringes and ampoules which littered the streets of the village. Many said they had seen the soldiers inject themselves in the leg or arm. They had stormed the village in a narcotic haze.*

From the APC on the road outside Samashky, a Russian soldier stared at the long columns of smoke rising from the Chechen village of Bamut, a few miles to the south which began at the foot of the mountains. Every few minutes the sound of large detonations broke, cracked and echoed around the mountains. The pristine white peaks mocked the Russian soldiers the way a society lady would laugh at her student lover. 'You've got this far,' the mountains seemed to say. 'I dare you to push through the forest skirts at my feet.'

The soldier spoke. 'We aren't near the end. Next comes the partisan war – the worst of all.'

I waited at Sleptsovsk airport in Ingushetia a few days later for a flight to Moscow. A young Ingush woman was also waiting in the stuffy departure lounge – more an airless classroom – with her sister and father. Their children wandered about or sat on heavy checked traders' bags piled up on a bare concrete floor. The family had lost their homes in first Grozny and now Samashky. She was travelling to Chimkent, an industrial town thousands of kilometres to the east on Kazakhstan's stony southern steppe, to start a new life. 'They say

---

* A brave reporter with Voice of America smuggled out the ampoules and had them tested in Moscow. The drugs were identified as Promodol, a narcotic, and Dimedrol, a tranquillizer, both found in army medical kits ('Russia's ugliest hour', *Newsweek*, 1 May 1995).

there's work there,' she said. On the jetliner, one of the boys slept across a couple of empty seats. His grandfather held his veined, mottled hand above his head to shade him from the harsh sunlight streaming through the porthole.

# A dog's death for a dog

Where a dog can pass, a Russian soldier can!

General Velyaminov, 1832

A RUSSIAN MILITARY column had stopped on the road near the settlement of Goragorsk, northeast of Grozny, in the middle of January 1995. Dead yellow grass at the top of the Sunzha Range was patched unevenly with snow. Fog pulled the sky to the ground. The column was headed away from Grozny. If it had not been for the tanks, the line of trucks, stacked with beat-up furniture, might have been a column of refugees. One of them towed a large field stove with a metal smokestack mounted on wheels. The men's faces were black with dirt, their hair matted. There was no chat. A jumble of sweaters and heavy coats had replaced part of their uniforms. Soldiers leaned against the wheel-arches of trucks and puffed on cigarettes, drawing in all the smoke and letting it out in straight blue lines through fish lips.

Vladimir, a senior lieutenant, and his men were from the elite Dzerzhinsky Division based in Moscow, part of the standing army equipped and fed by Russia's interior ministry, not its defence ministry, to enforce law in the empire. They had been pulled back to Mozdok for a couple of days rest, to wash their clothes and eat. They had spent a month living in *zemlyanki*, earth dugouts. Vladimir did not know where they would be sent afterwards.

'Nobody likes this war. We've lost about two thousand men.

I've lost friends. Nobody wants to fight.' Like so many Russian soldiers after battle in Chechnya, he had barely the energy – or desire – to string more than four words together.

Were Russian troops doing better in the city? The lieutenant shook his head in the negative.

A transport plane droned above the mist, probably bringing more troops and equipment to staging areas around Chechnya. At a checkpoint behind the column, a busload of Chechen women were arguing with Ossetian policemen wearing black balaclavas and wielding metal batons. The women wanted to head south back to their homes. The policemen wanted money to grant the privilege.

A captain, a tall young army doctor, said he was on his way back to Moscow. His grey combat trousers were supported by braces which bunched the shoulders of a dirty tan jersey like parcel string.

'We're hungry for news. We don't know what's going on.'

I had seen wounded soldiers lying on stretchers on the floor in a dark field hospital at Grozny's northern airport. They slept a morphine sleep waiting for helicopters to take them out. When I was waiting once for a flight out of an airport near Vladikavkaz, a Russian army medic let me sleep in one of the canvas cots at a makeshift trauma unit set up in a cavernous departures lounge, a metal stand to hang a drip standing sentinel at one end. A landing helicopter rattled the glass front to the lounge and woke me. A couple of soldiers carried a stretcher from the helicopter, lowering their heads under the whirling blades, wrestling to keep a bloodstained sheet from flying off a dead soldier.

The army doctor said his unit had battled to take the railway station. He had personally treated about a hundred injured in the city's cellars. 'There are a lot of civilian casualties – they're mostly Russians, there aren't many Chechens there. Many fighters are heading for the hills. There will be a partisan war. They will fight to the death,' he said, pulling on a cigarette. 'I'm not going back a second time.' He said a Grad missile attack on the unit by the Chechens near Goragorsk, where they had originally entered Chechnya the previous December, had killed many men.

The military high-ups told their men little. Companies emplaning in Siberia might be informed they were headed for winter exercises in the Urals, only to disembark at one of the North Caucasian airports. They would find themselves shortly afterwards guarding a remote rural crossroads in Chechnya. Their women – usually mothers as most conscripts had not got round to marrying – could only guess where they had gone. Soldiers at checkpoints would stop television crews and demand to play back tapes on the cameras, not to confiscate the material but because they wanted to see what was going on. If they had been posted to Chechnya after the first couple of months of fighting and had access to Russian television and newspapers, they knew what to expect.

Some Russian reporters drove across the lines to report on the Chechen side (they were automatically considered by the Chechens as spies) as well as with their own soldiers. Typical of the reportage was a front-page story printed on 8 February 1995 by the daily *Komsomolskaya Pravda*. The newspaper still proudly carried its Soviet medals – a Lenin and a hammer and sickle – on the masthead. The headline *'First-year Misha Yepifantsev won't be walking to school anymore . . .'* was run over a picture of a young boy lying on a hospital bed with both legs amputated above the knees, bandages clotted with blood, his mother crying into a handkerchief by his bedside. Misha's legs were ripped apart by shrapnel after he had left a Grozny cellar with a bucket to find water during the January bombardment. The journalist described how he had first met the Russian boy as he lay badly wounded in the back of a Chechen's car. The Chechen, despite the danger, was taking the boy to a hospital.

As in Afghanistan, returning soldiers who had fought for the empire were received at home with indifference or hostility. No home fires burned, there was no rallying of support, so crucial to the morale of a soldier at the front. There was no great sympathy for the Chechens but Russian opinion polls routinely showed opposition to the war. The soldiers endured months of terror, lost friends and perhaps a limb but had clung fiercely to life, only to come home and be told it was all for nothing.

Lermontov pinned down the gulf between the soldier and home in his violent narrative poem *Valerik*. The poet was sent by Nicholas I to fight in the Caucasus as a punishment for a duel he had fought with the son of the French ambassador in St Petersburg. Lermontov saw action on the River Valerik in Chechnya on 11 July 1840 and was mentioned in dispatches for his bravery. But Nicholas twice turned down recommendations for an award that would have freed him from service. In the poem the narrator describes in telegraphic metre how his unit advances towards the dark forest in the foothills below the Chechen village of Gekhi, about 20 kilometres southwest of Grozny. Imam Shamil's *murids* – his lieutenants and Sufi adepts – carry green Islamic standards and bellow war-cries, pouring musket fire onto the greycoats. The Chechens then clash face to face with the Russians for two hours in the river, sabres flashing against *kinzhaly*, until the waters flow warm and red. With the dead and the dying lying around him in the smoke at the end of the battle, the narrator is left empty and numb. He is snapped from his thoughts by a tap on the shoulder from his Chechen *kunak*, his sworn brother, who tells him 'Valerik' means, in his language, 'river of death'.

The poem takes the form of a letter to a lover who the narrator believes has long forgotten him. The missive is sent with no hope of an answer; the narrator is fated to go unheard at home. The poem speaks for the unheard generations who followed, the piles of dead in the bastions at Sebastopol in the Crimean War, the cruelties of the Civil War, the famines, the purges, World War Two, the Soviet soldiers left alive by the *mujaheddin* on the slopes of the Hindu Kush with their arms and legs cut off.

But the narrator is possessed, he must pour out the evil he has seen and taken part in, which goes over and over and over in his head like repeat footage on a 24-hour news channel. Writing to a friend from Fort Grozny after the battle in 1840, Lermontov imagined retelling all he had seen to people back home. In his make-believe audience a society lady drifts off to sleep, the head of the house ducks out on 'pressing' business and a baby sitting on the warrior's knee shits on his leg. Perhaps it was this invisible wall dividing his experience in Chechnya from the claustrophobia of a Petersburg drawing room that made him reckless. He quarrelled the following year with a fellow officer in Pyatigorsk. The two fought a pointless duel in which the poet was killed aged twenty-six. 'A dog's death for a dog' was Nicholas's verdict.

The Russian officers who battled Maskhadov's fighters had low expectations even before they were sent to Chechnya. They arrived having already survived unpaid for months, living in tents with their families after vacating barracks in former Warsaw Pact countries. Arms dealing – which in Chechnya took place at the lowliest post, with rifles and ammunition swapped for vodka along with a gentleman's agreement not to fire at one another – kept them from starvation. Raw recruits were often the victims of the Russian army's *dedovshchina*, the twisted hazing of recruits at the hands of 'grandfathers' near to demob that in one form or another has existed since Peter the Great, the founder of Europe's first modern conscript army. The news agency regularly put out briefs picked up from the Russian wires of soldiers in remote outposts who had been driven mad by the hazing, shooting comrades before turning a gun on themselves. General Lev Rokhlin, Babichev's commander who had pushed Maskhadov out of the Presidential Palace in Grozny in January 1995, lashed out the following year at Yeltsin, his putative commander-in-chief, as head of the Russian Duma's defence committee.

'Stronger than the American army? Nato? It's a lie,' he barked. He had swapped his general's uniform for a politician's suit, which diminished him. 'The factories which produce the weapons we need are standing idle. Our pilots, submariners and others have not been paid for four to five months. Yeltsin says not to worry, but nothing's been done in the last two years. We just don't believe him.' Rokhlin wanted the Duma to impeach Yeltsin.

The Soviet period, when the military industrial complex gobbled up much of the empire's resources, was something of an aberration for Russia's normally cash-strapped armed forces. Khrushchev, who bragged to the West 'We will bury you', balked even then at the cost, nicknaming the military, and the belching factories that fed them, the 'metal-eaters'.

In the nineteenth century the empire's soldiers were told to fend for themselves. A company of 300 men would include tailors, carpenters and stone masons in its ranks. Soldiers grew their own cabbages for their staple *shchi* soup and raised live-stock. Colonization was as much a means of survival as politics. A peasant family's son who was called up enlisted for 25 years. On the recruit's departure to his regiment, his family and neighbours would hold the equivalent of a wake for the young man. Dumas *père*, riding through the North Caucasus in 1858 *'dans les dangers et l'extrême rudesse d'un Far West russe'*, was amazed at the Russian soldier's mulish endurance, 'living on humid black bread, sleeping in the snow and dragging artillery, supplies and cannons on routes where man has never set foot, where the hunter has never trod, where only the eagle soars beneath the granite and snow. And for what kind of war? For a war without mercy, without prisoners, where all wounded are considered dead men, where the most ferocious of their enemies cut off their heads, where the mildest cut off their hands.'

After Yermolov left the Caucasus, Russian soldiers continued his scorched earth campaign in Chechnya, burning rebel villages and felling the thick forests of beech trees to deny the Chechens cover. On one of the Russians' first disastrous attempts to take the mountain village of Dargo in 1841, the beech trees lining the approach groaned with the weight of 30–40 *murids* in each, who sniped in deadly fashion at the approaching greycoats. 'The volleys of whole battalions failed to dislodge the garrisons from these improvised towers of defence,' wrote Baddeley.

So vital were the trees to the Chechens' defences that Imam Shamil fined his own people a cow or a bull for every one cut down without his permission, with the worst offenders strung up in the middle of their villages, their bodies left hanging for a week as a warning. General Tornau wrote in 1832 that the Chechens 'merited the fullest respect, and amidst their forests and mountains no troops in the world could afford to despise them.' The Russians were attacked and harried by the Chechens on their tree-felling expeditions with relentless monotony. 'Fighting went on from beginning to end of each march: there was the chatter of musketry, the hum of bullets; men fell; but no enemy was seen,' wrote Tornau. 'Puffs of smoke in the jungle alone betrayed their lurking places, and our soldiers, having nothing else to guide them, took aim by that.'

In 1995 I was given a contemporary flavour of forest combat by Isa Madayev, the Chechen commander in the village of Chiri-Yurt, 15 kilometres south of Grozny, and one of the directors of the cement factory there. He was in his forties, slim and fit and wearing cement-coloured combat fatigues. We had both narrowly escaped a Russian ambush when we were machine-gunned and shelled as we attempted to drive to a mountain village to follow a lead to the missing American aid worker, Fred Cuny (he was never found). The Russians had promised the search party a ceasefire about 15 minutes earlier. We stopped to take cover at first but as the shells ranged in towards us, we had to jump back into our cars and drive off as best we could. Madayev lost his jeep. He held up a beret he had left on the seat and put his fingers through holes torn by shrapnel. He remained defiant.

'They have orders to come up through the woods – but there are already plenty of soldiers lying around for the dogs and wolves to eat. Their armour and their aircraft won't help them here.'

In the nineteenth century the Chechens' obstinate resistance, witnessed by Lermontov on the Valerik, led to battles of sickening brutality. Kazi Mullah led the *ghazavat* between 1829 and 1832, with the young Shamil as one of his lieutenants. Hearing that he was in the vicinity of Germenchuk, a village about 18 kilometres southeast of Grozny, General Velyaminov sent troops commanded by General Tornau to storm it. The village lies on flat land and is not easily defended. A Chechen family sheltered me there for a couple of nights while Grozny was bombarded. When Tornau's men approached, there were few *murids* to defend the village but they hastily shoved their rifles through the loopholes of the village's clay walls and set about sniping at their enemies.

Russian sappers were sent in to set fire to the walls while two soldiers climbed onto the rooves and threw genades down the chimneys. Only the first two grenades exploded as the *murids* quickly learned to douse the fuses when they fell into the hearths. The fighting ceased momentarily while a Russian commander went forward to parley and called on the Chechens to surrender, promising fair treatment. A Chechen, blackened by gunpowder, walked out and told the officer: 'We want no quarter; the only grace we ask of the Russians is to let our families know that we died as we lived, refusing submission to any foreign yoke.' The Chechens then fired a hail of bullets at their attackers. The Russian soldiers succeeded in setting the entire village ablaze and the defenders were either burned to death or were cut down as they ran from flaming doors, firing pistols and waving their *kinzhaly*.

Tornau concluded while writing in his tent that night: '. . . maybe more than one [Russian soldier] in the depth of his being asked himself, why must such things be? Is there no room for all on this earth without distinction of speech or faith?'

Back on the Line, Dumas also noted how Russian officers stole from supplies to buy vodka. Second Lieutenant Tolstoy was reprimanded by his artillery commander at Sebastopol for balancing his detachment's mess accounts to show a credit, exposing all the other thieving officers. 'What on earth have you done, Count?' asked the flabbergasted general. 'You are making trouble for everyone.' Tolstoy, despite fabulous gambling debts, replied self-righteously that he thought the money belonged to the state.

Major Albert Mamedov commanded a company of paratroopers which held a wooded road near the town of Argun, about 15 kilometres east of Grozny, in the spring of 1995. The cheerful major was paid two dollars a day. I asked him what it was like for a Russian officer to be fighting on his own territory.

'I'm half Turkmen and half Azeri,' he said.

We sat round a pilfered table in a beat-up trailer. The major had decorated his makeshift officers' mess with a kelim nailed to the wall. A sabre hung from one of the nails. A copy of the army newspaper, *Krasnaya Zvezda*, 'Red Star', was pinned to a noticeboard outside.

A conscript brought in plates of steaming *shchi*, concentrating hard so as not to spill them. Major Mamedov opened some tins which contained a pungent, runny paste like watery cat food. A bottle of vodka appeared – my donation – and we tucked in, spreading the paste onto thick slabs of bread and slurping down the hot soup, the taste anaesthetized by the vodka.

Mamedov had served for 30 months in Afghanistan and later the imperial outpost of neighbouring Tajikistan. Despite their hardships, the paratroopers I had met across the Caucasus maintained pride in themselves as a fighting force. Their troops were comparatively well trained and fit. 'A para kneels for two reasons only,' the saying goes: 'to drink water with his hands, and to pay his respects to his dead friend.' Mamedov's company was no exception. The paratroopers scorned the sloppy discipline of the interior ministry troops. When we had walked round the camp earlier, his men had saluted him warmly. The well-dug entrenchments, men kept on lookout and a general sense of purpose showed an officer determined to keep his men alive. We stood in silence for the third toast, drunk to the memory of comrades killed in action. Mamedov then quickly refilled our glasses for the fourth.

'So that the third toast won't be drunk to us!' We all gulped down the thick, fiery water and bit on a piece of bread.

Mamedov took us on a tour of his Area of Responsibility in a truck. He stopped from time to time to give Chechen women hitchhikers a lift, useful protection as well as kind-heartedness. Truck-drivers hung their flak jackets over the doors of their cabs by way of armour. He shrugged off the difficulties in Chechnya. 'If this was Afghanistan, we wouldn't be sitting here,' he said. 'Argun was a dead town when we took it – we found one old *babushka* when we got in.'

Chechen fighters had defended a strip of buildings in Argun along the river of the same name. The smashed architecture and scorched tree trunks were Grozny's cathedrals of destruction in miniature. The one-sided fighting with bombs, shells and rockets continued as we spoke – the sound of jets followed by the blast of bombs and the deep, *whooshing* groans of Grad rockets going out to hit one of the villages in the foothills. On our return, a loud bang and a puff of white smoke signalled a gun being fired next to the camp.

'We have some fighting in the woods, especially at night. The Chechens served in our army and they were good. The Soviet army was a good school but if we saw a Chechen now face to face he wouldn't shoot,' he said. He spoke with the regular soldier's hatred for the insurgent who appears and disappears like the Cheshire Cat.

I spent the night with the unit in one of their *zemlyanki*. The earth hole was a large, low cave with wide boards set above the ground around the walls and covered with a jumble of grey blankets. The roof was reinforced with logs, stones and earth. While it was cold at night, the shelter was unbearably hot as a wood-stove was kept alight permanently. Yermolov slept in a *zemlyanka* which was preserved, according to Baddeley, in the centre of Grozny before the Revolution.

On entering the *zemlyanka*, I stared at a poster of a topless woman with pneumatic breasts. The soldier who showed me my quarters for the night tapped me on the shoulder. 'I wouldn't look at her if I were you,' he said. 'She's already spoken for.'

I lay down crammed in next to the earth wall. The heat, now compounded by two soldiers sleeping and farting next to me, made sleep impossible. A radio brought in static commands to a soldier on guard duty on the other side of a blanket which served as the door. The *piff-paff* of small arms fire poked at the night. I got up to find a lavatory. Through the blanket door the night was deliciously fresh and cool. The liquid moonlight was reinforced by flares fired into the sky in nervous relays above the black outline of the forest. The crapper was a rough cabin like a wooden telephone box over an earth hole, set at the edge of an orchard and right on top of the embankment behind which the camp had been dug in. I imagined that a hundred Chechen rifles were trained on me as I squatted over the black hole.

In 1895 a Christian sect exiled to the foot of the Caucasus, the Dukhobors, or 'spirit-wrestlers', refused to serve in the imperial army. Their lands were confiscated, their homes looted and four thousand were sent further south to mountain villages. Their leaders were imprisoned. Lev Tolstoy, whose long beard and plain peasant's *rubashka* gave him an Old Testament look, was outraged and set about campaigning to secure the Dukhobors' release. When Tolstoy heard that the children of another Orthodox sect, the Molokhans, or 'milk drinkers', had been separated from their parents on the grounds that they were not growing up to respect the official Orthodox church, Tolstoy penned a letter to Nicholas II, who had surrounded himself with reactionary advisers:

> Majesty, for the love of God make an effort and, instead of avoiding the matter and referring it to commissions and committees, decide, without asking anyone's advice, you yourself, acting on your own initiative, that these religious persecutions, which are causing the shame of Russia, must cease; the exiles must be sent back to their homes, the prisoners released, the children returned to their parents, and, above all, the whole body of administrative laws and regulations be abolished, as they are so complicated and obscure that they are just so many pretexts for illegality.

The children were returned to their parents but Tolstoy began receiving death threats. His wife feared they might be deported to Siberia. Tolstoy, who hankered after martyrdom, was slightly put out when no punishment came. The old sensualist hit back, tearing apart the Tsarist state in his novel *Resurrection*, the story of a prostitute condemned to exile and the worthless aristocrat who originally seduced her, with scalding descriptions of hypocrisy in the church and every other pillar of the rickety Tsarist edifice.

In 1901 the Orthodox clergy put up a notice on church doors across Russia declaring Tolstoy a false prophet and excommunicating him. Now, wherever Tolstoy went, crowds would form at railway stations, ports and city streets to cheer and applaud him. Telegrams and letters of support flooded into his estate at Yasnaya Polyana. The tsar's secret police forbade any mention of Tolstoy's popularity in the newspapers but word got around. A crowd admiring Repin's portrait of Tolstoy at an exhibition in St Petersburg burst into spontaneous applause and sent the author a letter reporting the occasion with 398 signatures. Suvorin, Chekhov's wealthy publisher, noted at the time: 'We have two tsars, Nicholas II and Lev Tolstoy. Which is the stronger? Nicholas II is powerless against Tolstoy and cannot make him tremble on his throne, whereas Tolstoy is incontestably shaking the throne of Nicholas II and his whole dynasty.'

In June of that year, Tolstoy caught malaria. The interior ministry sent coded instructions to provincial governors to prevent demonstrations in the event of the writer's death. The old count travelled to the Crimean coast to get his strength back. Recovered, he penned another letter to the tsar: 'Autocracy is a superannuated form of government that may suit the needs of a Central African tribe, remote from the rest of the world, but not those of the Russian people, who are increasingly assimilating the culture of the rest of the world.' The number of secret agents watching the borrowed villa was increased.

I want to speculate: that the Tatars who lived on the Crimean coast, their veiled women and the smell of the smoke of *kizyak*, animal dung burned as fuel there and in the Caucasus, conspired in old Tolstoy's head with Nicholas's cruelty to the religious sects to blow the dust from a long-forgotten debt.

The particular debt Tolstoy would have had in mind went back half a century to his Chechen *kunak*, Sado Miserbiyev. Although it is not mentioned in *The Cossacks*, the young artillery officer visited some of the Chechen villages near his Cossack billet which were less hostile to the Russian troops. The Chechens from the north of the territory, the area later favoured by Moscow's Chechen proxies in the guise of the Chechen opposition, had the worst time of it during the nineteenth-century Murid wars, trapped by Russian troops on one side and Imam Shamil on the other. To go over to Shamil brought the destruction of their *aouls*. To submit to the Russians brought the sharp axe of Shamil's executioner down on their necks.

Shamil had to be careful not to lose the independent-minded Chechens altogether. Such was his tartarly reputation that a dep-utation of four Chechens quaked with fear as they petitioned Shamil's aged mother for either adequate protection for their vil-lages or permission to sue for peace with the hated infidels. The *khanoum* left her son's rooms in tears. The four Chechen repre-sentatives feared the worst but Shamil came out of his residence and retired to the mosque to ask for guidance from the Prophet. For three days and three nights the doors of the mosque remained closed. When the doors reopened, Shamil walked out, pale and red-eyed with fasting and exhaustion. He then addressed the people of Dargo from the roof of the mosque. 'It is the will of Allah that whoever first transmitted to me the shameful inten-tions of the Chetchen people should receive one hundred severe blows, and that person is my mother!' The begum fainted after the fifth blow, at which point the Imam removed his own red robe and shirt to take publicly the rest of the 95 strokes for his mother. Afterwards, the Imam addressed the wavering Chechen deputation: 'Go back to your people, and in reply to their foolish demand tell them all you have seen and heard.'

Tolstoy's *kunak* was a wastrel youth much like himself who dropped by the northern village of Starogladovskaya to play the officers at cards. His mathematics could not keep up with the hastily chalked scores and he regularly lost. This offended Tolstoy's sense of justice, and he teamed up with the Chechen against his brother officers. Miserbiyev declared himself Tolstoy's *kunak* in gratitude. 'His father is quite a rich man, but he has buried all his money and won't give his son a cent,' Tolstoy wrote to his lonely Aunt Toinette (the same person he had promised to contribute, 'by the aid of the cannon, to the slaughter of the wild rebellious Asiatics'). He continued: 'To get money, the son goes over to steal horses and cattle from the enemy; sometimes he risks his life twenty times to steal something that isn't worth ten roubles; but he does it for glory, not because he covets the thing he steals. The biggest thief is respected here, and called a *dzhigit*, or brave. Some days Sado has a thousand silver roubles on him, others not a kopeck.'

They had colourful adventures. Tolstoy and Miserbiyev rode ahead of a Russian column to get to Grozny when a group of Chechen horsemen bore down on them, intent on taking them hostage. The two had swapped horses that day, Tolstoy riding the mountaineer's swift charger while Sado was stuck on the count's ambler. Tolstoy could have made a break for Grozny but he remained with Sado, the latter levelling a pistol he had forgotten to load at their pursuers while shouting wildly in Chechen. The bluff worked and the two made it to Grozny, unlike another companion who had his horse shot from under him and was slashed with sabres before a Cossack unit galloped to the rescue.

Despite all his resolutions to give up cards, gambling held a power over Tolstoy as strong as the outlines of the Cossack women. He had left Moscow with 4,000 roubles' worth of gambling debts. He lost another 500 roubles in a game against an officer, Knoring, at Stary Yurt in 1852. He went to bed on a cold January night with a fervent prayer to God to deliver him – somehow – from this debt. The next morning he received a letter from his brother Nikolay at another camp which contained the torn-up IOU slips from Knoring. Miserbiyev had beaten the officer at cards and called in his *kunak's* debt.

'Is it not astonishing to see one's desire fulfilled the very next

day,' Tolstoy wrote to Aunt Toinette, 'is there anything so astonishing as the divine goodness for a being who deserves it so little
as I? And is not this feature of attachment in Sado admirable?' He
despatched his aunt to Tula to buy Miserbiyev a revolver and a
musical box by way of thanks – 'if this does not cost too much'.

Decades later, the injustice of Russia's campaign of conquest
in the Caucasus haunted the scourge of autocracy in bast shoes.
Very well – he would write a story that would serve as a broad-
side on the arbitrary nature of power and, for the first time in
Russian literature, give voice to the millions of people added to
the empire at the point of a Russian bayonet. *Hadji Murat* is a
spare novel based on the career of the Avar warrior of that name
who turned against the dictatorial Imam Shamil and went over
to the Russians, only to find his treachery unrewarded. Tolstoy
was in Tbilisi at the time when Hadji Murat presented himself to
the viceroy, Vorontsov, but never saw him. As he wrote *Hadji
Murat*, he consulted 80 works and pestered veterans of the
Caucasian campaigns for their reminiscences, especially of
Nicholas I. 'I absolutely must find the key to him,' he wrote in a
letter in 1903. 'Mostly what I need are details of his daily life,
what are called the anecdotes of history: his intrigues at a masked
ball, his relations with Nelidova [his mistress], his wife's behaviour toward him. . . . Do not blame me, my dear friend, for
busying myself with such trivialities when I have one foot in the
grave.'

Tolstoy said the chapters on Nicholas and Shamil were meant
to contrast European and Asiatic despotism. But the way these
leaders treat their women and their enemies, and the fear and
flattery that reinforce their belief in their own religious infallibil-
ity, are virtually identical. The novel was published in a severely
censored form after Tolstoy's death in 1912. A stage production
of the book planned by the Avar National Theatre in 1988 was
banned by the Soviet authorities purporting to promote *glasnost*.
It is a work that many Chechens, despite its Russian authorship,
admire.

Tolstoy, I maintain, was paying back a debt to Miserbiyev and
the mountaineers for the unjust war he had helped wage against

them. There is even a character named Sado in the novel. Chapter 17, which describes the aftermath of a Russian raid, is only about five hundred words, the length of one of my agency stories:

> The village laid waste by the raiding party was the one in which Hadji Murat had spent the night before going over to the Russians.
>
> Sado, with whom he had stayed, took his family away to the mountains when the Russians approached the village. When he came back he found his house destroyed: the roof was caved in, the door and the post supporting the veranda were burnt, and the inside befouled. His son, the good-looking boy with shining eyes who had regarded Hadji Murat with such rapture, was brought into the mosque dead on the back of a horse draped with a cloak. He had been bayoneted in the back. The fine-looking woman who had waited on Hadji Murat during his visit stood over her son with her hair loose and the smock she was wearing rent at the chest to reveal her old, sagging breasts. She stood clawing her face till the blood ran and wailing without stop. Sado took a pick and shovel and went with his kinsmen to dig a grave for his son. The old grandfather sat by the wall of the ruined house, whittling a stick and gazing blankly into space. He had just come back from his bee-garden. The two small hayricks he had there were burnt; the apricot and cherry trees which he had planted and tended were broken and scorched; and, worst of all, every one of his hives had been burnt together with the bees. The wailing of women sounded in every house and in the square where two more bodies were brought. The young children wailed with their mothers. The hungry animals howled, too, and there was nothing to give them. The older children played no games and watched their elders with frightened eyes.
>
> The fountain had been befouled, evidently on purpose, so no water could be drawn from it. The mosque, too, had

been defiled and the mullah and his pupils were cleaning it out.

The village elders gathered in the square and squatted on their heels to discuss the situation. Nobody spoke a word of hatred for the Russians. The emotion felt by every Chechen, old and young alike, was stronger than hatred. It was not hatred, it was a refusal to recognize these Russian dogs as men at all, and a feeling of such disgust, revulsion and bewilderment at the senseless cruelty of these creatures that the urge to destroy them – like the urge to destroy rats, venomous spiders or wolves – was an instinct as natural as that of self-preservation.

The villagers were faced with a choice: either to remain as before and by terrible exertions restore all that had been created with such labour and so easily and senselessly destroyed, while every minute expecting a repetition of the same thing, or they could act contrary to the law of their religion and, despite the revulsion and scorn they felt for the Russians, submit to them.

The old men prayed and resolved unanimously to send envoys to ask Shamil for help, and straightaway they set about rebuilding what had been destroyed.

I was ordered by the agency to break my April vigil outside Samashky and sent west for a day to the autonomous republic of Kabardino-Balkaria to cover a visit by Yeltsin, his first trip to the North Caucasus since the beginning of the war. Aircraft landed ahead of him full of anxious, toadying officials. Special forces lined the route to the stadium where the local apparatchik was to present him with a Kabarda thoroughbred. Security was so tight that I had to argue for some time with the local police on the republic's borders to let me into Kabardino-Balkaria as an accredited correspondent.

I have no memorable quote in my notebook from Yeltsin on that occasion, other than a growled 'I love *Russian* Kabardino-Balkaria'. But the entourage, the way Yeltsin saw nothing of the war he had unleashed, a lackey opening the door to an expensive limousine, the tall figure and puffy white face (reminiscent of Tolstoy's Nicholas I) – all the trappings of arrogant power spoke for him. In Yeltsin's memoirs, *Midnight Diaries*, there is a detailed chronology that starts with his birth in 1931 in the Siberian village of Butka and ends with Vladimir Putin's election as president in 2000. From May 1994 to May 1996 – virtually the entire course of Yeltsin's war – Chechnya gets no mention.

# The English will rule

. . . we are still, with the grace of the Creator (may His name be
elevated), fighting these Russians.

Imam Shamil to the British Ambassador in Constantinople, 1858

THE KREMLIN dangled a two-week 'moratorium' in front of
the Chechen fighters at the end of April 1995 in the hope
there would be no embarrassing killing to spoil the visit by
foreign leaders due in Moscow for Victory in Europe Day. The
Chechens responded by shooting down a Russian reconaissance
plane which buzzed over the southern village of Serzhen-Yurt.
General Maskhadov, who kept appearing and disappearing at
this time like Aslan in *The Lion, the Witch and the Wardrobe*, made
a two-hour broadcast from the insurgent and peripatetic
Presidential Television station which all Chechens – at least those
who had television sets and electric generators – knew when to
tune in to.

'It's not possible to delude Clinton and the world. There's a
war going on here,' Maskhadov said, wearing combat fatigues
without rank or insignia. The broadcast, with a date in the
corner making it two days old, was scratchy.

We have sacks of identity tags of dead Russian soldiers.
Every day the fighters are slipping back into Grozny. As the
Russians let Napoleon into Moscow, we let the Russians
into Grozny. Stepashin [Chief of Federal Counter-
Intelligence] said it would take two months to end the war.
But I say even after twelve years the war will not have

ended. When you hear planes and helicopters you might think this is strength but it's not – morale is our strength. After the war we won't fight as we did before. We'll live in friendship, there'll be work. All those in the opposition, those who were on the other side, everyone must forgive each other and live in peace. If we unite, the Russians will leave.

Maskhadov let slip a shortage of men. 'Those who don't fight today will be ashamed tomorrow when we free the republic. Why aren't there more volunteers?' The broadcast ended with the Chechen national anthem.

Dudayev, in hiding for months, took up letter-writing again, with an epistle to the United States president printed on the front page of the rebel newspaper *Ichkeria*, a Chechen wolf prominent on the masthead. An extract:

Esteemed President Clinton,
Please do not think that the war in Chechnya is over just because the killing here is no longer shown on your television screens or that the Russian government claims that there is no military action. . . . Why, Mr President, does this nightmare continue in our country? In the last four months, 30,000 innocent and peaceful people have been killed and 50,000 people have lost their homes. Medical experts predict that this spring we shall be threatened with cholera and other epidemics. And we only total one million and 200,000 people. . . . When on the 9th May You will stand on the tribune to observe the victory parade, You will see soldiers who recently used their weapons against the civilian population of Chechnya. . . . Every day Russian artillery shells our country. At night the shelling is even worse. Every three-seven minutes new salvoes hit our aouls and our villages. It is a shame that You do not hear the sound of these salvoes, Mr President, the crying of the women, children and elders who have nowhere to escape to.

The newspaper also published a list, headed by Yeltsin, of Kremlin officials, jet pilots and helicopter crews wanted for political and military crimes next to a presidential decree appointing a new *Mufti*.

After dark, soaring flares followed by their wobbly descent, red tracer fire, muzzle flashes and the occasional explosion lit up Grozny's deserted streets and gutted buildings as if it were all a hellish nightclub. At sundown the beleaguered residents would close their gates and doors, some of which had chalked on them *Lyudi zhivut*, 'People live here'. The black smoke from a fuel dump sabotaged one night hung over the city for a day. As the sun set, at a Russian checkpoint in the south of the city Volodya, an interior ministry soldier, fired his rifle in the air when a car loaded with women and children did not stop to present their papers. The car jerked to a halt under the crimson Soviet flag flying at the post.

'Many people are leaving the city again. They fear an attack by the Chechen rebels.' Volodya was unshaven, tired and fed up. 'It's bad at night. They shoot at us,' he said, involuntarily clutching his assault rifle. 'But we never see their faces.'

The Chechen 'police' in the pay of the Russian-backed administration were of dubious loyalty. Working inside the system gave them intelligence and guns. I once witnessed a group of supposedly pro-Moscow Chechen police demand that the Russian commander of an APC in the centre of Grozny come to their headquarters for questioning after his armoured vehicle had run over a car as if it were a beer can. When the lieutenant refused, there was a rattle of bolts as the Chechen militia officers swung their guns up at the young Russian, who in turn shouted to his nervous men, his face red and covered in sweat, 'Stay in your places!'

I asked Aslanbek, a Chechen militia officer supposedly loyal to the Russians who was standing near Volodya, if he was not afraid of being shot as a traitor at his post by the fighters. The thick, green spring undergrowth around the post provided perfect cover for an ambush. Aslanbek replied with a cryptic smile:

'We have a role to play. Anyway, these attacks on command

posts are exaggerated. The Russians just get drunk and shoot at each other.'

In the spring of 1995, the Russian-backed administration had slipped in over the rubble to occupy one of the few administrative offices still standing in the centre of the city. A Soviet Neo-classical building, its yellow stucco scarred with shrapnel and bullet holes, it had once served as the Institute for Civil Planning. The handful of Chechen officials who worked there were ringed by razor wire, sandbags, armoured vehicles and flak-jacketed Russian soldiers who scanned their papers coldly. One of the jeeps parked nearby had painted on its tailgate: 'Patrol to hell'. The fox-eyed Chechen opposition politician, Khadzhiev, who now headed a 'Government of National Revival', appraised his position honestly, telling me in the security of the Russian army's Mozdok base in February: 'The government may not be legitimate in the strict sense of the word but someone has to do the job.'

In May one of his aides, Gersolt Elmurzayev, was bracing himelf for the VE Day celebrations. 'There are rumours that something will happen. But we're checking them thoroughly.' Elmurzayev was the conspiratorial type, a habitué of dark rooms with sad, bloodhound eyes. He had risen through the drudge ranks of the provincial Communist Party in the town of Gudermes, about 35 kilometres east of Grozny, making it as far as First Assistant Chairman of the Chechen-Ingush Republic's Council of Ministers before the collapse of Soviet power in August 1991. The Dudayev government's *Kto Yest Kto* ('Who's Who') gloated in 1994 that he was currently 'unemployed' but this was not entirely fair. He wrote an introduction entitled 'When words cure' to Chechnya's 'White Book', which printed harrowing interviews with the survivors of the 1944 deportations. He had hung about in Znamenskoye with the now all but forgotten leadership of Chechnya's Russian-backed 'Provisional Administration' the previous year.

Elmurzayev was not in a good mood as he laid out his plans to keep the city quiet on VE Day. 'We've called on the traders not to sell vodka and other spirits to the soldiers. What kind of security is there when soldiers are drunk?' For a time that summer, I slept in a dormitory above Elmurzayev's office. One night the firing was so intense around the building that a Russian agency reporter in the dormitory telephoned Moscow to report a rebel attack. Embarrassed Russian officials explained the next morning that the gunfire was the sound of a drunken celebration by a unit of Russian soldiers leaving Chechnya the next day.

Elmurzayev said he was working to give the Chechens a sovereignty which comprised jobs and security, a Chechen state with close ties to Russia. Elmurzayev was a product of the Soviet, Russianized elite and had prospered in the Party fold. I sensed his imagination had long ago limited itself to an existence within Party confines, and while names and flags had changed, the system, with Moscow at its centre, had not. But a politician to his fingertips, he hedged his bets with a safe jibe at Grachev. 'The defence minister said first it would take two hours to take Grozny – in January, he said three years. We hope Grachev will be mistaken again and it will finish by the end of the year. But if he continues using the same methods it will last a lot longer – this is the tragedy of our people.'

Zina Yashurkayeva didn't think any of the important foreigners due in Moscow for the anniversary would pay much attention to the war in Chechnya. She hauled buckets of hot water with a sulphurous smell which leaked from a rusting pipe above a natural spring near the Chernorechye resevoir and sloshed it into a tub to do her laundry. She took pleasure in the task, chatting to the other women with their skirts hitched up as they kneeded red kelims sodden with soap suds on a sunlit patch of grass next to the reservoir. The only black cloud in the sky hovered over the smoking remains of the Lenin refinery.

'We clean our children's clothes and our carpets here. But my hands,' she said, holding her arms out in front of me in rolled-up sleeves, 'it's a shame – I'm an accountant. It would be better if there was water in our flats – it's bad. There's been shooting the last three nights. My daughter clings to me in my bed with fright.' She paused before summing up: 'They've stolen my daughter's childhood.'

A couple of Russian soldiers walked up, toting guns, to fill an empty canister with some of the hot water. Yashurkayeva screwed up her green eyes to look up into the sunlight from her washing, her hair tied back in a white scarf. 'Write this: I don't want Dudayev or Yeltsin – I want somebody who comes to us in peace.'

The bodies in the open pits at the nearby Russian cemetery had been buried. In the recently turned earth, hundreds of tiny wooden crosses, each bearing a red number, were spread out in neat rows like saplings in a plantation. Only a bloated corpse and an empty stretcher broke up the lines. But the smell of the dead still travelled on gusts of wind like the odour that escapes an unwashed fridge.

For much of this time I was billeted on Natalya Grechenko in her tiny house on a street in the centre of the city which, miraculously, had survived almost intact. 'Aunt Natasha', as her guests called her, was a rangy old woman with a mop of badly cut brown hair. Her thin brown arms and legs jutted out at angles from a skimpy, rectangular cotton shift in summer. She had lost all her teeth. She explained that they had been gold and that before the war a couple of Chechen men had pinned her down and pulled them out. It gave her speech a watery lisp. The talkative woman spat slightly over the omlettes and salads she produced for me at table. Despite this rare lapse in presentation, the food was delicious, especially as my diet at that time consisted largely of Coke and Snickers bars. No matter that Chechnya was a remote, forgotten war zone. The *snikerizatsiya* of Russia's economy ensured steady supplies to the indomitable chocolate- and cigarette-sellers in Grozny's market.

Aunt Natasha had lived most of her life in Grozny, remembering the clatter and whistle of the trains during the nights of the deportations in February 1944. With so many Russians washed up on the edge of the empire, it never occurred to me to ask how she had got there or to probe too deep as to who might have persuaded her to stay. She lived on amicable terms with the Chechen families in the neighbouring houses set round a small, dusty courtyard, where she stretched her hunched, boyish body to hang out the washing.

In the summer of 1995 I was thinking the city's Chechen-Russian relations had got back to normal when a *pensionerka* selling newspapers – she, of course, received no pension – stated dramatically, 'They came in their tanks and killed Russians!' A Chechen man looked up nonplussed from a newspaper he was thinking of buying. 'Excuse me,' she said. 'Of course, they killed us both.'

Like all elderly Russians in Grozny, Aunt Natasha hadn't a kopeck. Like them, she could not leave the city for, even if she had managed to sell her house, the money would have barely lasted her a month outside Chechnya. At that time a three-bedroomed flat in Grozny – with all its walls – sold for about $400. A noticeboard next to the besieged Federal Migration Office was covered in tatty bits of paper like a cloth-covered tree at Bairam, offering flats and houses for sale. The Migration officials were unable to help much as other regions refused to grant residency permits, the dreaded *propiska* of Soviet times. But though she had lost her teeth and had no relatives or government to provide for her, this old Russian woman was cheerful, without a trace of self-pity and something of a coquette.

One evening she pulled from out of a cupboard a fabulous red négligée for me to admire. She said it had been a gift from one of my colleagues. She was also observant. As I lounged in her kitchen one day, Aunt Natasha, a scarf wrapped round her tousled head, came back from the market with tomatoes, eggs and spring greens peeping out of her shopping bag. 'I saw a Chechen with a gun on the top of a building!' she said, her eyes wide in ghoulish surprise. 'He had a gun and was crawling along like a snake!' She wiggled her hips to demonstrate the snake-like movement of the fighter, conveying something both terrifying and attractive.

There was a fitful peace the night before the foreign guests arrived for VE Day to watch the pomp and circumstance on Red Square: an average amount of tracer fire stapled Grozny's night sky while Yashurkayeva and her daughter tried to sleep; a Russian military report said only four soldiers had been killed and nineteen wounded in the previous twenty-four hours in Chechnya.

On the morning of the celebrations in Moscow, Russian soldiers turned out on parade at Grozny's Khankala Airport to mark the Soviet victory. Colonel-General Mikhail Yegorov took the salute. 'We must remember,' he droned in a weedy, deadpan voice into a microphone on the apron, 'that we are on Russian land, and that we will complete our task.' His call to the Chechen fighters to give up their 'pointless resistance' went uncheered by the soldiers. After an honour guard fired a volley of shots into a storm-grey sky, Yegorov picked cheap commemorative watches from a cardboard box held by an aide and handed them out among the ranks.

The army had managed to dust down some World War Two veterans replete with chests full of medals to attend the ceremony. One of them, seventy-one-year-old Vladimir Terekov, had driven a Studebaker truck during the war. He told me he was pleased with the food parcel and the twenty dollars worth of roubles he had been given by the defence ministry but added shyly that these were small compensation for his apartment which had been destroyed in the January shelling.

The next day Yeltsin held on to his guests as they were about to leave to tell them that operations in Chechnya were now simply police work. As he spoke, I watched four attack helicopters swerve in low from the north over Serzhen-Yurt, the forested village 35 kilometres southeast of Grozny where the Russian reconnaissance plane had been brought down. They drew fire from Chechens in the surrounding forest; the noise was like the spitting of Chinese firecrackers. The helicopters returned fire with rockets, bright white stars which spewed from their sides leaving trails of arrow-straight smoke. The explosions drummed the base of the snow-capped mountains, the sound a roar of frustration as it was unlikely the pilots knew what they were firing at. The helicopters' attack was followed by a salvo of Grad rockets. Russian army trucks loaded with ammunition crates drove fast up and down the road outside the village to resupply their guns. The drivers had slung their flak jackets over the doors.

I sat with Uwayis Neduyev, a thirty-nine-year-old farmer

wearing a red skullcap, in his house about a kilometre from the village. The teacups and plates on his kitchen dresser clinked and rattled as we spoke. 'Every day and night they're drunk,' he said. The Russian soldiers' heavy drinking and their bathing half-naked in public view in the rivers were deep insults to the Chechens' mores on alcohol and modesty. 'They're not soldiers, they're just looters. The Russians come up and ask for vodka, saying they'll blow up your house if you don't give it to them. The fighters don't drink. They practically don't smoke.'

He ran his fingers through a set of prayer beads. 'They've tried to move into the mountains for a month but with no result. Every night they shoot but this is the heaviest I've heard since the moratorium. Like Solzhenitsyn said, we will never submit.' Neduyev referred to a passage in *The Gulag Archipelago* in which Solzhenitsyn described the Chechens during their exile in Kazakhstan: 'There was one nation that would not give in, would not acquire the mental habits of submission – and not just individual rebels among them, but the whole nation to a man. These were the Chechens.'

Children on the road outside Neduyev's farmhouse jumped and shouted *Allahu akbar!* at the Russian ammunition trucks as they roared past.

I ate a delicious dinner of broth, eggs, fried *chirimsha*, and bread and honey washed down with gallons of black tea at a farmhouse tucked up in the forested mountains behind the village of Bamut, 50 kilometres southwest of Grozny. The honey had traces of comb in it from the hives on the farm which trapped the sweetness of the Alpine flowers that carpeted the meadows that spring.

On the route up through Ingushetia to the settlement, Chechen fighters hiked back and forth a few hundred metres out of sight behind a tented post manned by a meagre detachment of Russian border guards who, like the Roman legionaries in the *Asterix and Obelix* adventures, were not keen to patrol as they did not want to come across any crazy Gauls. The occasional tractor and trailer strained the other way along a barely passable mud track, carrying refugees. The fighters tramped through the forest or along the track to relieve comrades holding the lower half of Bamut, a village in the foothills of the North Caucasus range. The Chechen fighters defending the village sat under a constant barrage from a ring of Russian guns and armour camped a couple of kilometres back on the plain, spread out in a semicircle as in a medieval siege. I was taken out by one of the fighters the morning after my arrival to peer down from the mountains at the toy tanks and guns down below. Someone must have spotted a flash from the fighter's binoculars or some movement in the trees as we had to run from a hail of rockets which crashed into the woods nearby.

In the farmhouse I sat with the men, or rather kept getting up and sitting down in a mark of respect, as Chechen elders entered and left the kitchen. I asked the elders if they had heard of the prophecy which was repeated to me at odd moments all over Chechnya, that the English would rule them at some time in the future. They all nodded that their elders had told them that the English will rule, bringing with them a government which will be just to the Chechen people.

One of them, Kudin Dadayev, short but with an eagle's face underneath a tall karakul *papakha*, sat up straight in the best chair of the house, set on bare floorboards near the range. 'Ask anyone here and they'll know the sayings. The elders, they told us the English will come to power. We didn't believe the roads would come but roads and cars have come,' he said. The men, young and old, sat or stood round and listened in respectful silence. 'What to believe? Everything they've said has so far come true. They said a little country will destroy Russia. Our grandfathers and our great-grandfathers said it would happen. They're all concerned now whether the victory celebrations will be an embarrassment in Moscow. No country's helping us now. Our people are being exterminated.'

The Chechen men nodded vigorously to confirm the prophecy but they were short on details. One Chechen fighter, tongue in cheek, had told me the legend of the '*Enginoy*' *teip*, or clan, so named because its members were said to have wandered over the mountains in search of better pasture, wandered too far and ended up in England. Perhaps Britain had interests in Chechnya after all.

The most detailed description of the prophecy came to me from an Ingush forester who lived not far from the Russian border guards at their lonely forest crossroads. He had invited me in for tea while we waited for his son to come home – he would guide me past the guards' tent and on to Bamut. He wore the Soviet forester's uniform with oak-leaf flashes on his collar and heavy boots. He declined to give his name but unearthed a newspaper clipping he kept on the prophecy and showed me an old, colour-tinted photograph of a smiling elder with dark eyes, a white beard and a *papakha* on his head. The forester said the elder was Enni Taisam, a Chechen, the nephew of a sheikh from a village near Vedeno and the oracular source before his death in 1937 of events that had come to pass since: the 13-year exile of the Chechens and Ingush (the deportations); the bloodshed in the Prigorodny district (the 1992 fighting between Ingush and Ossetians); the absence of government in Chechnya in 1995. The elder also prophesied an event that would be dear to the Ingush – that the Ossetians would be moved to the Don.

The advent of English rule was expected soon and would be signalled by the arrival of a large black bull over the mountains at around the time the wheat and corn were harvested. The elder had not predicted which year. The English would rule for six years and would bring peace and prosperity to the Chechens. Turkey would then take over and the Chechens' fortunes would worsen. 'The Turks are more cunning – we'd be better off under the English. We know the English are Christians but that's no problem for us,' said the forester, who kept up with global events by listening to Radio Liberty and the BBC on shortwave radio. 'His predictions are one hundred per cent accurate.' The Chechens would eventually buy themselves out of Russian, English and Turkish rule with gold the elder claimed lay slumbering under the mountains.

Given 'perfidious Albion's poor record towards the Chechens, the strength of the prophecy is strange. The genesis of the prophecy is clouded, but much of Britain's supposed interest in the mountaineers can almost certainly be put down to the Victorian publicist and adventurer David Urquhart. Persuaded to travel in the east by Jeremy Bentham to fight ill health, the young Urquhart fought with the Greeks against the Turks from 1828 to 1829, securing the rank of lieutenant on the frigate *Hellas*. His freelance activities came to the attention of the British government, which sought his advice on relations with Turkey. Urquhart was particularly exercised by Russia's intentions in the Black Sea, urging a forward policy to ensure the Dardanelles remained open to British shipping and goods. The intrigues around Sultan Mahmud and the Pasha of Egypt, Mehemet Ali, concern us only so far as the intelligence-gathering mission on which Urquhart was sent by Lord Palmerston around the Near East in 1832, disguised as a 'commercial traveller'.

In July and August the following year, Urquhart travelled secretly along the northern shores of the Black Sea, landing at Anapa where he met Cherkess chieftains fighting Russian dominion on the western side of the North Caucasus. The Cherkess, or the 'Circassians' in Victorian popular imagination, while Moslems, are a distinct people from the Chechens. The feudally structured Cherkess tribes fought the Russians until defeated in 1864, when a large number of the population was deported by Russia to Turkey. In this instance the deportations worked, leaving only a small Cherkess minority divided today between the autonomous regions and republics of Adygeya, Karachayevo-Cherkessia and Kabardino-Balkaria. A handful of Imam Shamil's lieutenants fought alongside the Cherkess, but during the two Caucasian campaigns being fought simultaneously, the two sides failed to unite to form a common front against the Russian infidel.

The Cherkess chieftains told Urquhart they needed salt, gunpowder and lead, which they lacked owing to a Russian coastal blockade. Urquhart pleaded the Cherkess tribes' cause in notes to the Foreign Office, arguing that only a sixth of the six million tribesmen had submitted to Russia. He drafted a declaration of

Cherkess independence which he despatched to his patron, William IV. The mountaineers, with proper support, Urquhart argued, could check a Russian advance on Turkey. The theory that aid to the mountaineers could form a solid wall against Russian incursion into Persia, and eventually India, was repeated by British hawks for the rest of the century.

The British government got cold feet, accusing Urquhart of provoking the Cherkess revolt. This was unfair as the Cherkess were already up in arms. But even the king, reportedly much moved by the Cherkess declaration of independence, was wary of encouraging Cherkess hopes of British support for their cause. Urquhart returned to Britain to argue his hawkish policy to the British public in pamphlets and the newspapers, printing in his own journal the Cherkess independence declaration which he 'addressed to the courts of Europe'. He backed his arguments with trade figures to show how Britain was losing out to Russia on the bottom line. He even designed a flag for an independent Cherkess state. He set about provoking a crisis to try and enlist the British navy in the Cherkess cause. 'It was as though the soul of *Don Quixote*,' according to one historian, 'had wandered from the pages of Cervantes and found a new resting-place in the physical frame of an energetic Scotsman.'

He enlisted John Longworth, a foreign correspondent on the *Morning Post*, and a Captain James Bell to run guns to the Cherkess. The schooner *Vixen* was impounded – as Urquhart had hoped – by the Russian authorities in 1837, who accused Bell of shipping arms to the tribes. The British government protested that the cargo contained salt but in the event, and much to Urquhart's disappointment, the desired crisis was avoided and Urquhart was cut loose by his government. Baddeley slammed his efforts for 'encouraging the [Cherkess] with false hopes of British intervention; furnishing them with arms and munitions for war. The native successes were undoubtedly largely due to these efforts, but the unhappy mountaineers had no reason in the long run to thank their would-be benefactors.'

In 1858, however, a beleaguered Imam Shamil did not give up hope of British intervention in the North Caucasus. Shamil's long *ghazavat* on the eastern side of the Caucasus tied up hundreds of thousands of Russian troops. For nearly 30 years, first as a deputy to Kazi Mullah and then as the leader of the holy war himself, the learned Avar warrior, with enormous reserves of physical strength (it was said he could leap a ditch 27 feet wide), incited a war against the Russian invader in the mountains of Daghestan and the forests of Chechnya (with lightning incursions into Georgia and Kabarda).

The imam had survived several close calls. Surrounded in 1832 by Russian troops in the *aoul* of Gimri in Daghestan, nearly 100 kilometres southeast of Grozny and high in the mountains, he ran out of a *saklia*, or settlement, and leapt over the soldiers about to shoot at the entrance from which he emerged. It is said that the young *nayib* then turned round and cut down three soldiers with his sword, but was bayoneted in the chest by a fourth. He grasped the soldier's rifle, pulled it out and cut down his attacker, and fled into the forest. He was treated by his father-in-law who dressed the wound with wax, tar and butter.

In 1837, now Imam of Daghestan and Chechnya, the undisputed leader of the *ghazavat*, Shamil felt his forces sufficiently strong to turn down a meeting offered by the Russian authorities with Nicholas I, who was to visit the Caucasus that year. A *nayib* held back Shamil's arm when the Russian general sent to negotiate offered to shake hands. But Shamil's fortunes almost ran out again in 1839, when Russian forces captured the *aoul* of Akhulgo in mountainous Daghestan. A third of the Russian casualties were marked down as 'contused', wounded by rocks and wooden beams hurled down on them by the mountaineers. At a desperate moment in the battle, Shamil surrendered his twelve-year-old son Jamaluddin as a hostage to the Russians but the imam changed his mind and refused to submit (his son grew up a St Petersburg aristocrat). 'It is difficult to imagine all the scenes,' wrote Baddeley, 'of this terrible, fanatical struggle; mothers killed their children with their own hands, so only that they should not fall into the hands of the Russians; whole families perished under the ruins of their *saklias*.' Shamil escaped with one of his wives and a son on his back, crawling along a river bank while Russian soldiers fired at an empty raft he had sent downstream as a ruse.

He reappeared once more in the Chechen forests where he redoubled his efforts against the infidels. The villages under Shamil's imamate provided food, shelter and fodder for the highly mobile and lightly armed cavalry which the imam sent out on commando-style raids to harry Russian troops along the Terek. The commanders wore black *cherkeski*, the men yellow tunics while both wore green turbans. '. . . Those who showed cowardice in fight were distinguished by a metal ticket on their backs, if, indeed, they escaped mutilation or death.' The 1845 campaign to take Shamil's seat in Chechnya, Dargo, was led by the champagne-swilling staff of the newly appointed viceroy to the Caucasus, Prince Vorontsov, whose force was cut to pieces by Shamil's men, 'like a wounded stag that wolves have hunted down and brought to bay'. Vorontsov lost three generals, 195 officers and 3,433 men killed or wounded and was rescued by the skin of his teeth by a relief force under the command of General Freitag. Vorontsov tried to pass off the campaign as a success but old Yermolov could not resist a dig at the prince from retirement, writing to him: 'I do not dispute that if Freitag had not come up with fresh troops you would none the less have fought your way through. But how many of you?'

By 1858, however, Shamil's situation was again desperate. Axes, not guns, were his main enemy. Russian troops had cleared great swathes of Chechnya's beech forests (in the capture and clearing of the Argun defile, a Russian witness reported on the forebears of Grozny's indefatigable chocolate and cigarette traders who followed in the wake of the armed woodcutters: 'shops were opened, and booths set up by vendors of food and drink and every sort of petty trader'). From 1857 the greycoats – 200,000 of them in the Caucasus – were now issued with rifles in place of muskets. Chechen support for Shamil's *ghazavat* dwindled after decades of violent uncertainty between Russia's punitive expeditions and the imam's executioners. As soon as it became clear to a Chechen village that the Russians could take it, they now offered their submission.

As Shamil continued to lose territory, the imam penned a letter to Lord de Redcliffe, the British ambassador in Constantinople, in a request for help that must have stung the Avar's pride: 'The *ulama, ayan* and other dignitaries of our land have continuously suggested to me to introduce the other honourable rulers to the unprecedented anguish and oppression that have befallen us. Perhaps they will adorn the thrones of their rule with the jewels of virtue and humanity, and complement their crowns with moral chivalry by looking at our state and grievances with the eye of justice and fairness . . .'

The petition to Queen Victoria was never answered. The only Britons to go to the Caucasus were mountaineers in another sense, scions of the Royal Geographical Society who in their Victorian arrogance claimed to be the first to the summits of Mts Elbrus and Kazbek a decade later.* Shamil made his surrender in the Daghestan *aoul* of Gunib in 1859 but not before more than three-quarters of the remaining 400 loyal *murids* died in a last stand. When the imam rode out before the victorious Russian troops, they cheered. Mortified, Shamil turned his horse and headed back to the village. An Armenian in Russian service, Colonel Lazarev, ran after the imam and persuaded the proud, cruel leader that the *oorahs!* of the Russian troops were a mark of honour. Britain's main bulwark against an expansionist Russia went to live in 'honourable confinement' in Kaluga. He was allowed to make the *haj*, dying in Medina in 1871.

The fact that limited British support reached only the Cherkess, and even then only for a short time, did not worry the historians of the Stalinist era, who painted Shamil as 'the stooge of English colonialism and the Turkish Sultan'.

The mountaineers hoped once more for British intervention at the outbreak of civil war in 1918. Haidar Bammate, a Kumyk from Daghestan, was the Mountain Republic's foreign minister. When later an exile in Paris, he wrote a short account of the attempts by the fractious Caucasus nations to break from the

---

* A Cherkess hunter named Killar is recorded as having reached the summit of Elbruz in 1829.

empire. In a short review of Caucasian history up to his own time, he described Urquhart as 'one of the greatest political minds in Britain'. Bammate and his government were delighted when British troops were sent to fight the Bolsheviks. They were unhappy when British military advisors threw their arms and gold behind the rapacious Cossacks enlisted in General Denikin's White Army.

Colonel Rawlinson, the British officer sent to liaise with the White Army in the North Caucasus, issued a declaration in September 1919 which stated bluntly: 'Britain is helping General Denikin by supplying him with instructors, munitions, tanks, aeroplanes, cannon and machine guns, and will continue to supply aid until this goal [defeat of the Bolsheviks] has been achieved. He would regret being forced to turn his arms against the Mountain peoples, whose villages would be destroyed.'

The situation was understandably confusing but the British representative was either blind to – or determined to ignore – the battles between Denikin's Cossacks, led by the wantonly cruel Ossetian Cossack General Bicherakhov, and the mountaineers. As we have seen, the fighting fuelled Uzun Haji's *ghazavat* later that year, first against the Whites' attempt to keep the mountain peoples inside a Russia 'one and indivisible', and then against the Reds, who had imperial designs of their own. In June 1919 Bammate wrote to Lord Balfour, then foreign secretary, to apprise him of the situation. He warned him that Denikin could never hope to beat the mountaineers into submission. The Soviets, he argued, were winning over the mountain peoples, promising them all they wanted to hear and more, but without any intention of honouring pledges to recognize their sovereignty. He called on the British to order Denikin's withdrawal from the Mountain Republic.

'My government cannot believe that Great Britain,' he wrote, 'always considered a great friend of the North Caucasian people, having shown us its goodwill many times throughout the nineteenth century in our struggle for independence from the Russian Empire, should today be in favour of our total annihilation, caused by British military aid to Denikin. My government wishes to believe that the British High Command in the Caucasus is not acting in accordance with the intentions of His Majesty's government . . .'

The British ignored the warning. After the exhausted mountaineer fighters had expelled the Whites, their promised sovereignty was trampled into the ground under the boots of the invading Red Army in 1920. Bammate, now president of a shaky provisional government in Vladikavkaz, addressed his people by radio. He told them – as he had predicted – that the Soviets had swindled them. He used the address to make a declaration of his own: 'Considering that such a state of affairs contradicts the promises made by the central Soviet government and is likely to lead to a new period of anarchy, I demand the immediate confirmation of recognition of the Republic of [the] North Caucasus, and would ask you to give the appropriate instructions to your troops and agents.'

Bammate retreated south over the mountains to head a government in exile in Georgia in 1921, the Azerbaijan-North Caucasus Committee, until it was forced once again to escape the Soviets. Looking back from exile in Paris, Bammate bemoaned the lack of Caucasian unity which alone could have thrown back the Red Army. Fifty years earlier, Imam Shamil thought his own defeat was due not to Russia's superior forces but to disunity and treachery in his own ranks. Shamil put this down to Alexander the Great who, he said, had exiled all the criminals of the world to the barren Caucasus Mountains as a punishment. Bammate warned that, as with the Tsarist officers who wore Red Army uniforms to save something of their empire after the Revolution, the rude Soviet commissars' policy of expansion in the east was no different from that of their aristocratic forebears. With no world revolution in the offing in Europe, 'the Soviets turned their attention towards the East, where they believed they could strike an effective blow to their most feared enemy, Britain.'

Apparently undeterred by Britain's miscalculations during the Civil War, the Chechens refused to give up hope of a British *kunak* (in which Stalin might have had more grounds for the deportations than the trumped-up charge of collaboration with the Germans). The Chechen historian Avtorkhanov said the prophecy remained strong among Chechens even in 1942, when he was told a year before he left the Soviet Union: '"We are ready to stake our lives on it: it is not the Germans who will come but the *Ingiliz*, and they will not come from the West but from the East".' Avtorkhanov did not know where the prophecy originated. But he said it was believed with almost as much passion by the NKVD, who ascribed every uprising and 'bandit' group in Chechnya to British intelligence.

# Hostages

WE ARE ALL HOSTAGES OF THIS WAR

Headline in *Komsomolskaya Pravda*,
January 1996

IN JUNE 1995 Chechnya's most daring field commander, Shamil Basayev, seized hundreds of hostages, both patients and medical staff, at a hospital in Budyonnovsk, an unremarkable steppe town in southern Russia about 60 kilometres from the Stavropol region's border with Chechnya. Basayev said later he and his men had meant to drive further, but after spending thousands of dollars en route they had run out of money with which to bribe Russian checkpoints. The Russian authorities' fumbling attempts to storm the hospital, endangering those inside, and Basayev's audacious escape with his men back into the Chechen mountains took the war outside Chechnya's borders for the first time and forced the Russians to stop fighting.

For me, there are two enduring images: Basayev's floppy hat, a grey-green mushroom cap, as instantly recognizable in Chechnya as Montgomery's doubled-badged beret; and television pictures of the panicked Russian prime minister, Viktor Chernomyrdin, pleading with Basayev over a *spetsliniya*, shouting, 'Shamil! Shamil!' into a receiver pressed against his fat jowls. While the raid left Russians in shock, the hostage-taking brought hope to Chechnya and its war-weary fighters, who had been pushed further and further into the mountains after the capture in May of Vedeno, Basayev's home town (and also Imam Shamil's base of operations for a time more than a century earlier).

Peace talks began in June. A rough agreement was reached to swap Chechen disarmament for a Russian withdrawal, with Chechnya's ultimate status left hanging. Maskhadov tore across the countryside that summer to implement the agreement, bringing independent-minded field commanders like Basayev into line somehow to stop the fighting. Russian troops at checkpoints gawped as the Chechen commander sped past, protected by only a few Chechen fighters in green headbands. His Russian opposite number, General Anatoly Romanov, was just as keen to make the agreement stick.

Dudayev, still hiding out in the mountains, was suspicious of his chief lieutenant's strong rapport with Romanov. There were rumours that Romanov, as one of Maskhadov's former army commanders, had been assigned the task to try and 'turn' the Chechen commander and make of him a latterday Hadji Murat. Maskhadov was later unequivocal in his respect for Romanov: 'I remember well, for example, the condition of General Romanov who after this horror [of the war] truly wanted to save his soul on the path of peace. One day during the negotiations in the summer of 1995, he let me know openly that he would no longer fire on the Chechens. "Even if I have to leave the army," he said, "I will no longer kill Chechens."' But there are always those who lose in peace. Romanov was severely wounded when a bomb was detonated under his vehicle in October 1995.

Even as the ground was being prepared for negotiations, Russia's hardline interior minister, Anatoly Kulikov, did his best to undermine them from the start. After the war Kulikov moved to soften his hawkish image, writing in a US military journal in 1999 that he 'stood directly at the headwaters of the negotiation process as early as 1995. Even today I believe that all the critical issues must be solved with negotiations, not with cannon or machineguns.'

However, almost as soon as Russian and Chechen representatives met in a small house in Grozny the same month, I was driven to Kulikov's temporary headquarters at the northern airport in the metal bowels of an APC to listen to another Russian ultimatum. The hard little man, his blue uniform shirt stretched over a paunch and his eyes obscured by tinted pebble spectacles, waddled about in front of a large map of operations, fulminating against the 'terrorist' Basayev and demanding his immediate handover.

'The whole point of this action [Budyonnovsk], as estimated by the Russian government, was to reanimate Dudayev's criminal regime,' he told a small group of reporters, stabbing at the forests on the map around Vedeno where Basayev was presumed to be hiding. 'We have the right to start military action against these military bandits who are criminals. We expect an answer by the end of the working day to our demands. We can't sit at a table with people who carry out terrorism. Shamil Basayev, under Maskhadov, heads an illegal armed formation.'

The ultimatum was ignored, and shortly afterwards Chechen fighters under the command of Basayev's brother, Shirvani, invited Russian troops occupying Budyonnovsk to a working lunch in Vedeno to discuss the Russians' withdrawal. Shirvani wore a floppy hat, a little self-consciously, like his elder brother. The fighters had cut up two sheep which boiled away in large grey chunks over a fire in an iron cauldron large enough to cook a man, enveloping Basayev's back garden in a rich muttony cloud. A couple of Russian officers nervously accepted the Chechen hospitality and hesitantly joined Shirvani's toasts to peace with homemade *kompot*, or stewed fruit juice.*

But as the fighters slipped back into the villages they had been forced to abandon in the spring, hardliners like Kulikov started to regain their dominant place in the Kremlin. A scrappy, low-level conflict continued, with both Chechen fighters and Russian soldiers taking potshots at one another. Maskhadov and Romanov rushed about the Chechen countryside to try and stamp out the fires but the warring sides' continued proximity and a mutual fear of the double-cross gnawed away at any trust built up between the Chechen and Russian generals.

---

* The Russian journalist Anna Politkovskaya was told by Russian soldiers in 1999 that Shirvani Basayev was gang-raped by Russian soldiers when imprisoned in the Ingush capital of Nazran during Putin's war in Chechnya. The soldiers said the rape was videoed by the Russian security services for the edification of Russian troops serving in Chechnya (Anna Politkovskaya, *A Dirty War*, 2001, p. 107).

In mid-August I drove back to Achkhoy-Martan to observe the Chechen fighters handing in weapons, more theatre than any real intention to disarm. Shortly after I arrived, I was told a boy had been injured in a mortar attack. I found a Chechen doctor at the local clinic, sombre in his white coat, standing over the thin, tanned body of an eleven-year-old boy who had been playing in the street with a friend when a single round was lobbed into the town. A shrapnel fragment had spun into his back. The concertina pump on an artificial respirator squeezed air into his small chest but the boy's life was ebbing away. His father stood miserably in a cramped corridor outside the reanimation unit.

I left the doctor searching for words to speak to the father and headed for the weapons handover. On a leafy road on the edge of the village, a Russian officer sat at a small table with a typewriter and large bricks of roubles. He was guarded by sharpshooters. On the other side of the table was a small group of Chechen fighters. The officer read aloud the price for each weapon handed in – the equivalent of $227 for an RPG, $205 for a Kalashnikov and $34 for a hunting rifle. There was some haggling. The Chechens then produced from the boot of a car five ropy Kalashnikovs, a rusted shotgun and 30 anti-tank mines, laying them carefully on the road. The weapons amnesty that summer fared little better than the empire's attempts to do the same in the nineteenth century. 'Disarmament, too,' wrote Baddeley, 'was once more resorted to, but, as usual, ended in a farce – none but old pistols and inferior blades being surrendered . . .'

The officer was typing up a receipt for the scrap when a black Volga sedan pulled up next to the soldiers. The body of the boy I had just seen at the clinic was laid across the back seat, wrapped in a blanket like a pupa. His papery dead face lay inert on his aunt's lap. The woman was crying. The Russian commander at the weapons handover, Major-General Viktor Fyodotov, had radioed ahead for a helicopter to fly him to a field hospital in Grozny but it was too late. The Russians were shamed into a silence that oppressed everyone like the stormy summer weather. The fighters said nothing but their faces told everyone that nothing more could be expected while the Russians were there. General Fyodotov spoke to a Chechen elder in a long *bashlyk* by way of apology.

'This is why we have to withdraw.'

On the way back to Grozny the same day I passed a Russian column, the 503rd Motorized Infantry Regiment, and counted 160 armoured vehicles and trucks. The regiment raised a large cloud of dust as it headed out of Chechnya for its base in Vladikavkaz. A colonel stood next to his jeep by the side of the road to watch the column pass and count them out. He was in a bad mood. He said a reconnaissance team he had sent ahead the night before to check the route of withdrawal had been attacked.

'They're not keeping to their side of the agreement,' said the colonel, 'so we think we'll be back soon.'

I travelled back and forth to Chechnya to report on sniping, bomb attacks and shelling which continued into the autumn and winter. In November Basayev's group cached a small amount of radioactive caesium in a Moscow park and then told journalists where to find it to prove they could attack Moscow. The Kremlin moved to hold an election in Chechnya in December 1995 to give its puppet administration some shred of legitimacy. The Chechen administration-in-hiding warned Chechens that they would be punished if they voted. I caught up with Vakha Mirzhoyev, the Chechen field commander from Achkhoy-Martan. He had overseen the defence and then retreat from the village in the spring but he was back once more in the administrative building there. 'How can there be elections under artillery fire and machineguns? There's nowhere else where they've held elections under such conditions,' said Mirzhoyev, his beard still bushy but overall a little thinner. 'I agree with Maskhadov – "If we're men, there will be no elections". We had our elections in September 1991.'

During the voting in December polling booths were virtually empty. An American colleague who voted in one of them confirmed widespread irregularities and ridiculed the system. But this did not bother the Russian authorities, who declared a high turn-out, with more than 90 per cent of the imaginary votes cast for Moscow's Chechen quislings. The 'election' was quickly forgotten with the seizure of another hospital and 2,000 hostages in the town of Kizlyar in northern Daghestan.

*Wednesday 10 January 1996.* After a day of bluffing at checkpoints, false turns and confused information from villagers in Daghestan, I catch up with the hostage-takers. They are in the next village. A group of Chechen fighters under the command of Salman Raduyev, who is married to Dudayev's niece, have released most of the 2,000 hostages they held at the main hospital in the town of Kizlyar, mostly patients and medics as in Budyonnovsk. Raduyev calls his unit 'The Lone Wolves'. They aim to escape like Shamil Basayev from Budyonnovsk by travelling with over a hundred hostages in buses towards Chechnya, threatening to kill them if they are attacked. Pictures show Chechen fighters with RPGs standing at the doors wearing green headbands. White cloths hang from the windows.

But locals I speak to say the convoy has been attacked by helicopter gunships which blew away a bridge on the road back into Chechnya, and that the Lone Wolves have abandoned their convoy of eleven buses and two trucks and herded the remaining hostages into the small farming village of Pervomayskoye in Daghestan, just over the border from Chechnya and 50 kilometres east-northeast of Grozny. A unit of about forty Russian interior ministry troops near the village – most of them local people from Daghestan – have been attacked and disarmed at the same time by the Chechens, and the prisoners taken have been added to the hostages. Nobody gives the exact number of hostages but they are now estimated at more than 160. There are no exact figures either on casualties in Kizlyar.

Just before sundown military transport helicopters swoop down on the outskirts of Pervomayskoye. I watch them from about a kilometre away, in the village of Sovetskoye. The wind and snow render the engines almost silent. The soldiers who jog out of the back start digging as the icy wind whips the snow off the desolate fields surrounding the village, partially obscured by a black spinny. There is no contact with the village. Prime minister Chernomyrdin, who pleaded with Basayev the previous summer, talks tough. 'We aren't going to start frontal attacks, or act according to an eye-for-an-eye principle, since we feel convinced that death only brings death. But the bandits and terrorists will be punished.'

Dudayev telephones the Russian agencies from hiding and promises more Kizlyars, more apocalypse.

By nightfall Russian troops are dug in around the village, their shallow holes in the frozen ground lit by unearthly fires to heat their rations.

*Thursday 11 January.* Russian armour and troops start driving past the village of Sovetskoye, from where I am watching. They position themselves around the village in grey streaks across the fields. Trucks arrive towing artillery pieces. Helicopter gunships start flying incessant figures of eight over Pervomayskoye and Sovetskoye. To watch them, tails up and machinegun-laden noses down, makes one dizzy.

Yeltsin has gone to Paris for Mitterrand's funeral (he was in Halifax, Canada for a summit during Budyonnovsk).

An officer in dark interior ministry combat fatigues approaches several of us journalists and introduces himself as Major-General Alexander Mikhaylov. He says he is a spokesman for the Federal Security Service, the FSB, the latest acronym for the KGB. I have never experienced a Russian spokesperson volunteer information, especially in person, in the field. He has a sandy moustache hanging uncertainly on his upper lip. A black commando ski-cap rolled down tightly over his head looks like a condom. He says there are 150 fighters in Pervomayskoye holding 103 hostages, 37 of whom are interior ministry troops taken hostage on the way there. We ask how negotiations are faring to free the hostages.

He answers: 'These bandits must be annihilated.'

The Daghestan authorities say 40 were killed in the raid on Kizlyar and 50 wounded. Dudayev, who has telephoned *Komsomolskaya Pravda*, says the raid on Kizlyar was aimed at destroying a helicopter base from which the dragonflies regularly fly to strafe and bomb Chechnya. The fighters have apparently only the food and drink they took with them from the hospital. Red Cross officials waiting to enter Pervomayskoye with food and medicines are turned back. The temperature has sunk to minus five degrees centigrade and it is cold to stand for any length of time to watch the siege.

'Our orders are to stand and wait,' says a young Russian lieutenant wearing white camouflage. He pulls on a cigarette beside the light tank he commands about half a kilometre east of Sovetskoye. He stands and waits.

The predominantly Muslim Daghestan villagers are angry with the Chechens. 'I expect them to destroy the fighters so this will never be repeated,' says sixty-three-year-old Gaudzhi Zaudinov. He has had to abandon his home in Pervomayskoye and is now watching to see what will happen from Sovetskoye.

Journalists who have walked into Pervomayskoye say the hostages have been spread out among different buildings in the village, including the mosque and the school (I set off down the empty road for the village but I turn back, spooked by the helicopters, which loop their figures of eight at a height where you can clearly see the pilots' faces). Raduyev says he will release the hostages if foreign aid workers and journalists take their places.

'If they are not ready to solve this problem in a peaceful way we are ready to fight,' Raduyev tells them, 'until the last round, the last drop of blood.' My colleagues quickly leave the village again when they feel the fighters eyeing them up as potential hostages.

*Friday 12 January.* There is fog so there are no gunships up this morning. But there is considerable military activity on the ground, with reinforcements arriving to strengthen the siege. Russian agencies say Raduyev will release 30 hostages if he and the Lone Wolves are granted safe passage back to Chechnya. They then demand that well-known politicians and generals take the hostages' places.

A doctor who was allowed into the village to treat some of the hostages yesterday is turned back by Russian soldiers. The pregnant woman he helped out of Pervomayskoye has delivered a baby boy overnight in a nearby hospital.

The fog lifts and the helicopters restart their incessant figures of eight. Women and children climb into buses in Sovetskoye as the village elders have decided to evacuate them.

'We just don't know what to expect,' explains Rajab Baddrudinov, the head of the village administration. The temperature drops to ten degrees of frost. Russian troops continue to dig in. Russian agencies say Chechen refugees have started to flee Kizlyar, fearing reprisals.

General Mikhaylov saunters up to inform us that the fighters have released eight hostages: four women, three children and one interior ministry officer. Eight other women refused to leave their husbands behind. The general, bending over slightly as he taps and shuffles his feet, gives no explanation for the release. The Daghestan government has told Russian agencies that some of the hostages are suffering from frostbite.

At nightfall the lights of tanks lance the darkness. It is impossible to say where they are going, what they are doing. My agency wants me to know where they are going, what they are doing. Fires flicker in Russian foxholes like chains of oil lamps. The next day's edition of *Izvestiya* comments on the trenches, camouflaged armour and gun emplacements now surrounding the village. 'Judging by this powerful buildup of men and matériel, the authorities are clearly preparing for a final "dialogue" with the terrorists. Then, it seems, nobody will have time to think about the hostages.'

*Saturday 13 January.* At first light the helicopters are up, buzzing back and forth over Pervomayskoye and Sovetskoye, their fuselages so low you can almost reach out and touch them. Across the snow-covered fields, Russian brass hats make an inspection.

My journalist colleagues and I keep struggling with the

changing mathematics of this hostage crisis. First there are 103 hostages but after eight have been released, there are now 116. Hungry for information, like fledglings with their beaks wide open, we gather round General Mikhaylov, whose condom cap sets off a Pavlovian response, telling us it is feeding time. We hope he will regurgitate a fat, juicy worm of information. We are disappointed.

'Strategically, our aim is to free the hostages and punish the criminals. But tactically, the terrorists are the ones with the strong hand, it is they who are making the demands.'

Russian soldiers set off an explosion by a bridge near Pervomayskoye but the bridge remains intact, their intentions unclear. Grad rockets are heard crashing into the forest in neighbouring Chechnya. A Chechen demonstration appears on one of the roads around Pervomayskoye in solidarity with the kidnappers. 'Our people have been blown to bits, our hospitals bombed, our homes and cattle destroyed, but nobody says anything about that,' says one of the protesters.

Russian agencies quote General Mikhaylov's FSB chief, Mikhail Barsukov, as saying: 'If even one hostage is shot, I will act immediately.' He does not say how he will act but sets a deadline of ten am the next day for the hostages' release and the fighters' surrender.

The journalists I have commandeered a house with now scavenge for food. Ever since the women of the village were evacuated, everything has gone to pieces. We set a routine. The photographers search for food after sundown (they cannot work any more) while the reporters write. The reporters cook when they have filed. Dish of the day is spagbol, made from Iranian spaghetti and tins of *tushonka*, cans of beef stew. The men of the house can still run to tea and bread. The spaghetti dissolves on boiling into wallpaper glue.

I send an urgent telex to the Moscow office requesting hams, cheeses, chocolate, biscuits and a bottle of whisky, a winter hamper to be dispatched with another stringer which we dream about for the next 48 hours. There have been no working telephones in Chechnya for months but my agency does not see the need to provide me with satellite equipment so I have bought my own. The telex machine sits in an attaché case. To watch its green lights flash as the words fly up to the Indian Ocean satellite and down to the Moscow bureau in a triangle via a dish in Holland is a Euclidean pleasure. Only the agency staff forget to look at their telex printer and I have been hurried out of some areas by angry Chechens who think I am using the equipment to guide in Russian rocket strikes.

Jets start flying at night. At ten pm they release brilliant rings of flares, much brighter than those dropped over Grozny in December 1994, which light up the snow-blanketed countryside for kilometres around Pervomayskoye.

*Sunday 14 January.* At dawn hundreds of Russian troops march out of the fog and past our house in Sovetskoye along the exposed road towards Pervomayskoye. They look like ghosts, the line of the road they march along the only part of the landscape in crisp focus. Snow and sky dissolve together in the mist. In an open field between Sovetskoye and Pervomayskoye, Russian troops pitch a large, square canvas tent with a red cross on the side and walk in and out to fill it with bandages, medicines and stretchers. General Mikhaylov appears to explain the situation.

'We are preparing the operation. There is a deadline of ten am. We start then.'

The fog lifts and the helicopters start swerving back and forth, as if to hypnotize the fighters.

The deadline elapses with promise of an extension. There are no further details save that the FSB chief and the interior minister, General Anatoly Kulikov, are said by Russian agencies to be on their way to Pervomayskoye to take command. The Russian troops march back again, slogging through the mud and snow with snipers' rifles or anti-tank rockets slung across their shoulders. They sit inside buses to keep warm.

'We'll move back if we're ordered,' says the commander of one unit, his crash helmet wired with the radio equipment of

Russia's special forces. A loudspeaker broadcasts a message over and over again across the frozen fields:

'FREE THE HOSTAGES – YOUR LIVES ARE GUARANTEED!'

General Mikhaylov reappears to inform us that the Russian authorities have been thinking ahead: there will be no pardon for Raduyev. 'He has a lot of blood on his hands.' The interior ministry in Moscow tells Russian news agencies that their men have been fired on by the fighters. We have heard no shooting. Daghestan's local interior ministry condemns the Moscow report as a 'provocation'.

*Monday 15 January.* I am asleep in an upstairs room in the house when I dream I am caught and twisted in an enormous explosion, spun about as if trapped in a breaking wave. I wake up shouting. A Russian jet has broken the sound barrier low over the village, the sonic boom blowing out the glass in the windows of my borrowed bedroom. The glass lies in slivers on my blanket when I start up from the bed. Flares fall in chains of burning orange-white balls.

At nine am, the Russian storm begins. We watch like nineteenth-century generals at the edge of the battle. Small arms fire crackles. White flashes and smoke pour from Pervomayskoye, explosions sounding every second as artillery pieces pound the village. The helicopters are up in the air and are finally allowed to let fly their unguided rockets, streaks of white smoke cutting into Pervomayskoye. The noise is deafening as the helicopters hover above our house when they fire. The ground shudders under my feet. I see the roof of the school building in Pervomayskoye blown off in a direct hit.

Suaybat Aliyeva, a nurse, watches with the journalists from a mound above a ditch at the edge of Sovetskoye as her village is blown apart. Her thoughts are not with the hostages. 'I spent thirty years building our home – our cattle, our clothes, everything is there.'

General Mikhaylov, holding his gloved hands together, delivers the public explanation for this display of overwhelming force, reading out a statement in the name of his chief. The FSB, he says, have intercepted a Chechen order to execute the hostages. He says two have already been killed.

'On the 14th of January at four pm, the terrorists opened fire on federal troops and began to kill hostages. The federal powers cannot tolerate these illegal acts any longer and have been obliged to resort to the use of force to free the hostages.' He tells the Russian agencies that the two people executed were Russian interior ministry soldiers and that six more of their number were executed just before the storm.

We ask how many hostages have been freed.

'No hostages have been freed yet!' he says crossly.

The beat of helicopter rotors sings in my ears as the light fails. Russian armour burns on the outskirts of the village. The nature of the fighting is unclear. A tired special forces officer wearing his radio helmet explains: 'They are clearing the village. This is more delicate as there are many fighters still alive – we have to finish before the night.'

A soldier helping a wounded comrade to the field hospital fires his assault rifle into the air to gain the attention of the medics inside. The medics hurry out with a stretcher.

Movladi Udugov, in hiding in Chechnya, calls the Russian news agencies to deny there was any order to kill the hostages, or that any of them have been executed. A reporter from my agency arrives that night with the food hamper, inebriated. He has drunk the whisky but left some of the food.

The Daghestan men of our house, abandoned by the women, are also drunk. Late at night there is a sound of rasping breath as a sheep has its throat slit on the threshold. The blood runs off the step into the mud and snow in the yard. The house is then filled with the smell of boiling mutton.

*Tuesday 16 January.* Intermittent shooting continues during the night under the giant, incandescent posies tossed into the sky by the jets. Helicopters are up in the day, despite a snow flurry. The Russian agencies are reporting that 30 workers at an electric power station near Grozny have been taken hostage. An explosion has gone off near the remains of a Grozny cinema. All traffic in the city is banned for fear of Chechen attacks.

General Mikhaylov looks taciturn this morning. He says Russian troops have 'freed' 16 hostages. He later changes the number to 24. The more likely explanation is that they managed to run away in the confusion.

We are not allowed to speak to the hostages, kept locked up in a small administrative building in Sovetskoye, while General Mikhaylov's intelligence colleagues start to question them to make sure they are not fighters making an escape. They have been given canned food to eat and have been allowed to wash their hands. Through the windows of the building, the hostages look dazed. They are bundled by Russian officials onto a bus which they say is bound for Kizlyar. One of the men is distraught.

'My daughter is in there!' he shouts, motioning towards Pervomayskoye. 'I can't leave!'

Gunmen sympathetic to the Lone Wolves have seized a ferry in the Turkish port of Trabzon, bound for Sochi on Russia's Black Sea coast. The masked gunmen, assumed to be Chechens, are demanding freedom for Chechnya. They are armed with automatic weapons and have taken 120 passengers and 45 crew hostage, Turkey's Anatolia news agency reports. They have threatened to kill all Russian passengers if the ship does not leave port.

There is no further word on the fate of the 30 power station employees.

The interior ministry admits losses – four dead, including the commander of a rapid reaction unit, and 20 wounded. The ministry claims to have killed 60 rebels. All I can construe from this is that in what appears to have been close-quarter fighting, the Russians have come off badly. As darkness descends over Pervomayskoye, General Mikhaylov appears on the edge of Sovetskoye, the battle raging across the fields behind him. We quiz him on Chechen losses. He says something that my colleagues and I have to double-check three times to make sure we have heard him correctly.

'We're not counting them in terms of corpses – we're counting them in terms of arms and legs.'

A journalist returns from the tented field hospital where he has talked to a Russian special forces soldier having his arm bandaged. We swap notes and my colleague says the soldier has told him that he has lost six comrades, saying Chechen sniper fire is especially deadly. He adds that the radios in their special helmets do not work. The soldier tells him: 'We've been had.'

General Mikhaylov is losing patience with his journalist clients. Explosions and flames throw an evil light from Pervomayskoye as darkness falls once more over the village. When we ask the general what next, he replies menacingly: 'Annihilate the fighters.'

Esman, a twenty-year-old Russian trooper, humps crates of shells up to a field gun set up near to where I watch the battle. Shells are loaded and the breech is slammed shut. The battery crew then kneel down and stick their fingers in their ears. The gun jolts back as the round is fired into the pall of flames and smoke boiling up over Pervomayskoye. Esman shrugs when questioned. 'War is war.'

*Wednesday 17 January.* A Russian who has escaped from the Trabzon ferry says that fellow passengers have been wounded while the Anatolia news agency says one passenger has been killed. The gunmen's leader, Muhammed Tokcan, and the ferry captain say there are no casualties. 'This is a warning to Yeltsin,' Tokcan, who claims allegiance to Shamil Basayev, tells Turkish television. Turkish officials say Tokcan is a Turkish national who has fought with the Chechens. He has threatened to blow up the ship in the Bosporus straight, with all Russian passengers on board. The Turkish authorities say they do not think the ferry has enough fuel to get to Istanbul.

The search continues for the 30 workers reportedly taken

hostage from a power station near Grozny. A report that several construction workers have been taken hostage in Achkhoy-Martan is dismissed as a wild rumour by the authorities there.

This morning three Zil trucks carrying Grad rocket-launchers park near the artillery emplacements between Sovetskoye and Pervomayskoye. General Mikhaylov, condom cap rolled down low over his ears, rubs his hands and then holds them together for warmth before depositing a fat worm into our hungry mouths. He repeats in a deadpan, take-it-or-leave-it voice: 'Because the situation is becoming more complicated, we have decided to conclude the operation.' This explains the Grads.

And the hostages?

'We have little hope for them,' he says quietly.

The Russian troops are withdrawn. They climb back into their buses. One of their officers mutters quietly that the Chechens, who have pinned them down for three days in the icy fields, are fighting better than his own men. He says his unit has suffered heavy losses.

The Grad launchers start to conclude the operation, the rockets leaving sheets of flame in their wake. Helicopters clatter up overhead and fire more rockets into the village. At sundown, as gusts of snow are blown across the marshy fields, the chatter of a heavy machinegun signals continued Chechen resistance. The Russian agencies claim an old man, a hostage, has escaped from the village and has said there is noone left alive inside. It is even more difficult to know what to believe as my colleagues and I have been expelled from Sovetskoye by interior ministry troops. ORT, Russia's main state television channel, cancels light entertainment because of the fighting in Daghestan.

*Friday 19 January.* The gunmen who hijacked the *Avrasya* ferry have surrendered to the Turkish authorities. There are no reports of casualties among the 242 crew and passengers. The whereabouts of the 30 power workers remains a mystery.

Yeltsin defends the storming of Pervomayskoye from the Moscow Kremlin: 'Mad dogs must be shot down.'

An aide to the Russian-backed administration in Chechnya says Raduyev has escaped to Chechnya.*

*Saturday 20 January.* Nurses and doctors are sweeping up the glass blown out of windows at the Central District Hospital in Kizlyar. A freezing January wind blows through the corridors, the stairwells and the wards, carrying away the cloying hospital smell of old bandages and iodine. White sheets and towels, waved at Russian troops by the hospital staff and patients in a plea to hold their fire, still dangle from trees and open windows.

One of the nurses clearing up, forty-eight-year-old Lyudmila Rogalyova, says she was asleep when Chechen fighters in green headbands burst into her home at five-thirty am on 9 January. They forced her, her husband, son, daughter-in-law and grandson at gunpoint to the hospital nearby. 'There was machinegun fire as we were being brought into the building. I saw two bodies on the street.'

Khayruddin Gadjiev, an anaesthetist from Daghestan, stares into space, his face unshaven, doing nothing. He was on duty at the hospital when the fighters arrived, telling them: 'You are now prisoners of Dudayev's army.' Gadjiev says he cannot wake from the shock. Two of his colleagues were killed. 'It's a nightmare which plays over and over in my mind. We looked after the Chechens and fed them when they came as refugees.'

A laboratory assistant who is also helping to clear up the debris of dressings, soiled mattresses, old food and spent cartridges says she held up a blanket around two women giving birth during the siege at the hospital. 'They were screaming in pain. We were trying to give them some privacy.'

A young ambulance-driver was forced to join the fighters' convoy which was halted at Pervomayskoye. He is lying in a bed at another hospital across town, his face grey. He says he tried to run from Pervomayskoye during the final Russian assault on the

---

* Raduyev was eventually captured, and in December 2001 was found guilty by a Russian court on counts of terrorism and murder and sentenced to life imprisonment.

Thursday. 'The fighters tried to get us out.' He points to his legs under the sheets. 'These are Russian bullets.'

*Sunday 21 January.* The houses in Pervomayskoye, built of mud and reeds, are reduced to charred, timber skeletons. A cold soup of fog hangs over the scene. Deep trenches have been left behind by the fighters, the lines running through what were once the living rooms in some of the houses. The trench lines zigzag for maximum protection against shelling. The ground next to the recently built mosque is strewn with sharp, twisted shrapnel. The mosque is roofless. The iron cylinder of the minaret lies flat on the ground. A brick chimney stack is all that remains of the school. Livestock lie dead and bloated on the frozen, rutted tracks in the village. One cow lows, her stomach hanging out of a gash in her flank. Circles of grey ash in the snow show where stacks of winter hay have stood. A long row of burned steel carcasses is all that remains of the convoy of buses that set off from Kizlyar.

A few villagers have returned to try and salvage what they can from the ruins with tractors and trucks borrowed from relatives. The men gather in small groups and debate whether they should try and rebuild the village or abandon it altogether. One of the women, in her sixties, lifts up her arms and bends over, sobbing. 'Nothing's left – no animals, nothing. What am I going to do? I'm old.'

Detonations signal the presence of Russian sappers clearing mines and booby-traps in the village. Workers in red overalls from the Emergency Situations Ministry clear corpses. Four dead fighters lie on one of the frozen tracks. One is wrapped in a parachute from a flare. Another has a green headband tied around his waxy, pale forehead, his nose pinched in the sharp angle of death. A young villager pulls the blanket off one of the fighters, turns his head and spits. 'Why did he have to come and fight here?'

Chechens and Russians suffered their own hostage crises every day during the war and continue to do so as I write. Early on in the war, Chechen men's freedom of movement was severely limited, even if they were not fighters, as they could be stopped and arrested at Russian checkpoints on a whim. Their mothers, wives and brothers were told nothing if one of their men disappeared. They could only presume that he had been taken to a 'filtration camp', where the Russian authorities 'filtered' Chechnya's male population to check if they were fighting in 'illegal bandit formations'.

The Russian defence and interior ministries refused to say where these filtration centres were. Chechen women (it was often too risky for the men to go and search) would follow rumours of filtration camps inside and outside Chechnya to track down their missing men. The camps were anything from a requisitioned railway carriage to a soldiers' tent.

The most notorious filtration centre in Grozny was PAP-1, a bus depot which had been requisitioned to encamp a unit of interior ministry soldiers. The windows at the depot were bricked up and the walls were topped with bushes of razor wire. The Russian authorities denied its existence and sentries at the gates warned enquirers off. I met one Chechen who had spent six weeks incarcerated in one of PAP-1's eight cells. He had been arrested at a checkpoint in December 1995 after visiting a sick aunt in hospital in Kizlyar. We sat in the room of a cramped flat in a town to the east of Grozny. He was stiff with pain, wincing as he lifted a cigarette to his mouth.

He said there was no light or heat in the cells, just a mattress and a blanket. If relatives found out their men were imprisoned there, they could supplement the single daily ration of buckwheat porridge with food brought from home – at a price. 'It's a real mafia that runs the prison,' the man said. At night, the prisoners were made to line up against a wall, spreadeagled. Interior ministry troops then beat and kicked them until they were unconscious. 'The beatings usually happened at night, when they were drunk.' He said the unit's guard dogs were also set on the prisoners.

In February 1995 I drove to Mozdok, the site of one of the filtration centres – always officially denied – with Sergey Kovalev, a biologist and political prisoner in Soviet times and now the head of Moscow's independent Institute for Human Rights. The sparely built, grey-haired *intelligent* had spent days sitting with the Chechens in the bunker of the Presidential Palace the previous month in an attempt to shame Yeltsin into halting the bombing.

Yeltsin praises Kovalev in his *Midnight Diaries* as 'a worthy person, a democrat', but in the same breath accuses him of 'siding with the separatists' and says he forced himself to ignore his and others' 'excessive, unfair criticism'. In an extraordinary feat of self-delusion, Yeltsin writes off the war as 'a new disease: a total negativity, a complete lack of confidence in ourselves and our strengths. We Russians had come to dislike ourselves. And that is a historical dead-end for a nation.' Kovalev saw clearly that it was the war in Chechnya, ordered and sanctioned by Yeltsin, that was driving Russia back to the Gulag and later resigned his post as the Presidential commissioner for human rights.

Before his resignation, Kovalev arrived at the muddy gates to the tent city in Mozdok to see for himself the conditions under which Chechen men were being held. He was given a sarcastic welcome by an interior ministry information officer, a colonel who grinned like a slavering jackal, the *shakal* of Chechen contempt.

'Welcome, friend of the Chechen people!' he said, adding a contemptuous bow. The colonel, smiling as we walked between the lines of tents below the fog, kept spouting difficulties and insults such that Kovalev lost his temper.

'I can't stand lying and you're a professional liar.' The grin was momentarily wiped off the colonel's face.

'The general,' said the officer, who did not name any general in particular, 'told me clearly that we could not meet your request. I'm telling you what he told me.' The colonel contorted his face from anger back to its jackal grin. 'I was told to get you the hell out or get shot.'

Kovalev did not appear overly concerned with this last possibility. 'I can't stand liars and especially those that do it for a living.' The jackal withdrew and Kovalev was shown some detention cells while we were made to wait outside but he saw nothing of import, as he was the first to admit.

The international Red Cross had an efficient-sounding break-down of the missing in Chechnya: those killed in the bombardments and whose bodies were never recovered; those arrested at checkpoints and taken to filtration centres; a tiny fraction who had used the war to change identity and escape an old life; and those who were 'disappeared', in the Latin American sense of the word. But both the Red Cross and local organizations which attempted to track the missing lacked the most basic information. They flashed black and white passport photographs of faces in special programmes on the local Russian-backed television station, a shamanistic act of faith in the hope that some of these human beings might magically reappear.

Hussein Hamidov, chairman of a Chechen group called Casualties of War, issued a report in November 1995 to make concrete, with examples and figures, the war of the missing. He said many Chechen men were dying of beatings in the filtration centres.

> Unlawful detention of Chechen citizens and searches of private dwellings continue to the present day, violating all norms, without approval from a prosecutor, without the presence of official witnesses and without drawing up protocols describing the results of the search. Searches are accompanied by beating of those searched. Subsequent to detention, evidence of criminal activity is falsified; weapons and narcotics are planted on those being searched.

The missing in Chechnya became a lucrative business for the Russian troops, who traded in both Chechens and their own men. Hamidov's report explained: 'Russian federal forces now demand arms or the release of Russian prisoners in exchange [for Chechen detainees]. Chechen citizens are reduced to having to hunt for federal soldiers or to buy weapons to procure the release of their relatives.' Chechens kidnapped even Russian Orthodox priests to use as bargaining counters.

The report detailed accurately a Hobbesian breakdown in law and order, where the lives of those in Chechnya were now 'poor, nasty, brutish and short'. Of the small minority of Russian soldiers who looted or murdered and who were actually investigated, most were let off with a slap on the wrist. The Russian authorities falsified lists of the missing with lists of convicted criminals in Russian gaols. Shooting from checkpoints at night, potshots fired at cars, mortar rounds lobbed into areas where children played, reckless driving that killed pedestrians and damaged property, continued looting and theft of cattle, the imposition of 'toll payments' at checkpoints – the Russian troops sent in to restore constitutional order in Chechnya, through their own fear, hunger and lack of discipline, created a hellish vortex into which anyone, innocent or guilty, could be sucked, with little hope of resurfacing.

Hamidov concluded his report: 'For three hundred years the Chechen people have struggled for freedom against the colonial policy of Russia. Hatred for the colonists has been transmitted from generation to generation.'

The former interior minister, General Kulikov, rejects such a view and speaks for much of Russian officialdom, writing: 'At one time or another, most peoples of the Caucasus have voluntarily expressed a desire to join Russia. It was Russian involvement and support that allowed these people to preserve and develop their political system and economic base, particularly crucial for those who had been living at an essentially primitive-communal level.'

In 1722 Peter the Great entered Derbent, in Daghestan, to acknowledge submission of the Caspian port, a minor earthquake shaking the town walls as he entered. 'Lo!' he declared, 'nature herself gives me a solemn welcome and makes the very walls tremble at my power!' Inland, however, some of the tsar's cavalry which had gone ahead to occupy the Chechen village of Enderi were driven back by the Chechens, who harassed the largely Cossack detachment in thick beech forests, a skirmish that augured ill for both the mountaineers and the empire. Chechnya, earlier a hostage of the tsars and the Soviets, has continued as a hostage of the Russian Federation, but ever since Peter's time the Chechens have never voluntarily submitted to the lawlessness of tsar, commissar and now president.

The Missing Persons Search Service was located in a shoebox of an office near the centre of Grozny, the war-damaged interior boarded over with cheap plywood. In February 1996 the room was crammed with women bundled in heavy coats. Their tales of the missing steamed the windows. Kurason Kharzhgeriyev sat at a small desk to listen to each tale in turn, taking affidavits from wives, fathers, mothers, anyone who had lost someone.

'We get several new cases every week as many men are being arrested at military checkpoints. We have no explanation for why it's being done but of course it spreads fear.' Kharzhgeriyev, short, stocky and middle-aged, had video film of about 400 corpses which he showed to relatives in case they recognized one of them. He said he had managed to pin down where 129 Chechens had been imprisoned. He then put his hands on the small desk and sighed. After that, it was an information black hole.

One of the women waiting in Kharzhgeriyev's office said FSB agents had broken down her door in Argun in April the previous year and arrested her sons, both in their twenties, pushing them into the belly of an APC. Tears of frustration and anxiety spilled down her cheeks. 'I've been to the military, the Red Cross, everywhere, but I have no information. I wait, I hope to find them alive. They're not to blame. They didn't fight.'

The tales poured and heaved out of these anxious, loving, exhausted women. Madina Magomedova was searching for her younger brother Shamsa. He had been arrested by Russian troops when the two of them were carrying the body of their elder brother, Maula, out of Grozny on 9 January 1995. Maula had been killed in the Russian bombardment. 'I've been to Moscow, all the agencies, and nobody helps,' she said, shaking with sobs, the tears forming like wet diamonds around her creased, red eyes which she stabbed with a handkerchief. She had bribed a Russian interior ministry official the previous June who told her that her brother was imprisoned in the interior ministry's No. 5 gaol in the town of Stavropol. She set out for the town, a few hours' drive away, and waited for two months

outside the prison. The prison officials refused to tell her anything.

'Tell all the women in the world what it is to wait and wait and
know nothing.'

The war of the missing also brought mothers of Russian soldiers from Siberia, the Altai Mountains and from all over Russia
to Chechnya to find their missing sons, fed up with hearing no
information from the authorities at home. They took what little
money they had, sleeping in railway stations and airports. Their
determination did not stop at Chechnya's hazy front lines, for
these women would turn up in areas held by the fighters asking
for their sons. A typical tale was that of Taya Kuprienko from
Stavropol, who had travelled to Grozny to track down her nineteen-year-old conscript son.

'They [Russian authorities] told me my son was a deserter, not
a hostage,' she said. She pieced together the real story. Her son
and two comrades, she said, were sent out by their commander
from a checkpoint to find vodka. Chechen fighters took them
prisoner. Even if the women found their sons, they were unable
to pay the middlemen – Chechen and Russian – who began to
take cuts. The price of a brother or son at that time was about
$6,000 and an automatic rifle, a fortune for an ordinary Russian
family.

Hope burned in these tired, abused women who went to sleep
each night in an empty bed or an empty flat. Tamara Elzayeva's
husband had been arrested in January 1995. The thirty-five-
year-old Chechen woman's tears willed her husband to come
back to her and her children.

'I don't believe he's dead. I feel him somewhere.'

In the spring of 1996 I joined a group of journalists to
interview Dudayev in hiding. I had not seen the
general for over a year. We were met by a field commander in the village of Goyskoye, 20 kilometres southwest of
Grozny, on a sunny afternoon. We were told to leave our vehicles and climb into the back of a military truck; the fighters

closed the canvas tarpaulin so we could not see where we were going. We were jolted and bumped around in the back for what seemed like hours. A fighter sat with us, but through a chink in the canvas I caught the occasional glimpse of an orchard or patches of snow that still lay on the foothills somewhere in southern Chechnya. I also heard the occasional cry of *Allahu akbar!* from young boys who ran out of the fields to see the truck.

At one point the truck lurched at a crazy angle, almost tipping over in a deep muddy rut. We were ordered out of the back and told to wait. Armed fighters stood about in a small orchard by the side of the track. We were then transported in UAZ jeeps to a village I did not recognize and told to wait in a house. We sat on the floor for several hours. We were moved to another house. Darkness fell and at about nine o'clock we were ushered into a living room with a low ceiling. A Chechen flag was pinned up behind a chair.

Dudayev walked in with a bodyguard. He deposited a couple of walkie-talkies on a small side table next to him, standing them upright next to a bunch of plastic flowers. He looked taller in a pair of heavy Soviet paratrooper's boots (those favoured by the late Afghan warlord Ahmed Shah Masood). He wore a neat but plain combat uniform with the Chechen coat of arms on his sleeve and a forage cap pulled tight over his forehead. The moustache was neat but had greyed and looked as if it received less attention than in previous times. He carried a pistol and a knife in his belt. The 52-year-old air force general sat with a straight back, legs planted open and square in front of him, arms resting on the sides of the armchair. He hardly moved from this position for the next four hours while I kept shifting in my chair to stop my legs from going to sleep.

He was angry with us, haranguing us as representatives of 'cowardly' western states that had not lifted a finger to stop the bombing and killing in Chechnya. 'Here, I must tell you, a people is being killed through the terrorism and banditism of the Russian government. It is international terrorism meted out by an illegal regime. Your leaders ask quietly to hurry up and finish the war in Chechnya.' As he talked, he stiffened in anger, bringing his hand down in a karate chop on the side of the armchair to underline the evil propensities of the Russian infidels and the spineless west cowering before them.

Before the war, I would have walked away from the interview laughing at Dudayev's millenarian tones. But that night, against the backdrop of the apocalypse in Chechnya, his words were tragic. The village of Sernovodsk, where the women from Samashky had wept on the green before the mosque the previous spring over the horrors they had escaped, had since suffered the same fate as its neighbour. And Samashky would suffer a second Russian storming that spring to push out Commander Mirzhoyev's men who had once again crept back in. Dudayev was in one sense a hostage-taker, responsible for locking the Chechens into an unequal battle to defend a tiny territory with little more than the audacity, courage and fathomless bloody-mindedness that Tolstoy noted in trying to pick a tough Tartar thistle in the opening and closing pages of *Hadji Murat*. In another sense, he led the life of a hostage, rarely appearing in public, constantly on the run. One of the journalists asked him to describe a normal day-in-the-life of Dzhokhar Dudayev.

'How can I tell you how I live? I've lost my childhood, I grew up without a father and an elder brother and this has been with me all my life. How many thousands of us are without arms and legs? They want us to be killed, to kill our future.' His eyes reddened. It was unnerving to think that this straight-backed man, whatever one's view of him, might break down and cry. He could not answer the question properly at first, instead mixing up his own life with the destiny of the Chechens. And how could it be otherwise, a leader who, like Moses in the Book of Exodus, escapes death in February 1944 as a days-old babe in arms, only not in a basket of reeds but in an unheated cattlewagon which dumps him and his family near the Kazakh town of Pavlodar, his mother's milk containing only the nourishment from potatoes the family has managed to find in the snow. His family leaves behind in Chechnya relatives who are locked in a barn by the NKVD along with 500 Chechen elders and infirm who are then burned to death. Like Moses, he grows up in the lap of the Pharaoh's family, becoming a successful Soviet pilot who lies about his nationality to advance (entering 'Ossetian' on his papers) and marries a Russian woman he is too shy to tell his family about until the birth of their first son. 'Russian history is one of barbarism, stealing from the people, especially here. We carry this history in our genes.'

I could not understand at first why Dudayev had a portrait of Sheikh Mansur on the wall of his ninth-floor office in the Presidential Palace, a more obscure hero and of more doubtful provenance than the better known Imam Shamil. One story crops up repeatedly in Western European accounts, that Sheikh Mansur, who in 1785 preached Chechnya's first *ghazavat* against Russia, was really an eighteenth-century Italian adventurer by the name of Giovanni Battista Boetti, who ran away from home aged fifteen, became a Dominican missionary at some point during his travels and scandalous escapades throughout Asia Minor, and reappeared as a Muslim prophet in Kurdistan. Another account points to the sheikh's beginnings as a learned Tatar from Orenburg. Both Russian and mountaineer accounts, however, point to Chechen beginnings, with Mansur born in the Chechen village of Aldi and educated at one of the medressehs in Daghestan. For Dudayev, Mansur was a Chechen, not a Daghestan Avar like Shamil, but above all a warrior prophet who marked the first in a long line of leaders who called on a fractious people never to submit to Russian rule. In an account of Sheikh Mansur published in Russian in Istanbul in 1924, written anonymously by someone who claimed to be the sheikh's descendant, Mansur is said to have 'slept in his coat fully armed. He would explain this strange habit by saying that it was shameful for an honourable Chechen to sleep undressed since, in his opinion, a Chechen must always be prepared for every eventuality and must never be accustomed to comfort.'

And so it was with Dudayev. He detailed some of his near scrapes with death at our prompting: a shell through a window, his office mortared, a shell which landed four metres away from his car on the road. He was given a knife as a gift which he discovered contained a tracking device. 'I've lost count of the number of attempts on my life. Dudayev's not dead yet. I'm an idiot of a believer, I'm a believer,' he said, raising his hand and chopping it down with a quiet thud. 'Life depends on the Creator who gave it to you. Otherwise you go out of your mind, you don't want to walk out of the door or look out of the window. I change places not because I'm running away from death. I'm in different places because I have to be there. I've a place in the mountains no bombs or special forces can get to.'

We asked him for details of his security. He cracked and popped his knuckles by way of an answer. 'I look after my own security. I keep fit. Everyone is his own bodyguard.'

Dudayev said some whacky things that night, promising the Chechens would soon unveil a weapon that could cause death and destruction on any continent. When we asked him what it was he replied like a child speaking of an imaginary friend: 'It's our secret – if the world knew, if this secret became known, it would be very difficult for you.' But much of what Dudayev said was prophetic and the words he had used to denounce the 'Satans in the Kremlin' at the start of the war now rang true. There *was* something diabolical in the Kremlin's determination to push Chechens and Russians through this horrible meat-grinder, like the horned, blackened devils stoking the fires underneath naked bodies at the bottom of a Renaissance trip-tych, cruelty that would never square the circle of contradictions that surrounded its crumbling empire.

Dudayev's reading of Yeltsin's war in Chechnya was identical to the historian Avtorkhanov's summation of Stalin's crimes: 'The struggle between good and evil, between democracy and totalitarianism, was being enacted in the Caucasian mountains for decades while the outside world remained largely ignorant and indifferent.' When he was asked how he might go down in history, he said that all he wanted to see under the letter 'D' was the word *dom,* the Russian for house, 'so that everyone has a house for their children. How many homes are there without blood? It's a military testing ground here. Only Satanic forces can do this. It's not human. This is already dangerous – for you. *Russianism* is a Satanic force and you don't want to see this. You support a totalitarian regime from your fear of Russia.' He scowled. 'You are cowards.'

Dudayev was not as ruthless as Imam Shamil but his refusal to compromise – 'Peace not on their terms but a peace on the terms we set' – had helped set Chechnya's villages on fire. He had no voice from the clouds throwing down plagues or parting the seas to help his people out of Egypt. If Chechens wanted independence, they had to die for it. We asked him if the cost of this war had sown any doubts in his mind.

'It is the will of the people, with the forces we have, to fight this terrorism. How could this small Ichkeria [Chechnya] fight against this giant for one and a half years? It's amazed you, me and everyone.' He smiled a small proud smile. 'The Chechens are a very strong people. When we came back in 1957, there was no food on the road back. In one year, we built 40,000 homes with our own hands, without any help from the state, only their interference. We are a strong people, in the mountains we have the defence towers,' he said, referring to the five-storey stone towers the Chechens built centuries ago to protect their homes and villages, a handful of which still guard some of the narrow mountain defiles. 'These people stand with just a knife in front of a tank. I am proud of how people make their own anti-tank weapons. My role in this is practically nothing. I haven't taught anyone how to fight.'

It was past midnight and his audience was flagging. 'Am I boring you?' he asked, bright and alert, opening and closing his fists and cracking his knuckles.

'No, no,' we replied politely, and then quickly asked him where we should dateline the interview.

'Wherever you want.'

'But what if there's a reprisal?'

'There probably will be.'

# Epilogue

**Tartarean**: of or belonging to Tartarus in Greek mythology; pertaining to hell or to purgatory; infernal; hellish.

*Shorter Oxford English Dictionary*, 1993

A MONTH AFTER the interview with Dudayev, he was killed. In April 1996 a missile locked on to the signal sent by his satellite telephone as he spoke in a field. I did not return to Chechnya, reporting only on an increased number of Chechens arriving in Kazakhstan in the summer of 1996 when I took up a post based in former Soviet Central Asia for a different news agency. The Chechens recaptured Grozny in August 1996. The Kremlin grudgingly signed a peace deal and in January 1997 General Aslan Maskhadov was elected president. There was a feeling of optimism among the Chechens, even if the territory's political status was left hanging. The causes behind the dark times that followed Russian withdrawal and before the second war – the killings and kidnappings of foreign aid workers, the beheading of four British and New Zealand telecom workers in 1998, Maskhadov's failure to install any semblance of postwar order in Chechnya – are fogged in conspiracy theories and too complicated for the scope of this book. What is important is the result.

Journalists feel less safe in covering the Chechen story, fearing kidnap or death at the hands of Chechen criminal gangs, Sergey's former colleagues at the Federal Security Service (FSB), or a combination of the two. Russia's new president, Vladimir Putin, has tamed much of the country's media, taking over the management of the independent NTV television station in April 2001 and closing down the independent weekly *Itogi*.* The Russian public now hears much about 'decisive victories' on the part of Russian forces in Chechnya. But while the intelligentsia hold as much store by these reports as those coming out of Soviet-occupied Afghanistan a decade earlier, the scepticism of such a minority is not enough to balance the damage the Chechen wars have done to the weak fabric of Russian civil society.

The lack of information means few Russians have any inkling of what is being done in their name in the second war in Chechnya, named 'Putin's war' but restarted by Yeltsin only months before his abdication in December 1999. Talk of 'terrorists' and 'Islamic fundamentalists' means few Muslims can feel safe in what is left of the Russian empire. In October 2001 a Russian mob hundreds strong, wearing paramilitary insignia, ran through a Moscow market-place where there are many Muslim traders from southern Russia and the Transcaucasus, beating stallholders with iron bars. Three traders were reported killed. Moscow police were called in to stop the violence but mob law is not far removed from official Russian policy. As in 1994, the authorities in Moscow expelled 15,000 *LKN*, the derogatory acronym for people of Caucasus nationality, and forced a further 69,200 to reregister in September 1999 in 'Operation Foreigner'. To be a Chechen in Moscow is to be a Jew in 1930s Berlin.

This is not my analogy but Anna Politkovskaya's, a courageous Russian journalist who writes for the bi-weekly newspaper *Novaya Gazeta*. She was one of the few independent voices left in Putin's Russia until November 2001 when she fled to Vienna after receiving death threats. In her book *A Dirty War* Politkovskaya describes how a Muscovite woman nearly loses her Chechen fiancé who, on turning up to reregister at their local police station, has heroin planted in his pockets and is then detained for the possession of illegal drugs. His fiancée fights for his release but her intended is told by fellow Chechens that he is

---

* As this book went to press, Russia's last national independent television station, TV6, was closed down, the authorities maintaining its closure to be a 'business matter'. The Kremlin now controls all television in Russia for the first time since the collapse of the Soviet Union.

lucky the police did not plant explosives on him – this would have incurred a far more serious terrorism charge. 'The theory of the criminal nation was particularly fashionable in Nazi Germany. Then they targeted Jews and Gypsies,' Politkovskaya writes. 'Filtration and concentration camps were opened for them everywhere, and they were also confined to the ghettos. There seems to be little to choose between that and what is now going on in Moscow with our mute (or in some cases vociferous) participation.'

The week-long 'Operation Foreigner' (no change here from *inorodtsy*, the label of imperial times) followed the start once more of hostilities in the North Caucasus: first over the Chechen field commander Shamil Basayev's incursion into neighbouring Daghestan with the Bedu adventurer 'Khattab' in August 1999, and secondly over the mysterious apartment bombings across Russia which killed almost 300 people the following month. Basayev's and Khattab's incursion into Daghestan, where they held a clutch of villages near the border with Chechnya for a few weeks before being forced out by massive Russian firepower, was disastrous for the Chechens. Basayev's motives are not entirely clear but the villages were strategically worthless and spoke more of Basayev's and Khattab's restlessness and vanity than their self-professed patriotism.

The apartment bombings are of a different order, however, with suspicion that the FSB were themselves linked to the bombings, manufacturing their own Reichstag fire. Politkovskaya's newspaper reported in September 1999 that residents in a block of flats in Ryazan called in bomb disposal experts to diffuse a powerful explosive device in the cellars. The FSB said soon afterwards that this had been one of their own training exercises. A parliamentary enquiry was blocked by deputies loyal to Putin, once an obscure KGB officer of Sergey's generation who was lifted to power on a wave of public hatred of the Chechens. The widespread desire for a 'strong-hand' in Russia, with the Chilean general Augusto Pinochet as role model, sees a Russian public apparently happy to trade their new freedoms for a modest amount of stability.

Fighting in Daghestan and the apartment bombings triggered the second war in Chechnya. In October 1999 over 90,000 Russian soldiers, twice the amount deployed in 1994 and with a significant contingent of mercenary *kontraktniki*, invaded Chechnya once more. 'For American readers to understand how unthinkable a metamorphosis has taken place,' wrote Sergey Kovalev in February 2000 in the *New York Review of Books*, 'let them imagine for a moment that in, say, 1978, the president of the United States resumed the war in Vietnam. And furthermore that this action was applauded by all Americans – from miners and farmers to university professors and students. Inconceivable? Of course it's inconceivable. Nonetheless, this is precisely what has happened in Russia today.'

The Russian authorities claim the war is over (again). Since January 2001, Putin has put the FSB in charge of pacifying Chechnya, much as Stalin did when he left the NKVD to do the job in the Thirties and Forties. Unlike the case of Kosovo or East Timor, there is no official moral outrage expressed in the west on behalf of the Chechens. War crimes, according to the United Nations tribunals set up to investigate them, are committed only by citizens of the former Yugoslavia and Rwanda. Russia, despite repeated violations of the European Convention on Human Rights (to which it is a signatory) had its voting rights restored at the Parliamentary Assembly of the Council of Europe in January 2001.

The attacks on New York and Washington on 11 September 2001 have further endangered the Chechens. Kovalev, along with a handful of other Russian human rights activists, published an appeal in November 2001, again in the *New York Review of Books*. While condemning the terrorist attacks on America, the appeal's authors fear they will be used by the Kremlin to hit Chechnya even harder. 'As human rights activists in Russia, we are particularly concerned about the predictable intent to use the new world situation to justify the resolution of the Chechen problem exclusively by force. Our view on the subject remains the same: the only way out of the dead-end situation in Chechnya is a peaceful settlement reached through negotiations.

The resolution of complex problems by force can only lead to an escalation of terrorism.' Worryingly, many western news organizations have been reporting Chechens as fighting for Al-Qaeda in Afghanistan despite the lack of any conclusive evidence that this is the case.

The Chechen war of 1994–96 was a war of repeats. Had no one in the Kremlin or the power ministries read Tolstoy? Politkovskaya's reports show how these mistakes are being repeated once more. Chechnya stands as a warning to ordinary Russians – and to the West – who buy into Putin's brand of security, one handed down by Yeltsin and the Soviet and Tsarist apparatchiks who came before him: that lawlessness, the absence of constitutionality, arbitrary power – all ingredients of the Kremlin's war against the Chechens – stand to ricochet back against the whole Russian population.

Every fifty years, say the Chechens. What can the next generation expect? Are the Chechens condemned like Prometheus – chained by Zeus to the summit of Mount Kazbek where an eagle swooped down and tore out his liver, the immortal demigod's tattered viscera growing back overnight, ensuring the torture was repeated the next day? What are the parents and elders teaching Chechen children in the Tartarean remains of their villages, abandoned railway carriages or freezing refugee camps rife with tuberculosis (a disease which is on the whole entirely curable), once more cast as a criminal nation and exiled from any vestige of normal, human existence?

As I write, fireworks are going off all over London to celebrate Guy Fawkes night. The cracks and bangs bring back nights in Grozny. They are sounds a Chechen child born after 1994 has heard most nights of his or her young life. Politkovskaya visited a Chechen tent school at a refugee camp in Ingushetia in March 2000. A Chechen teacher handed her a sheaf of short essays by her eight- and nine-year-old pupils on the theme, 'My Homeland'. This is one pupil's composition:

*I love my homeland, the village of Urus-Martan, because it is the most beautiful village in the world. Now I miss it very much. At*

night I dream that I am running with my satchel in my hands and
my girl friends to our own school.

Here in Ingushetia planes and helicopters often fly past and I get
scared, as though I am at home again. During the last war the soldiers from Russia killed my father. Mum searched for him everywhere. Finally she found a dead, mutilated body buried in the
ground. I was six then, my brother was eight and my younger sister
was eleven months old. After everything that happened I thought,
the war has ended for good. But in a short time it all started again.

Now every day I hear the grown-ups weeping and telling of
their murdered relatives. I would like to live under a peaceful sky!
But will there be such a thing?

# Glossary

| | |
|---|---|
| *Allahu akbar!* | God is greater! |
| *aoul* | mountain village in the North Caucasus |
| *bashlyk* | cloak of camel-hair |
| *BMP* | Russian initials for a light fighting vehicle used by airborne forces |
| *BTR* | Russian initials for APC, or armoured personnel carrier |
| *cherkeska* | tunic with cartridge pouches in lieu of breast pockets |
| *chinovnik* | bureaucrat |
| *chirimsha* | a type of wild spring onion rich in vitamins |
| *DGB* | Dudayev's security police |
| *dzhigit, dzhigitovka* | North Caucasian horseman with chivalric characteristics; riding tricks |
| *FSB* | see *KGB* |
| *FSK* | see *KGB* |
| *GAI* | the Soviet Union's traffic police |
| *ghazavat* | holy war |
| *giaour* | infidel |
| *gorets, gortsy* | mountaineer, mountaineers |
| *Grad* | Russian type of multiple rocket-launcher (literally 'hail') |
| *izba* | Russian equivalent of a log cabin |
| *KGB* | the Soviet Union's Committee for State Security (preceded by the *Cheka*, *OGPU* and *NKVD* in Soviet times and succeeded after the Soviet collapse by first the *FSK* and then the *FSB*) |
| *khalat* | long robe |
| *kinzhal* | short, double-bladed Caucasian sword without a hilt |
| *Komsomol* | Soviet youth organization |

| | |
|---|---|
| *kontraktnik* | mercenary, often from prison |
| *kunak* | sworn friend |
| *kvevri* | Georgian amphorae |
| *LKN* | initials for the racist Russian term 'person of Caucasus appearance' (*litso kavkazskoy natsionalnosti*) |
| *Mufti* | a senior Muslim cleric |
| *murid* | member of a Sufi order and a warrior in the holy wars of the nineteenth century |
| *nayib* | synonym for *murid* |
| *NKVD* | see *KGB* |
| *NTV* | Moscow-based television station, which was independent during the 1994–96 Chechen War but was brought under government control in 2001 |
| *OGPU* | see *KGB* |
| *papakha* | tall karakul cap worn by the mountaineers |
| *PTT* | Post, Telegraph and Telecommunications, i.e. Post Office |
| *RPG7* | Russian type of rocket-propelled grenade |
| *rubashka* | Russian peasant's shirt |
| *shapka* | Russian fur hat |
| *Spetsnaz* | Russian special forces |
| *stanitsa* | Cossack village |
| *tamada* | Georgian toastmaster |
| *zikr* | collective prayer by Sufi adepts in the North Caucasus, who chant prayers aloud while jogging in a circle |

# Sources

Contemporary quotations and accounts of current events are based on my own notebooks of the time, the news pieces I wrote for The Associated Press and longer pieces for the London-based journal *Russia Briefing* unless otherwise specified. The following is a short summary of my sources for the main subjects treated in this book, followed by a bibliography.

Among new material on the Russian Empire and its contradictions, essays published in the *Central Asian Review* (including original accounts by the mountaineers), Marie Bennigsen Broxup's *The North Caucasus Barrier: The Russian Advance towards the Muslim World* and Daniel R. Brower and Edward J. Lazzerini's *Russia's Orient: Imperial Borderlands and Peoples, 1700–1917* (following in the footsteps of the late Alexandre Bennigsen) proved invaluable. I used general histories of the empire by Orlando Figes, Geoffrey Hosking and Dominic Lieven (listed below).

Background on the film *Passport to Pimlico* is from George Perry's *Forever Ealing*.

The Baddeley Bequest at the London Library reveals few details of John Baddeley's life. Impatient marginalia pencilled in some of the books he left the library, a membership slip of the Royal Geographical Society (for which he wrote a monograph on the Ricci Map in the society's New Map Room) and a short obituary in *The Times* in 1940 add little more. However, his own book *The Rugged Flanks of the Caucasus* gives some account of the life he led riding through the Caucasus Mountains at the beginning of the twentieth century, while *Russia in the 'Eighties: Sport and Politics* tells much of his early life as a journalist in Imperial Russia. His *Russian Conquest of the Caucasus* remains the classic historical work on the subject.

On Pushkin, Lermontov and Tolstoy, along with their own work, I used Henri Troyat's biography of Tolstoy, excerpts from Tolstoy's letters and diaries and translations of Pushkin by W. Morison, A.D.P. Briggs and C.M. Bowra. In Lesley Blanch's *The Sabres of Paradise*, a tour of the nineteenth-century Murid Wars, I found material on the presence of Russia's literary giants in the Caucasus. Susan Layton's *Russian Literature and Empire: Conquest of the Caucasus from Pushkin to Tolstoy* is a fascinating account of Russian perceptions of the Caucasus through its writers.

For wolf lore, I am indebted to Barry Lopez's *Of Wolves and Men*, George Caitlin's *North American Indians* and I.Yu. Aliroyev's *Yazyk, istoriya i kultura Vainakhov* [Language, history and culture of the Vainakh].

The literature on Stalin is vast. I chose to source much of my material from the work of the late Dmitry Volkogonov, a former hardline Soviet army general with unprecedented access to Communist Party archives and who later, as a senior defence adviser to Yeltsin, saw first-hand the weakness of the new civil society he championed. I also used Chechen sources published in Russian in the early 1990s recording oral accounts of the 1944 deportations, alongside Robert Conquest's *The Nation Killers*.

On Chechen hopes of English rule, articles by early twentieth-century mountaineer leaders published in the *Central Asian Review* were again invaluable. G. H. Bolsover's 'David Urquhart and the Eastern Question, 1833–37: A Study in Publicity and Diplomacy', published in *Journal of Modern History*, 1936, and Moshe Gammer's 'The Imam and the Lord' in *Israel Oriental Studies*, vol. XIII, were also extremely useful.

Other accounts of contemporary events in Chechnya that I referred to include Carlotta Gall and Thomas de Waal's *Chechnya: A Small Victorious War*, Anatole Lieven's *Chechnya: Tombstone of Russian Power*, and Anna Politkovskaya's *A Dirty War*.

### BIBLIOGRAPHY

Svetlana Alexievich: *Zinky Boys: Soviet Voices from a Forgotten War*, London 1992

I.Yu. Aliroyev: *Yazyk, istoriya i kultura Vainakhov* [Language, history and culture of the Vainakh], Grozny 1990

Lucy Atkinson: *Recollections of Tartar Steppes and their Inhabitants*, London 1971

John Baddeley: *The Russian Conquest of the Caucasus*, London 1908

—— *The Rugged Flanks of the Caucasus*, London 1940

—— *Russia in the 'Eighties: Sport and Politics*, London 1921

Alexandre Bennigsen and S. Enders Wimbush: *Mystics and Commissars: Sufism in the Soviet Union*, London 1985

Paul Birukov: *Leo Tolstoy: His Life and Work*

Lesley Blanch: *The Sabres of Paradise*, London 1960

Akhmed Bokov: *Uzkiye vorota* [The narrow gate], Grozny 1994

# Sources

A.D.P. Briggs (editor): *Alexander Pushkin*, Everyman's Poetry, London 1999

Stephen Brook: *Claws of the Crab: Georgia and Armenia in Crisis*, London 1993

Daniel R. Brower and Edward J. Lazzerini: *Russia's Orient: Imperial Borderlands and Peoples, 1700–1917*, Indiana 1997

Marie Bennigsen Broxup (editor): *The North Caucasus Barrier: The Russian Advance towards the Muslim World*, New York 1992

George Catlin (edited by Peter Matthiessen): *North American Indians*, London 1989

John Channon: *The Penguin Historical Atlas of Russia*, London 1995

Chechen Republic of Ichkeria: *Ternisty put k svobode* [The thorny path to freedom], Vilnius 1993

Robin Collomb and Andrew Wielochowski: *Mount Elbruz Region*, Reading 1992

Robert Conquest: *The Nation Killers: The Soviet Deportation of the Nationalities*, London 1970

Kharon Dadayev (editor): *Belaya Kniga: Iz istorii vyseleniya Chechentsev i Ingushey 1944–1957* [The white book: from the history of the Chechen and Ingush populations 1944–1957], Alma Ata 1991

Norman Davies: *Europe: A History*, Oxford 1996

Alexandre Dumas: *Au Caucase*, Paris 1969

Orlando Figes: *A People's Tragedy: The Russian Revolution 1891–1924*, London 1996

Carlotta Gall and Thomas de Waal: *Chechnya: A Small Victorious War*, London 1997

Mikhail Gorbachev: *On Lenin*, Moscow 1990

Che Guevara: *Guerrilla Warfare*, London 1975

Stephen Handelman: *Comrade Criminal: The Theft of the Second Russian Revolution*, London 1994

Geoffrey Hosking: *Russia: People and Empire 1552–1917*, London 1997

Nikita Khrushchev: *Krushchev Remembers* (translated by Strobe Talbott), London 1971

Susan Layton: *Russian Literature and Empire: Conquest of the Caucasus from Pushkin to Tolstoy*, Cambridge 1994

M.Yu. Lermontov: *Stikhotvoreniya, Poemy, Geroy nashego vremeni* [Lyric and narrative poems, *A Hero of our Time*], Moscow 1993

Anatole Lieven: *Chechnya: Tombstone of Russian Power*, Yale 1998

Dominic Lieven: *Empire: The Russian Empire and its Rivals*, London 2000

Barry Holstun Lopez: *Of Wolves and Men*, New York 1995

Osip Mandelstam: *The Noise of Time* (translated by Clarence Brown), London 1988

Aslan Maskhadov: *Chest dorozhe zhizni* [Honour is dearer than life], Chechnya, 1997

Vladimir Nabokov: *Lectures on Russian Literature*, London 1983

George Perry: *Forever Ealing*, London 1981

Anna Politkovskaya: *A Dirty War: A Russian Reporter in Chechnya* (translated and edited by John Crowfoot), London 2001

Roger Rosen: *Georgia: A Sovereign Country of the Caucasus*, Hong Kong 1999

Kurban Said: *Ali and Nino: A Love Story* (translated by Jenia Graman), London 2000

Alexander Solzhenitsyn: *The Gulag Archipelago 1918–1956: An Experiment in Literary Investigation*, London 1978

V.A. Tishkov (chief editor): *Narody Rossii* [The peoples of Russia], Moscow 1994

Leo Tolstoy: *The Death of Ivan Ilyich and Other Stories* (translated by Rosemary Edmonds), London 1960

——*Master and Man and Other Stories* (translated by Paul Foote), London 1977

——*Twenty-three Tales* (translated by Louise and Aylmer Maude), London 1906

——*War and Peace* (translated by Rosemary Edmonds), London 1982

Henri Troyat: *Tolstoy: A Biography*, New York 1967

Dmitri Volkogonov: *Stalin: Triumph and Tragedy* (translated by Harold Shukman), London 1991

——*The Rise and Fall of the Soviet Empire: Political leaders from Lenin to Gorbachev* (translated by Harold Shukman), London 1999

Boris Yeltsin: *Midnight Diaries*, London 2000

Other contemporary news sources and journals

Casualties of War, Grozny: Hussein Hamidov, Chairman, *Report to the November 4th Round Table*, 1995 (author's copy)

Institute of War and Peace Reporting, website

*Military Review*, Fort Leavenworth: General Anatoly Kulikov, 'Trouble in the North Caucasus', July–August 1999 (accessed via the Internet)

Reuters, London, News and Business Information